WRITING THE GHETTO

Writing the Ghetto

Class, Authorship, and the Asian American
Ethnic Enclave

YOONMEE CHANG

Rutgers University Press

NEW BRUNSWICK, NEW JERSEY, AND LONDON

Visit our Web site: http://rutgerspress.rutgers.edu

Manufactured in the United States of America

LIBRARY OF CONGRESS CATALOGING-IN-PUBLICATION DATA

Chang, Yoonmee, 1970–

Writing the ghetto : class, authorship, and the Asian American ethnic enclave / Yoonmee Chang.

p.   cm.

Includes bibliographical references and index.

ISBN 978-0-8135-4801-2 (hardcover : alk. paper)

1. American literature—Asian American authors—History and criticism.   2. Asian Americans in literature.   3. Asian Americans—Intellectual life.   4. Poverty in literature.   5. Ethnic groups in literature.   6. Social life and customs in literature. I. Title.

PS508.A8C53   2010

810.9'895073—dc22

2010004656

A British Cataloging-in-Publication record for this book is available from the British Library.

A book in the American Literatures Initiative (ALI), a collaborative publishing project of NYU Press, Fordham University Press, Rutgers University Press, Temple University Press, and the University of Virginia Press. The Initiative is supported by The Andrew W. Mellon Foundation. For more information, please visit www.americanliteratures.org.

For my parents, Sang Gill and Woon Suk Chang

CONTENTS

ACKNOWLEDGMENTS

Writing a book is a blessing. It is the good fortune of being able to spend your time indulging your ideas. Writing is another kind of blessing; the ability to give shape to blank pages is, for me, a humbling gift from the divine. More tangible graces shepherded me along the way. They are the people without whom I would have more dearly suffered self-doubt and discouragement. I offer special thanks to Houston Baker Jr., who welcomed me as a graduate student at the University of Pennsylvania. He has been my teacher all these years, as well as my friend. Eric Cheyfitz saw this book through its early phases and remains someone whom I can count on. Joseph Clarke offered incisive readings of the previous versions of the manuscript. Faculty and fellow graduate students at the University of Pennsylvania kept me on track: Eiichiro Azuma, Mark Chiang, James English, Kendall Johnson, Grace Kao, Rosanne Rocher, and Karen Su. My colleagues at Indiana University provided me with the warm welcome necessary to clear my head and get writing: Catherine Bowman, Patrick Brantlinger, Melanie Castillo-Cullather, Margot Crawford, Nick Cullather, Susan Gubar, Angela Pao, and Joan Pong-Linton. George Hutchinson warrants special mention for showing me that in the life of the intellectual there is room for compassion and kindness. In the field of Asian American studies, I have been supported by colleagues across the nation, who offered their feedback, but most of all created a community. I have already mentioned some of them, but they also include Daniel Kim, Crystal Parikh, Min Hyoung Song, Cindy Wu, and Ji-Yeon Yuh.

At George Mason University, I am indebted to the Mathy Junior Faculty Fellowship for giving me time off to complete my manuscript, and especially to Keith Clark, Devon Hodges, Deborah Kaplan, Robert Matz, Paul Smith, and Scott Trafton. I also thank the many students who have passed through my classrooms and enriched my research. I am grateful to the anonymous readers who took the time to read my manuscript and offered rigorous feedback. At Rutgers University Press, I thank the staff and editors, especially Leslie Mitchner and Rachel Friedman, who made this book a reality. The same gratitude goes to the American Literatures Initiative for their commitment to cultivating literary scholarship. A version of chapter 4 previously appeared in a special issue of *Modern Fiction Studies* ("Asian American Fiction" 56.1). I thank the journal editors for allowing me to reprint the essay, as well as the issue's guest editors, Donald Goellnicht, Paul Lai, and Stephen Sohn.

Love and gratitude to old and new friends: Jane Ackerman-Gaffin, Lauren Choi, David Hsu, Sharon Kim, Clifford Lee, Sunyoung Lee, Christine Oh, Christopher Regan, Ju Yeon Ryu, John Yang, and Min Jung Yang. The support of my parents, Woon Suk Chang and Sang Gill Chang, and my grandmother, Chang Hee Koh, put my work into perspective. They reminded me of the importance of my project, but also of the importance of laying it aside. Many more have supported me. It is as much my shortcoming not to be able to thank them all personally as it has been my good fortune to have these individuals in my life.

All these blessings cannot allay one regret. My regret is that my father, a writer himself, who was eager to see his daughter publish a book, passed before he was able to do so. I dedicate this book to him, and to my mother who, during difficulty and celebration, has sustained us with her faith.

WRITING THE GHETTO

1 / Introduction: The Asian American Ghetto

What images are evoked by the phrase "Asian American ghetto"? Is this phrase an oxymoron in that Asian Americans, long considered a model minority, would hardly be thought to live and work in ghettos? Yet the Asian diaspora has seen the creation of spatially defined, racially demarcated clusters of Asian American residence and work in the United States. The urban spaces are familiar to us through names like Chinatown, Koreatown, and Little Tokyo, and their gritty conditions can be described through the vocabulary of "ghetto." But are these spaces ghettos? Aren't they more like cultural communities? Aren't they spaces of densely woven cultural practice, where immigrants and diasporic travelers convene to partake in the comforts of their Asian culture, and where tourists visit to get a taste of it? If they are, and despite that inhabitants of and visitors to these spaces experience and witness poverty, labor exploitation, and residential squalor, wouldn't these spaces be more aptly called "ethnic enclaves," a less pejorative term, which, while denoting racial difference and segregation, does not carry the same sense of social deracination as "ghetto"? What language has been favored in describing racially segregated Asian American spaces? How do these linguistic choices reflect the ways that Asian American racial and class experiences are understood—and refuse to be understood?

Writing the Ghetto examines these linguistic choices, the tension between "ghetto" and "ethnic enclave"; the Asian American spaces, mostly urban, but also suburban, that these choices are used to describe; and the literature through which these spaces are articulated and imagined.

To put it another way, this is an interdisciplinary study of the tension between class and culture, between "ghetto" on the one hand, which I define as a space of structurally imposed, racialized class inequity, of involuntary containment to racialized poverty and blight; and "ethnic enclave" on the other, a term that draws a rosier picture of racial-spatial segregation, and that in reference to Asian Americans foregrounds a sense of cultural community and culturally driven segregation, that is, voluntary, culturally chosen segregation. For Asian Americans, "ethnic enclave" and its vocabulary of cultural community have been preferred over "ghetto" to describe their racially segregated, economically impoverished spaces. This preference reflects a denial that racialized class inequity exists in America. This denial applies to different racial groups in varying degrees, but it is particularly keen in reference to Asian Americans. The language of "ghetto" is not eschewed for all racial groups. Indeed, it readily conjures up images of and is heavily relied upon to describe African American spaces. What produces these different lexicons for different racial groups? What produces the resistance to the lexicon of "ghetto" for Asian Americans? What is it about the specific ways that Asian Americans experience, or are said to experience, race and class that lends itself to this resistance?

At stake is how Asian Americans are made legible or, more to the point, illegible in terms of class inequity. The illegibility of Asian American ghettoization is central to shoring up larger national investments in denying class inequity, in legitimating the myth of America's exceptional classlessness. Asian American ghettoization is made illegible through what I will detail as "culturalizations" or "culturalist epistemologies," ways of imagining Asian American subjectivity and experience primarily through the lens of culture. In general, culturalizations reconfigure and attribute externally formed social dynamics into and to a group's putative cultural values and ethics. Regarding economic dynamics, culturalizations, as Arif Dirlik notes, attribute external, structural dynamics of political economy to interior, private workings of culture (265). Of concern here is how this attribution recasts the structural pressures that shape Asian Americans' class positions, relations, and possibilities into expressions of Asian culture. This is emblematized in the preference for the term "ethnic enclave" over "ghetto." By recasting the ghetto as an ethnic enclave, by recasting a space of structurally imposed class inequity as a cultural community, the structural pressures of race and class that create racialized ghettos recede from view and are replaced by culture, by the idea that Asian American ghettos are voluntarily formed cultural communities. This cultural recasting obfuscates the structural processes of ghettoization, as well as reconfigures and naturalizes structural class inequity *as* cultural expression—class is turned into culture. The culturalization of class is not exclusive to Asian Americans, but it is particularly pronounced for them. It is the cause and the effect of the especial usefulness of Asian Americans in legitimating the nation's cherished ideals about class, in the service of which they have become a racial yardstick and object lesson through which the myth of American classlessness is measured and vindicated.

By focusing on the topic of class, specifically, its relationship to culture, but also as an important subject in itself, I draw more attention to this naggingly present, but often silenced aspect of American life. Class is America's embarrassing secret, a "touchy subject," in Paul Fussell's words (15), that is deeply felt as a structuring factor of American life, but is as deeply buried in everyday conversation to national debates on legislation and public policy.[1] This is the result of the uncomfortable truth that we must acknowledge about the national claim to exceptionalist egalitarianism, especially to color-blind egalitarianism, vis-à-vis a sustained examination of national class hierarchies and inequities. "The denial of class," as Paul Lauter and Ann Fitzgerald write, is the "defining feature of American life and ways of thinking," not the exceptional condition of classlessness that is routinely claimed in order to fuel that denial (2). *Writing the Ghetto* contributes to the emerging body of American and ethnic studies scholarship that is dissatisfied with treatments of class, whether because class is neglected or omitted, or because it is treated as the perfunctory or epiphenomenal third in the "race, gender, class" triad. Here, I take class as a central axis of inquiry, making it seen and heard as a central structure, process, and relation of American life.

In doing so, I focus on Asian Americans because their experiences of class inequity are muted beyond the usual silence. Asian Americans are not unique in being subject to race-based class inequities. Some of these are structurally similar to those experienced by other groups, while others are unique to the racial position of "Asian American." However, as a specific racial group as well as part of a racialized collective, Asian Americans are distinctly and exceptionally invisible in terms of class inequity. For one, Asian Americans are illegible in the already inadequately voiced subject of class inequity because of the black-white binary that continues to frame discussions of race. Race has long served as a metonym for class inequity, but primarily in reference to blacks (for whom the conflation of race and class inequity engenders its own problems). Asian Americans are omitted from discussions of class inequity insofar as they are omitted from discussions of race. Given no place in black-white racial discourse, they fall out of the corresponding discussions of class. At the same time, Asian Americans do have a racial and class position of their own, that of the model minority. But if the model minority myth distinguishes Asian Americans in terms of race and class, it does so to claim that they do not suffer class inequity, but on the contrary, that they readily transcend it. Asian Americans' distinction in terms of race and class is the distinction of being a racial group that does not experience class inequity.

This is not merely a call to insert Asian Americans into the race and class formulations of the black-white binary. For instance, it would be insufficient to contest their position as the model minority, which makes them honorary whites (subjects who are not white, to be sure, but who are aligned with the class advantages of whiteness), by more insistently likening them to African Americans. Though Asian Americans share important similarities with African Americans, they are not adequately understood as belated blacks or their echoes, who need only be mapped onto African American–centered models of class. Likewise, Asian American class inequities are not sufficiently understood by likening them to another class of whites, that is, the white working class around whom other prevalent models of class disadvantage have developed. Rather, efforts to understand—and acknowledge—Asian Americans' experiences of class inequity are productive opportunities to unsettle and reshape the common racial scheme of black and white and its corresponding models of class. How do Asian Americans exceed the category of the working class, which has developed around Anglo and ethnic, immigrant whites? What do prevailing racial models of class, focused on African Americans, fail to capture? How is class inequity not only silenced for Asian Americans, but also how is it inadequately spoken?

One of my central goals, then, is to construct a hermeneutics of race and class that is specific to Asian Americans, that recognizes their relationships and intersections with other racial groups, yet captures and acknowledges the distinctions of their racial and class experiences. To this end, I confront a claim about how race uniquely functions, or is said to function, for Asian Americans, a claim that puts race in a different relation to class for this racial group. This different relationship is what has produced the illegibility of Asian American class inequity. This different relationship is the idea that race does not have negative class effects for Asian Americans but that, on the contrary, race *improves* their class situations. This is most evident in the model minority myth. If the model minority myth suggests that Asian Americans are honorary whites, insofar as it aligns them with the class advantages of whiteness, it does so by always reminding us that they are racially Asian. The model minority myth has different valences for Asian Americans, sometimes construing them as virtuous and at other times vicious (or both at the same time).[2] I detail the specific incarnations of this myth throughout the following chapters, but point out here that at the core of the myth is the belief that Asian Americans possess unique, productive cultural values and ethics, such as of hard work, devotion to family, and commitment to education, that distinguish them as a race. This racial distinction makes them a group that distinctively does not suffer under class inequity but readily, and inherently, transcends it. The linear relationship between race and class inequity, that being racially different has negative class effects, is derailed for Asian Americans. For Asian Americans the conventional relationship between race and class inequity is inverted.

Writing the Ghetto examines this derailment closely, untangling the inverted relationship between race and class inequity, an inversion that is false and misleading. Race and class inequity are deeply interwoven—even for Asian Americans—and though class cannot be reduced to race, and race to class, as Stuart Hall points out, race is "the modality in which class is 'lived,' the medium through which class relations are experienced, the form in which it is appropriated and 'fought through'" (55). This well explains how race has come to be a metonym for class inequity for blacks. But how has race come to signal just the opposite for Asian Americans?

We can understand this by returning to culture, the other central topic that I will be examining in close relation to class. For Asian Americans, the visibility of the relationship between race and class inequity is derailed by the intervening and mystifying effects of culture. Culturalizations or culturalist epistemologies have heavily imprinted the understanding of Asian Americans so that other facets of their lives have been absorbed under them, turning, for instance, class into culture, and their ghettos into ethnic enclaves. We need not look far to witness this primacy of culture in understanding Asian Americans. It is evident in how discourses of Orientalism, broadly construed as discourses that attribute the behavior and ontologies of Asian peoples to a radically non-Western mode of behavior and being—to some Oriental culture—stubbornly continue to permeate the ways that Asian Americans are commonly understood. A result of this high focus on culture is that the understanding of Asian American racial lives moves away from the externally imposed and socially structured—away from imposed processes of racialization, toward the internally driven and inveterately inhabited, toward the dispositions of culture. Borrowing Hall's vocabulary, we might say that culture is the modality of race through which Asian American racial positions are articulated. This foregrounding of culture in understanding Asian Americans' racial lives leads to the erasure of class by culture. This is precisely what is at work in the model minority myth. Its distinction of Asian Americans as a race that possesses values of hard work, family cohesiveness, and so forth is a cultural distinction, of the inner values and dispositions that they inherently possess. Through this culture, Asian Americans as a racial group are said to transcend class inequity, to use their culture to trump the negative class effects of racialization. If race is the "modality through which class is 'lived,'" then culture is the modality of race through which Asian American experiences of structural class inequity and ghettoization are made illegible.

How can Asian Americans make their experiences of racialized class inequity more legible? How can they write themselves into the polity in a way that acknowledges the damage to and straitening of their class possibilities, as well as the structural racializations that cause this damage? In seeking greater class legibility for Asian Americans, I turn to their textual legibility, the expressions of their class experiences in Asian American literature. These forms of legibility intersect in the notion of authorship. How do Asian American writers through the literary project of authorship contribute to the process of authoring Asian Americans' class positions and possibilities in the polity? How do Asian American textual bodies help write their places in the social body? This is not to take Asian American literature as transparent historical or sociological records of Asian Americans' class experiences. Their textual bodies do not merely express and reflect the class experiences of their social body. They do the social work of imagining and creating those experiences, of making available the languages and vocabularies through which class can be recognized, contested, and lived differently. This is not to suggest that transparent class critique, and sociopolitical critique more generally, are readily found in Asian American literature. On the contrary, this study is centrally concerned with the ethical quandaries underwriting Asian American authorship—does all Asian American literature have to offer sociopolitical critique? The complex body of Asian American literature does not uniformly do so. One of my goals is to show that Asian American literature has been historically written under pressures to mute sociopolitical critique, rendering many Asian American authors and texts complicit with the silencing of their class inequities. Thus, while *Writing the Ghetto* is animated by a desire to chip away at the silencing surrounding Asian Americans and class, it also explores the shape of that silence, including how Asian American texts and the social formations they represent perpetuate that silence themselves. By examining the shape of this silence, I construct a political-aesthetic genealogy of Asian American literature, a mapping of the political-aesthetic pressures that have conditioned the forms and conventions of this corpus. Asian American literature has been produced under what I call the "ethnographic imperative," explicit directives and implicit pressures to create superficially informative and exoticized "insider's views" of Asiatic culture. The result is a body of literature that serves as a simplistic "tell-all" ethnography that reduces Asian American life to Orientalist caricature and turns Asian American literature, in Frank Chin's terms, into "food pornography" (3). The ethnographic imperative is a literary expression of culturalization or culturalist epistemologies. Reducing and telescoping Asian American experience into cultural caricatures, it absorbs other facets of that experience into emanations of a simplistically rendered culture. Focusing on texts that are set in Asian American ghettos or that thematize forms of Asian American ghettoization, I show how the pressures of the ethnographic imperative absorb the imposed experiences of ghettoization under the rubric of culture, how they recast the ghetto into a cultural community or ethnic enclave. To put it another way, I show how Asian Americans' empirical experiences of ghettoization are obscured by the ghettoization of their literature to the genre of cultural ethnography. The title of this study means to capture this relationship between empirical class structures and their discursive representations, between Asian Americans ghettos, where class inequity is viscerally lived, and the ethnographic literary body, through which class inequity is discursively erased. Asian Americans' relegation to literal ghettos is obfuscated by the confinement of their authors to literary ones.

I focus on several forms of Asian American ghettoization within their various historical contexts and their representation through several subgenres of Asian American literature that are produced under the ethnographic imperative. These include Seattle's Little Tokyo in the years surrounding World War II in Monica Sone's coming-of-age autobiography *Nisei Daughter*; San Francisco's Chinatown in the late twentieth century in Fae Myenne Ng's "anti-bildungsroman," *Bone*; an imagined Koreatown during the 1992 Los Angeles riots, comprised of a network of Korean American mom-and-pop shopkeepers, which references the physical Koreatown in Los Angeles, but focuses on what I detail as the ghetto of small business ownership in Chang-rae Lee's spy novel *Native Speaker*; and the paradoxically intensified ghettoization constitutive of the "ethnoburb" or suburban ethnic enclave in S. Mitra Kalita's *Suburban Sahibs*, a "corrective ethnography" set in the early twenty-first century Little India of Edison, New Jersey. The introduction establishes the shape of Asian American literary ghettoization from the late nineteenth century through the twenty-first, with a focus on the work of the Chinese–North American Eaton sisters, and the conclusion reflects on one form of freedom from literary ghettoization, through the postracial aesthetic grappled with by the Vietnamese-raced narrator in Nam Le's short story, "Love and Honor and Pity and Pride and Compassion and Sacrifice."

The chapters follow two main arcs: the texts' ethical relationship to the ethnographic imperative, and Asian Americans' movement from ghettoization toward upward mobility. The texts' responses to and negotiations of the ethnographic imperative span a range of ethical positions. Sometimes the texts readily comply with the ethnographic imperative, and sometimes they subvert and critique it. Other times, critique is hindered by complicity, or complicity produces subversion. At still others, we see anguish at not being able to settle into a clear-cut ethical stance toward the ethnographic imperative and its obfuscations of class inequity. The chapters follow a progressive sequence toward upward mobility, beginning with Little Tokyo as a clearly structurally imposed, institutionalized form of ghettoization vis-à-vis the Japanese American internment, and moving on to Chinatown, also a form of structural ghettoization, but an emblem of its denial as such. I end with two forms of class mobility: Korean Americans' upward mobility through small business ownership, and Indian Americans' creation of and settlement in an "ethnoburb." These paths to upward mobility offer alternatives to spatial and economic impoverishment, but they are also alternative forms of ghettoization. The conclusion continues this arc, the movement toward intensified ghettoization in the putative movement toward freedom from ghettoization.

Each of the spaces under discussion illuminates ghettoizations specific to an Asian ethnic group and a historical and geographical context. These spaces do not exclusively or entirely represent the scope of Asian American ghettoization, but they tap into several key contexts of it, such as the Chinese Exclusion Era, the Japanese American internment, the development of Chinatown under late global capitalism, the 1992 Los

Angeles riots, the contemporary emergence of the "ethnoburb," and the Vietnam War. This historical and ethnic scope offers important overlaps and points of connection, but I do not suggest that it creates one fixed or generalizable idea of Asian American ghettoization. Nor do I suggest that the relationship between the form of ghettoization and the ethnic group under discussion is essential, that the ethnic group's racial-cultural characteristics give rise to that specific form of ghettoization (though structural contexts do produce forms of ghettoization that become attached to specific ethnic groups). Rather, by looking at the shape of ghettoization across a few historical periods and Asian ethnic groups, I benchmark some ways that the ghettoization of Asian Americans, of their social as well as textual bodies, has developed and shifted from the late nineteenth century to the early twenty-first.

Methodology and Keywords

Writing the Ghetto is an interdisciplinary study that draws upon sources in law, public policy, sociology, history, and mass media in order to illuminate the readings of literary texts. I do not merely juxtapose or collate discipline-specific texts, but offer a blended methodology that shows how Asian American experiences of class, and our social condition more generally, exceed the vocabulary of any one particular discipline. The nonliterary texts are not merely supplementary or background material, but literary documents themselves that impel their own readings, of the narratives and fictions that these putatively factual records create and sustain. In turn, the literary texts, which are more than documentations of Asian American class experiences, have nonetheless been instrumentalized as transparent records of social life. Vis-à-vis the ethnographic imperative, Asian American literature has been proffered as a kind of social science, reminding us that literary study requires attention to the supra-aesthetic perspectives through which literature is so often read and manipulated.

My investigation of class is keyed to national narratives and ideologies, concerned as it is with the distinctly American denial of class. But it is necessarily contextualized within the transnational migrations that create Asian American ghettos in the first place. The idea and the physical space of the Asian American ghetto embody what Kandice Chuh describes as the "transnational imaginary," the push and pull of the national and extranational that structure Asian America (76). An emblematic example of this in relation to the Asian American ghetto is evident in how U.S. Chinatowns are constructed as simultaneously national and extranational spaces. Often described as foreign cities within American cities, they are nonetheless claimed as national landmarks and icons of the American urban landscape. Moreover, Asian American ghettos are, on the one hand, spaces that have been created to manage and contain Asian American foreignness, yet, on the other, are paradoxically often located within the heart of American cities. Thus my examination of the Asian American ghetto does not exclusively focus on either the national or the transnational, but on both in interrelation, on how they are deeply, and at times, counterintuitively interwoven.

Keeping with this attentiveness to interrelation, though I foreground the distinctiveness of Asian American class experiences, I take a comparative approach, looking at the intersections of Asian American ghettoization with the ghettoization of other racial groups, especially with that of Latinos and African Americans. These groups are not merely distinguishing foils or coeval social and hermeneutic formations. Rather, their racial experiences are thickly woven in the process of Asian American ghettoization, sometimes to the extent that terms like "Chinatown" and "Koreatown" tend toward catachresis. This is not to resubmerge Asian Americans into other racial models of class or suggest that racial intersections are so imbricated that racial distinctions have become meaningless. It is to apprehend that imbrication as an uneven and variegated surface from which we can make out distinguishable, racial group–specific shapes whose borders, though jagged and irregular, can be focalized into protean forms of specificity.

A few words on key terms: "ghetto" and "ethnic enclave" are contested terms whose attributes and empirical referents have shifted and continue to shift in scholarship and the social imagination. I define ghettos as sites of racialized, spatially segregated, externally imposed—that is to say, structural—class inequity. This definition derives from well-known sociological scholarship, such as that by William Julius Wilson, Adolph Reed, and Douglas Massey and Nancy Denton. These scholars disagree on what social, economic, and political arrangements are primarily responsible for ghetto formation, but they concur that ghettos are structurally imposed phenomena.[3] Although I draw my conception of the ghetto from these scholars, who all focus on black ghettos, I do not equate Asian American ghettos with African American ones. The following chapters detail the important differences between the structural arrangements that lead to Asian American versus African American ghettoization, and between the resulting forms of ghettoization. What makes it productive to draw from studies of the African American ghetto, however, is that in these studies the structural analyses are pronounced, whereas this emphasis has been lost, I argue, in reference to Asian American spaces of class inequity.

The structural emphasis is lost via the use of "ethnic enclave." I define "ethnic enclave" as a term that obscures the structurally formed character of the ghetto by reconfiguring it as a space that is voluntarily and, especially, culturally formed. This kind of reconfiguration is evident in the discourse of the "culture of poverty" that is used to privatize black ghettoization. However, for blacks, though this reconfiguration changes the attributes of ghetto formation, it does not change the basic nomenclature—the black ghetto is still referred to as a ghetto. In contrast, for Asian Americans, the privatization or culturalization of ghettoization has changed the nomenclature to "ethnic enclave." On the one hand, even with this name change, "ethnic enclave" can connote a "culture of poverty," the idea that Asian Americans, like blacks, are culturally inclined to ghettoization. On the other hand, the change to "ethnic enclave" changes the valence of these spaces. As ethnic enclaves, class-segregated Asian American spaces are turned into spaces of positive and productive culture—they are turned into cultural communities. This latter use of "ethnic enclave" derives from the "ethnic enclave economy theory" developed by Kenneth Wilson and Alejandro Portes, and applied to Asian Americans by Min Zhou. This theory has been the source of much contention, making the term "ethnic enclave" unstable. Acknowledging this instability, I hew to a concept of the term that foregrounds the ethnic enclave economy theory's weighting of cultural community and cultural agency. This is not to conflate "ethnic enclave" with "cultural community" in every instance, but to highlight the close association of these terms in both the pronouncements and critiques of the ethnic enclave economy theory.

Chapter 2 details the lineage of the terms "ghetto" and "ethnic enclave," as well as the rationale for my particular usages. My uses foreground the counterpull between the terms—the ghetto as structurally formed, and the ethnic enclave as voluntarily, culturally formed—and the obfuscation of class inequity that results from the preference for the latter over the former. This is not to suggest that "ghetto" and "ethnic enclave" are mutually exclusive terms, nor to suggest the same for the concepts and lived experiences of class and culture. For instance, Asian American ghettos are not only ghettos. Asian Americans, among other racial groups, have cultivated rich cultural practices there—have created ethnic enclaves—even in the meanest of conditions. However, I parse these terms in this way, and seek to call attention to "ghetto" over "ethnic enclave," in order to right an imbalance. Culture and class are certainly interwoven, and culture can be richly practiced in the ghetto, but the problem is not that this has gone unrecognized. The problem is that culture in the ghetto is *over*-recognized, to the extent that Asian American ghettos cease to be acknowledged as ghettos and are turned into ethnic enclaves. Culture certainly exists in the ghetto, but I choose to create a fuller recognition of the ghetto as a class formation rather than to flesh out depictions of culture, because the ghetto is said not to exist because of culture. This is not to say that ethnic enclave models with their cultural focus are denuded of structural analysis; the ethnic enclave is not only an ethnic enclave. However, the weight that "ethnic enclave" gives to culture can, and does, result in the erasure of Asian American ghettoization.

Structural arrangements do not only produce ghettoization. This is evident in that in the later part of the twentieth century, the U.S. economy's embeddedness with Asia has transformed spaces like Chinatown into vibrant hubs of transnational investment and economic opportunity. However, the invigoration of Chinatown, to continue this example, by global capitalist development is partial and uneven. It benefits the few at the cost of many others. Investment in Chinatown often comes from a class of wealthy, jet-setting Chinese transnationals who have the financial wherewithal and social networks to reap the rewards of globalization. Yet they often do so by relying upon and deepening the labor exploitation of less fortunate co-ethnics. This certainly complicates the Asian American ghetto; it is an intra-ethnically, class-divided space, a structuring that is well worth attention and that I detail in chapter 4. But it should not be lost that the advantages of a few are not metonymic of the class condition of the collective, and that such a metonym would add another layer of illegibility to Asian American class inequity. The improvements in Asian American ghetto conditions, partial and uneven as they are, make the recognition of Asian American ghettos as ghettos more, not less, urgent. Partial improvements can cover over the class inequity that persists despite—and often because—of them.

The ethnographic literature produced under the ethnographic imperative is, as mentioned, a reductive form. It is not attuned to the sea changes in ethnographic practice, which as Robert Emerson notes, has moved over the course of the twentieth century from imperious "naturalistic observation" to methods in participant observation, some more immersive than others; to a "reflexive turn" in which the relationship between the ethnographic field and its written representation is keenly understood as not isomorphic, and in which the ethnographer's mediating, privileged position is not naively or disingenuously denied (2, 20). The kind of ethnography demanded by the ethnographic imperative is one of participant observation, in which the ethnographer, or author, in this case, is deeply immersed in the community at hand, in that she is a community insider, in short, a native informant. As such, she is expected to provide "naturalistic observation" that does not reflect self-consciousness about the power imbalances inherent in the ethnographic project. In other words, in investigating ethnography and its methods, and while cognizant of the complex and sophisticated forms of ethnography being produced, I focus on a form and method that are stunted in their development. This is not to suggest that Asian American literature is stunted, but to show how it is commanded to be so stunted by the ethnographic imperative, to eschew the reflexive and critical.

By focusing on the concepts of class and culture, I tread into the treacherous territory of attempting to define and capture the scope of these unwieldy terms. I use "culture" primarily to refer to "ways of life" in the anthropological sense (Williams, *Keywords* 90), which is different from culture as zeitgeist, artistic expression, and social refinement, though not extricated from the latter usages. More specifically, I use "culture" to refer to racial group–specific culture, to social practices associated with or assigned to a racial group that thereby distinguish that group. At times I use "culture" interchangeably with "ethnicity," as the latter denotes both racial and cultural difference. But I usually favor "culture" over "ethnicity" in order to call attention to an important difference between race and culture. "Race" is a physical condition of difference that leads to social ascriptions, to racializations, external impositions of identity, belonging, and possibility. In contrast, I use "culture" to refer to values and behaviors that are assumed to be internally created or inhabited. "Ethnicity" can also be used to denote this definition of culture; this term is often equated with culture as such. But "ethnicity" is also bandied about as equivalent to "race." As a result, on this shared ground of "ethnicity," differentiations between race and culture become blurred. That is, "race" can lose the sense of external ascription and be associated with the inhabitations of "culture." I prefer "culture" in order to call out the difference between external impositions of racialization encoded in "race," and the connotations of self-will and nature that adhere to "culture."

I put forth culture as a vehicle of damage, as an epistemological lens that obscures and naturalizes class injustice. In doing so, I depart from the more common perspective in American and ethnic studies, which is that racial group–specific culture is not a problem, but a solution. A main impulse in these fields is to identify and uphold marginalized groups' culture as a central means of agency, self-worth, and subversion, as a means of creating meaningful lives under domination, and of contesting that domination through compelling social and aesthetic practices. This is especially, and importantly, the case when marginalized groups have few other channels to contest their domination, for instance, when government and public institutions cannot be relied upon to rectify social injustice because they are the sources of it. Culture, as that which can be, or at least attempt to be, cultivated outside the terms of state and institutional domination, has thus emerged as a prime ground and means of protesting, critiquing, and subverting structures of power, leading influential scholars like Lisa Lowe to declare that "if the state suppresses dissent by governing subjects through rights, citizenship, and political representation, it is only through culture that we conceive and enact new subjects and practices in antagonism. . . . [It is] by way of culture that we can question these modes of government" (22). Lowe does not claim that culture is the only means of contesting injustice (though from her standpoint it is the primary one), nor is she putting forth an essentialized notion of culture that reentrenches racialized groups' marginalization by naturalizing them as odd, primitive, and foreign. Rather, she conceptualizes culture as deeply contextualized and historically attuned. It is a "repository of memory, of history," and a truer one at that. A more accurate embodiment and expression of social lives that are subject to injustice, culture creates counternarratives that give the lie to official narratives of states and social institutions that deny social inequity (22). From this perspective, culture productively contests class inequity. Lowe writes with David Lloyd that marginalized groups' cultures are a gnarling of political-economic pressures with social practices, dialectical excesses that emerge from between the pressures of, for example, the labor exploitation of racialized groups and those groups' resistance to capitalist exploitation. Culture cannot be fully "refunctioned" by capitalist rationality; culture engenders contradictions and excesses, in fact, exists as those excesses, through which racialized groups can reclaim agency and subjectivity under class inequity (1–2).

Culture can certainly and effectively work in this way, and there are both a need for and an urgency to this conceptualization of culture. But it is also worthwhile to look at culture's limitations, to ask a different question—what happens when culture does not embody and express sociopolitical protest, but obstructs or substitutes for it instead? My focus on the limitations of culture partly stems from a difference in the type of culture under study. Critics in Lowe's vein examine the culture that Asian Americans claim as their own, often but not always with sociopolitical critique in mind. I focus on the culture that is claimed for and assigned to them, namely the caricaturized culture of Orientalist exotica that is produced under the ethnographic imperative. However, the line between these types of culture is not so easily drawn. Asian Americans do not have a uniform ethical relation to their culture. They do not uniformly seek to produce oppositional and subversive culture but, for instance, often claim and reinforce the Orientalist caricatures imposed on them. In the literary field, this receptiveness has much to do with the conditions of literary production, how market pressures and available social vocabularies constrain Asian American literary voices. The point here is that Asian Americans' self-constructions of culture cannot be readily schematized into ethical binaries. There is a spectrum of Asian American ethical positions in relation to culture. These positions may hew to one extreme or another, but they also oscillate between the poles of the spectrum in ambiguous gray areas. Here, I address the gray areas, the variety of ethical positions, not to evacuate the usefulness and interventions of culture, but to examine culture in its fuller complexity. To this end, the following chapters are framed along the literary texts' ethical bearing toward the ethnographic imperative, along the complicity, the resistance, as well as the muddier positions in between of Asian American literature in using culture to obscure class inequity. To be sure, my goals are to make Asian American class inequity legible and to articulate a sociopolitical critique, but in a way that nuances prevailing American and ethnic studies methodologies and ethical assumptions, so that they can attend to a fuller range of racialized subjects' ethical and political positions.

The definitions and usages of "class" are likewise various and untidy. Rather than try to alight upon or mandate a strict definition of the term, I define class by its indeterminancy, exploring rather than straitening the confused and confusing ways that class is defined and its categories parsed and lived. This follows the approach of class scholarship that "presse[s] past the definitional issue," in Lauter's words ("Under Construction" 64), or, as John Russo and Sherry Lee Linkon write, that is able to understand class as a "homograph," so that the study of class does not seek pat agreements and resolutions, but embraces the complex and contradictory meanings of class, as an analytical category as well as an element of social life (11). The meanings and experiences of class shift across time and space, especially for Asian Americans, which makes their experiences a productive lens through which to examine the equally flexible forms that national class ideologies take in order to deny structural class inequity. The indeterminacy of class is enriched by the intersectionality of class, the weaving of class with race, as well as with gender and sexuality, in ways that make it difficult to pin down in stable forms, even within what at first glance appears to be readily identifiable class categories.

Some parameters, however, will be helpful. First and foremost, class is a system of economic inequity, which can be measured by common sociological indices like income level and its related causes and effects, such as education level, occupational status, and place of residence. In this sense, class refers to positions and relations within a hierarchy that are identifiable and structural. They are identifiable in recognizably different forms of social experience (e.g., living in an urban tenement versus an expensive suburban house), and those experiences are not necessarily chosen, but are created and perpetuated by embedded social structures (e.g., individuals do not choose to be poorly paid wage laborers, but often have little other choice since they cannot afford the higher education that would qualify them for better-paying jobs. More to the point, racialized subjects, with or without high levels of education, tend to have restricted access to the best jobs because of racial discrimination). These positions and relations are usually categorized under the familiar rubrics of "underclass," "working class," "middle class," "upper class," and so forth, categories that will be useful here, but that also have limitations, especially in relation to Asian Americans. Class positions and relations are also measured by a combination of economic and social capital. Both forms of capital are crucial to my discussion, particularly in chapter 5, but I caution against losing sight of class as being at the root an economically determined hierarchy.

At the same time, class is more than an aggregation of sociological indices. Class structures the hierarchies of the literal economy, but it is also structured by and as symbolic and semiotic economies whose workings cannot be captured by statistical measures. Rita Felski points out that there are emotional and psychological dimensions of class, a class "feeling" that is generated by and gives shape to positions in economic hierarchies, but is irreducible to "the sum of material relations" (39). Eric Schocket and Amy Schrager Lang model the importance of the semiotics of class, the languages and forms of expression created by the working and underclasses, as well as used and manipulated by those who try to speak for or silence them. In other words, while class structures result from a system of economic exchange, they are lived through the circulation of language and symbols. This often has paradoxical effects; for instance, David Roediger and Eric Lott show how the symbolic compensation of white racial pride and masculinist gender privilege has psychologically soothed, but materially aggravated, the economic injustice experienced by the white working class.

Likewise, I delve into the symbolic, affective, and semiotic dimensions of class, into how material inequity is thickly woven with less quantifiable social relations. My arguments are premised on this inextricability: focusing on how the recasting of the ghetto into the ethnic enclave in the realm of language, social imagination, and literature effaces the recognition of Asian American class inequity, my underwriting claim is that symbolic and semiotic expressions have material class effects. Regarding the relationship between economic structures of class and their representation in the symbolic economy of literature, Schocket puts it this way: "[C]lass [is not] antecedent to textuality." It is not something that "has already happened . . . [as] a set of identities, structures, or, at best, relationships that have determined the 'social background' that texts then 'reflect' with greater or lesser degrees of fidelity." Class is, instead, *made to happen* through textuality and other discursive acts (17). This approach is not to reduce class to a poststructuralist product of language and acts of representation, as Schocket notes; class is not just a construct of language and discourse. But it is to say that the ways that class is lived, understood, and aggregated as "class" necessarily happen through discourse and representation. In turn, discourse and representation are shaped and filtered through the realities of economic injustice that representation has taught us to recognize as class. The symbols and meaning structures of language and literature are not dispassionate vessels of historical or sociological documentation, but a constitutive part of class relations that must be "held accountable" for their role in shaping how we understand them, for how they make class experiences imaginable and thereby livable, or recognized as intolerable (Schocket 20–22, 11).

A moment here on how I will *not* be defining and using class: attentiveness to the mixture of material and nonmaterial economies of class is reflected in the methodology of the emerging field of "new working-class studies." In a recent anthology by that name, editors Russo and Linkon write that this field, redressing the neglect of class studies as well as moving it in innovative directions, aims to transcend purely economic analysis; conventional sociological indices; narrow workplace, masculinist industrial and unionist models; and Marxist teleologies. New working-class studies, while "almost always begin[ning] with some [account] of the power relations" that form class-stratified societies, "put[s] the working class, in all its varieties, at the center . . . asking questions about how class works for people at work, at home, and in the community" (10–11). Lauter's contribution to the volume specifies this claim: to study the working class is not to limit inquiry to work and macroeconomic processes and categories, but to apprehend the psychical, intellectual, and affective templates—the "sensibilities"—that shape and are expressed by those who are or have been at some point constrained by class ("Under Construction" 64). What partially results is a foregrounding of *class culture*, culture in the sense of social practices as well as aesthetic expression, with the goal of recuperating the neglected or discounted social contributions of both. Essays in Russo and Linkon's volume work toward this goal through studies, for instance, of working-class poetry, music, and vernacular.

Though I will also be addressing class through a form of aesthetic expression and while the symbolic and semiotic economies of class that I examine might be categorized as part of class culture in that they reflect social practices and investments, I take the pointedly different stance of not gathering these together to construct some form of unique and recognizable Asian American class culture. For Asian Americans, such a move would not be recuperative, but disabling. For one, ghettoized Asian Americans have a very different relationship to culture than other class-stratified groups. The white working class or impoverished African Americans, for example, are more often than not denied a culture, of meaningful everyday social practice and aesthetic expression, so that recuperating it is an important and necessary project. However, Asian Americans have hardly been denied a culture, but on the contrary are imagined as seeming to have only culture, in the sense of social practices, which, as I noted, does little to call attention to their class situations, but rather obfuscates and naturalizes them. This is also not a project of codifying an Asian American class aesthetic, for reasons I discuss below.

Second, the construction of class cultures risks valorizing something akin to class identity. Turning class into an identity is especially unproductive. It mires class in the usual bugbears of identity politics, and in doing so produces at least one very different and important effect. Class as identity can essentialize class, suggesting that class hierarchies reflect some natural ontological ordering. Class as essentialized identity thereby reentrenches the very class disempowerment that class studies seek to contest. When race is a factor, class as identity risks becoming doubly essentialized, as natural to a racial social order. Additionally, class as culture and identity is unproductive because class is fundamentally not equivalent to other common modes of identity. Schocket explains: "Whereas race, gender, and sexuality can, arguably, name social relationships that are not structured by an unequal distribution of power (this is the dream of pluralism after all), class—by any definition—can only name a structure, process, or position of inequality" (18). What end would it serve to imagine and live class as an identity? Why would we seek to construct—and celebrate—a class identity, when the salient need is to eradicate class stratified positions, not to settle more deeply into them? An answer to the last question has to do with the pluralist impulse that Schocket invokes and that animates much of American and ethnic studies. Schocket notes that the pluralist impulse folds class into a diversity or "cultural 'mosaic'" model, a model that is provisionally useful elsewhere, but in terms of class does the strange work of reappropriating economic inequity as a valuable condition (17, 20–22). This is not to say that class culture cannot be constructed in an anti-essentialist way, or to discount the meaningful social practices and aesthetics lived under class inequity. But it is to keep sight of class as being at the root a system of economic injustice that needs to be recognized—in all its symbolic, semiotic, and cultural complexity—so that it can be dismantled, not reified.

I also do not seek to reify a class-based literary identity. This is not a project of recuperating an Asian American class aesthetic, for instance, of constructing a canon of Asian American working class literature. It would be difficult to create such a canon because conventional class categories like "working class" are inadequate. They are useful to make broad and real social differentiations, but they ultimately cannot capture the full scope of class experiences gathered under them. This is particularly the case with "working class," a catch-all term and a main category used to reference class disadvantage, often to avoid the term "lower class" and its pejorative connotations, as well as the painful reality of class stratification that the latter term so baldly announces (i.e., that in America one can be "low"). However, the working class is itself stratified. Some members are poor, others make what is described as "moderate" income, while still others make fairly high incomes, but are categorized as working class because their occupations are not prestigious. How do we categorize the entrepreneurial plumber, whose occupation lacks prestige, but brings in revenues that rival the salaries of doctors and lawyers to whom he easily affords to live next door? How do we capture that the plumber, wealthy as he is, might not be welcome at his neighbors' dinner parties? We might conclude that class is a matter of social rather than economic capital; indeed, it is a combination of both. But as important as social capital is in this discussion, moving too far in this direction risks denuding class of the main concern here—economic injustice. "Working class" also fails to capture that its poorer members are poor because they do not work, even as they aspire to, but find themselves, particularly because of racial discrimination, unemployed or underemployed.

The limitations of conventional class categories are magnified for Asian Americans. For instance, the nature of work in a common Asian American economic niche, small business ownership, might characterize them as working class. Yet, as workers in atomized mom-and-pop businesses, they are not tapped into the union or labor-advocacy networks commonly associated with the term "working class," and have been historically excluded from such networks because of racial discrimination. At the same time, because Asian Americans are often the managers and owners of their businesses, they can be described as part of the professional-managerial class. Yet being part of the professional-managerial class by virtue of the often gritty field of small business ownership is hardly equivalent to being part of that class by virtue of being, say, a corporate executive. Other Asian Americans are less ambiguously economically disenfranchised. They are exploited laborers with few avenues for advancement, which makes it more appropriate to characterize them not as working class, even as they work, but as an underclass. Yet as an underclass they are better-off than the standard referent of "underclass," African Americans who experience extreme spatial and social ghettoization, are caricaturized as idle or criminal men and teen welfare mothers, and who have been discarded as socially unsalvageable (Wilson 20–62; Reed 179–96). The Asian American underclass that I discuss is at least valuable to capitalist development.

For these reasons, I use a variety and combination of class categories to describe the forms of class inequity addressed in this study. This approach demonstrates the limits of existing class vocabularies, but also productively underscores the instability of class categories. This approach enables a focus on the ambiguity of class itself in order to gain a richer picture of the complex and contradictory ways that class works. One of my goals is to show how Asian Americans confound rather than stabilize class categories. In the same way that they are not perfect fits for terms like "working class" or "underclass," they impel a rethinking of "middle class." They impel a rethinking of not only the class situations that need to be transcended, but also of the class situations that are aspired to and desired.

It would therefore be difficult and unproductive to create a canon of literature that corresponds to a tidy scheme of class categories. Studies of literature and class have puzzled over what constitutes, for instance, working-class literature. Does it primarily include texts written by the working class? If so, must the subject matter be working-class life, or can it address any subject as long as the author characterizes herself as working class? Or, does the working-class author, by having entered the high-culture realm of literature, cease to be working class? The answer, again, is that definition is not the goal, but that honoring a number of responses to these questions yields complex and nuanced insights about class, and about the relationship between literature and class.

Finally, to try to construct a coherent body of class literature, of Asian Americans and others, can assume an ethical bearing of texts and authors, inasmuch as the point of collating this canon is to make visible and challenge class inequity. This risks assuming that an identifiable class aesthetic is axiomatically an aesthetic of class resistance. I choose instead to focus on the range of authors' and texts' political-ethical desires, to complicate our understanding of class by complicating our assumptions about class resistance, to preclude the construction of a facile ethical-aesthetic notion of class resistance, so that we can confront the barriers erected by our allies as well as our opponents, and uncover what we did not expect or would just as soon rebury.

Chapter Summary

Chapter 2, "'Like a Slum': Ghettos and Ethnic Enclaves, Ghetto and Genre," maps the language and vocabulary that has been used to describe—and deny—Asian American ghettoization. Mapping the resistance to calling the Asian American ghetto a ghetto, I trace the genealogy of the term "ghetto" in sociological studies, as well as the genealogy of the turn to "ethnic enclave." The latter term provides a means of empowerment for ghettoized Asian Americans, but ironically privatizes their experiences of class inequity by turning the ghetto into a space organized and driven by culture. I also trace the genealogy of the relevant concepts of "culture." The potential empowerment of "ethnic enclave" hinges upon an empowered conception of culture, the conception of culture as a form of ethnic agency and political protest. I show how culture has come to be used as such, but also how this use can backfire, namely by culturalizing class. I outline the specific shape of the culturalization of class for Asian Americans through the model minority myth and American Orientalism. That the former culturalizes class has been well discussed, but at the core of American Orientalism is also a culturalizing class scheme that obfuscates Asian Americans' structural ghettoization. I then turn to the relationship between culture and class in Asian American literature. Mapping how the ethnographic imperative has ghettoized Asian American literature to the genre of what Frank Chin calls the "Chinatown book" (3), I trace how Asian Americans' literary heritage is deeply shaped by the pressure to obscure and culturalize class as is mandated by this genre. Asian American literature turns ghettos into ethnic enclaves too.

Chapter 3, "The Japanese American Internment: Master Narratives and Class Critique," brings together issues of internment and class in Monica Sone's coming-of-age autobiography, *Nisei Daughter*. The Japanese American internment is a canonical topic in Asian American studies, an emblematic example of institutional racism against Asian Americans. Here, I show that at the heart of the internment is a class narrative. Sone's autobiography is a conciliatory text that iterates justifications of the internment, as well as abides by the class obfuscations of the ethnographic imperative. It is through this faithfulness to "master narratives," however, that the text subverts internment justifications and class obfuscations. The archives of the War Relocation Authority, the federal agency that created and managed the internment camps, show that a central extenuation of the internment was keyed to class. The agency asserted that the internment was beneficial to Japanese Americans because it removed them from the Little Tokyos in which they were ghettoized before the war. *Nisei Daughter*'s "subversion through faithfulness" makes visible the narrative manipulations necessary to construct this claim, which relies on an astonishing denial and reconfiguration—the claim that the internment was not an internment, but a socioeconomic assistance project.

Chapter 4, "Chinese Suicide: Political Desire and Queer Exogamy," focuses on San Francisco's Chinatown in the late twentieth century, an iconic site of Asian American ghettoization as well as of its disavowal, in Fae Myenne Ng's *Bone*. Scholarship on *Bone* by and large reads the text as an anti-bildungsroman. The novel's loosely backward, antichronological temporal structure, shot through with the failed resolution of a suicide, is read as reflecting how a ghettoized Chinatown family is excluded from the linear fiction of the American Dream. The text is also read as an anti-ethnography that rejects Chinatown's exoticization. I argue that the novel's refusal to resolve the Chinatown family's story in a tidy narrative of upward mobility and emotional peace bespeaks the refusal of a different kind of resolution. The novel's competing voices and failed resolution trope the failures of an ethical fantasy of ethnic studies, the fantasy of what Viet Nguyen describes as "racial-political essentialism," the belief that racialized subjects share a uniform, oppositional political desire (145). Racial-political essentialism counteracts the racial-cultural essentialism that exoticizes Chinatown, but fails in unifying Chinatown voices against their culturalization. In light of this failure, I turn to what I call "queer exogamy," a model of politics that looks beyond the creation of a political family based on race and, moreover, that accounts for the multiracial character of Chinatown. Queer exogamy accounts for the Latina presence in Chinatown that *Bone* brings to light, and does not perpetuate what I show are the gendered, heterosexual assumptions of racial-political protest.

Chapter 5, "Ethnic Entrepreneurs: Korean American Spies, Shopkeepers, and the 1992 Los Angeles Riots," focuses on Chang-rae Lee's spy novel, *Native Speaker*, to examine one solution to the problem under discussion. How can Asian Americans move beyond their economic and spatial ghettoization? I look at Asian American upward mobility through ethnic entrepreneurship, focusing on Korean American mom-and-pop shopkeepers. These shopkeepers' road to upward mobility is culturalized, their economic activity conflated with their cultural identity. As "ethnic entrepreneurs," they are not merely entrepreneurs who happen to be ethnic, but are entrepreneurs *because* they are ethnic. This conflation naturalizes what I argue is the inadequacy of upward mobility through ethnic small business ownership, which is characterized by economic enfranchisement stripped of social and political enfranchisement, a condition that I describe as the "fracturing of class spheres." This fracturing might have remained an imperfect, but relatively privileged condition had not the 1992 Los Angeles riots and the attendant "black-Korean conflict" demonstrated its violent consequences. In *Native Speaker*, the protagonist's job as a spy, which I describe as a form of authorship, figures the ethical quandaries and anguish in abiding by the ethnographic imperative and culturalizing Korean American ethnic entrepreneurs. The protagonist's ethical quandaries impel a rethinking of what constitutes class and class mobility, and makes visible that ethnic entrepreneurship is a form of ghettoization.

Chapter 6, "Indian Edison: The Ethnoburbian Paradox and Corrective Ethnography," looks at another form of compromised upward mobility in S. Mitra Kalita's *Suburban Sahibs: Three Immigrant Families and Their Passage from India to America*. Kalita's text is a "corrective ethnography." Rejecting the culturalist obfuscations of the ethnographic imperative, it provides a class ethnography of an Indian American community in Edison, a suburb in New Jersey. Edison is an "ethnoburb." This term was coined by Wei Li to describe wealthy, suburban ethnic enclaves. The ethnoburb is an emblem of Asian Americans' move toward economic middle-class status and wealth. However, this wealth can be sustained only through the invisible labor of ghettoized co-ethnics. Kalita's corrective ethnography makes this labor visible, rendering the ethnoburb as a paradoxical space in which increased upward mobility and privilege are attended and sustained by intensified ghettoization.

The conclusion, "The Postracial Aesthetic and Class Visibility," examines the postracial aesthetic, a radical form of freedom from the ethnographic imperative that implies an attendant freedom from the racialized class inequity that the imperative obscures. In Nam Le's short story "Love and Honor and Pity and Pride and Compassion and Sacrifice," the Vietnamese-raced writer's dilemma over whether to write an ethnic story or to hew to transcendental, postracial, post-class themes delineates the pitfalls and possibilities of the latter aesthetic. The core of his dilemma is that even as ethnic aesthetics are moving toward the postracial and post-class, toward an unfettering from the pressures of the ethnographic imperative, from the ghettoization of ethnic writers to the genre of the ethnic story, Asian American social formations have not been correspondingly released from class inequity. The dissonance between the direction of ethnic aesthetics and the direction of ethnic class formations impels us to ask: Does the postracial, post-class aesthetic enable the increased social presence of Asian Americans because it writes them into the polity beyond racial-cultural and class parameters, or is this aesthetic just a different way, insofar as Asian Americans remain racialized and ghettoized subjects, to denude their legibility?

2 / "Like a Slum": Ghettos and Ethnic Enclaves, Ghetto and Genre

In a sociologist's survey of the quality of life in San Francisco's late twentieth-century Chinatown, residents and workers remark upon the difficult conditions of their lives, of the crowded, dilapidated housing conditions; the demanding but poorly paying, dead-end jobs; the inability to find better work and housing elsewhere because of racial discrimination; and the damage that these material conditions impose on their psyches. This portrait tells us that Chinatown is a ghetto, a racially segregated space that is formed by and developed under social and economic structures that create a spatially contained Asian American underclass. One survey response gives pause. The respondent, noting the ghetto conditions in which she lives, describes the space as "*like* a slum," as if Chinatown were not an actual slum, but an approximation of one (qtd. in Loo 79, emphasis added). Perhaps this is just an offhand use of simile, but it hints at deeper, perplexing processes of social imagination, desire, and language that resist naming Chinatown, and other Asian American ghettos more generally, as slums or ghettos. What are the processes of social imagination, desire, and language that generate this impulse, the resistance to saying simply that Chinatown *is* a ghetto or slum? If Chinatown and other racially segregated sites of Asian American class inequity are not ghettos, what are they instead?

The resistance to calling the Asian American ghetto a ghetto bespeaks a denial that Asian Americans experience structural class inequity. It also bespeaks a more general denial of class injustice in America. Asian

Americans have become an especially useful group to fuel this denial. This is evident in that the Asian American ghetto in particular has been recast into an "ethnic enclave," which obscures and naturalizes Asian American experiences of class inequity. "Ethnic enclave" is broadly synonymous with "cultural community." Rejecting the negative connotations of "ghetto," "ethnic enclave" redefines racially segregated spaces of Asian American class inequity into productive communities infused with and driven by ethnic culture. "Ethnic enclave" constructs spaces like Chinatown as unique repositories of Asian culture, an esteemed and valuable culture that is and should be productively cultivated, and that engenders and organizes meaningful and rewarding social relations. This evaluation of Asian culture is important, and offers solace to ghetto dwellers whose social, spatial, and economic disenfranchisement often leaves them with little else but their culture. However, the recasting of the ghetto into the more positive ethnic enclave displaces a structural assessment of ghetto life onto the terrain of culture. This recasting makes the de jure and de facto economic and class structures that cause Asian American ghettoization recede from view, replacing an account of how Asian Americans are structurally limited by race and class to spaces like Chinatown with a portrait of these spaces as ethnic communities that are formed, developed, and organized by culture. The substitution of the term "ethnic enclave" for "ghetto" obscures class with culture.

Structuring ghetto life through culture also turns class *into* culture. When elements of ghettoization are recognized, such as poor housing, joblessness, and labor exploitation, they are assimilated into the cultural portrait and reconfigured as cultural phenomena, suggesting that the conditions of ghetto life are natural expressions of Asian culture. This culturalization of class—the reconfiguration of structurally produced hierarchies of class into internally produced expressions of culture—is evident in some of the claims made about the original Chinatown ghetto in San Francisco. Chalsa Loo points out that late nineteenth- and early twentieth-century studies of San Francisco's Chinatown attribute tenement living not to the legal and social exclusion of Chinese immigrants from better housing choices, but to the assertion that "it is almost their universal custom to herd together as compactly as possible. . . . [T]rained in centuries of stifling gregariousness . . . they like crowds and clamor and elbow-jostling" (Dobie 6–7). Likewise, the San Francisco Health Officer's Report of 1869–1870 attributes the filth and squalor of Chinatown to a "Chinese mode of living," neglecting to mention that sanitation and street-cleaning services were regularly withheld from the area (Loo 44).

Another study, Loo notes, states that Chinese Americans "apparently delight to exist in . . . dense conditions of nastiness" (Farwell 4).

These uses of culture on the one hand deny that Asian American ghettoization exists at all, and on the other, recognize its existence, but render it as part of a natural race and class order. This obfuscation and naturalization can be mapped in sociological studies of the Asian American ghetto, as well as in Asian American literature that is written under the pressure of the "ethnographic imperative." The ethnographic imperative straitens Asian American literature to the genre of reductive, cultural ethnography, which, like the reconfiguration of the ghetto into an ethnic enclave, obfuscates and naturalizes Asian American experiences of class inequity. The ethnographic imperative rewards an aspiring writer like Ahn Joo Cho, in Patti Kim's *A Cab Called Reliable*, with classroom literary prizes when she writes about village wells in Korea, *hanboks*, and jade hair pins, but makes illegible her other kinds of writing, such as the magic-markered signs that display the price and spiciness of half-smokes that are sold in her father's food truck (79, 76). The cultural ethnography that Ahn Joo is expected to write makes illegible her class experiences as an immigrant child who spends her after-school hours toiling for meager profits in her father's food truck and later at his slum carry-out restaurant.[1] The only canvas on which she can articulate her class experiences is the dusty wall of that truck, onto which she writes, "Ahn Joo was here" (83). Scrawled onto a symbol and physical site of her family's economic struggles, this declaration is a plea for the recognition of her presence as a racialized, classed subject. But who will be able to write, much less read, this plea when literary adulation comes from submitting to the pressures and desires for cultural ethnography in Asian American literature? How do Asian American writers negotiate the ethnographic imperative and its culturalist obfuscations of class? How can an Asian American writer like Ahn Joo make her "here" in terms of class be seen, heard, and read?

I respond to these questions by beginning with a mapping of the language of "ghetto" in sociological studies of racialized, urban, socioeconomic segregation, in general as well as in reference to Asian Americans. For Asian Americans, the language of "ghetto" has given over to the language of "ethnic enclave." On the one hand, this move empowers and gives agency to the Asian American underclass. On the other, it ironically diminishes attention to the structural class inequities that "ethnic enclave" can empower ghetto workers and residents against. At the center of the recasting of the Asian American ghetto into an ethnic enclave is a culturalization of class. The culturalization of class is not unique to

Asian Americans, but it distinguishes Asian Americans as a racial group whose structural ghettoization is insistently obscured. This is evident in two main discourses of class culturalization that are specific to Asian Americans, the model minority myth and American Orientalism. Both distinguish Asian Americans as a racial group that does not experience structural class inequity, either by suggesting that Asian Americans are culturally immune to it or by denying that class inequity is structural, asserting instead that it is a natural expression of Asian culture. That the model minority myth disavows Asian American experiences of structural class inequity has been well discussed, but this disavowal is less apparent though equally at work in American forms of Orientalism. At the heart of American Orientalism is a class discourse that culturalizes Asian Americans' class experiences.

The culturalization of class is echoed in the genealogy of Asian American literary production from the late nineteenth through the twentieth centuries. This corpus has been shaped by the political-aesthetic pressures of the ethnographic imperative, which ghettoizes Asian American literature to a genre of cultural ethnography that obfuscates class with culture. The relegation of Asian American authors and texts to literary ghettos perpetuates the obfuscation and naturalization of class inequity that Asian Americans experience in literal ones.

Plantesamfund: Ghettos and Ethnic Enclaves

That racialized subjects in America are often ghettoized is hardly deniable. Asian Americans are no exception, but for this racial group the term "ghetto" has been avoided and left off for "ethnic enclave," making Asian American experiences of racialized class inequity more difficult to see. The preference for "ethnic enclave" over "ghetto" has some positive effects, given the vexed history of the concept of "ghetto" in sociological scholarship and in the American social consciousness. The etymological origins of "ghetto" are unclear, but its earliest usage is said to come from *gietto*, the name of a sixteenth-century Venetian cannon foundry around which Jewish settlement was restricted by law (Wirth 2). The term has come to be used more capaciously, referring generally to spatially confined, urban spaces that are segregated by racial or ethnic difference, whose residents comprise a socially, politically, and, most important, economically disenfranchised underclass. In African American studies, Douglas Massey and Nancy Denton see the late twentieth-century ghetto as a racial phenomenon, produced primarily by racial discrimination in the labor and housing markets. William Julius Wilson sees it as produced by class transformations, by the outmigration of working- and middle-class blacks from the inner city, enabled by civil rights legislation, which left a concentration of the most disadvantaged individuals in the urban core (Massey and Denton 83–114; Wilson 56–62). Despite their differences, these scholars agree that, though contemporary American ghettos are not created by legal dicta, like the Venetian Jewish settlement from which the ghetto concept derives, they are created by social and institutional arrangements. The causes of ghettoization are structural. Ghettoization is not caused by the individuals who are ghettoized, nor is it overcome by their efforts alone.

This conception of the ghetto enables structural critique and helps incite structural reform, but it also strips ghetto dwellers of agency. Ghettoization "happens" to them, suggesting that they are passive victims, shadow people living in the economic and spatial margins of society with little power to do otherwise. This construction engenders two main frames of ghetto research: the examination of how ghetto dwellers are detrimentally isolated from larger society, and the formulation of prescriptions for how they might beneficially integrate themselves into the mainstream. Both framings are versions of the same assumption, that the ghetto is a categorically irredeemable space that lacks productive and meaningful social relations.

Contravening this dim view of the ghetto and its residents is the keystone ghetto research of Robert Park, the leading figure of the 1920s and 1930s Chicago school of sociology. Park's theory of the ghetto has been overhauled by contemporary sociologists, but it is often the reference point from which their revisions proceed, and its broad strokes continue to inform popular understandings of ghettoization. Park's model of the ghetto nuances the pejorative assumptions and connotations described above, but it ultimately reinforces the negative constructions of the ghetto and its residents. Park uses the term "ghetto" interchangeably with "immigrant colony," describing the latter as a segregated space that immigrants, often but not always racialized,[2] naturally and spontaneously form to ease their transition to a new country, for instance, through the comforts of shared language and culture, as well as of proximity to co-ethnics. The ghetto is also a space formed in response to structural, racial-cultural discriminations that immigrants confront, like discriminatory laws and hostile social attitudes. These structural discriminations relegate immigrants to a spatial, social, and economic underclass—to the ghetto—the best, if at times the only, option for immigrants who are barred from work or residence elsewhere. Thus ghettoization is both self-imposed and structurally imposed—it is a way for immigrants in a hostile host country to take control of their lives, a productive survival mechanism vis-à-vis the structural hostility to their race and culture (*On Social Control* 60–61, 114–20). Park's model of ghettoization thereby gives positive value to the ghetto and its residents. The ghetto is structured by meaningful and necessary social relations, especially ethnic-cultural relations, and those relations are possible because ghetto dwellers have positive agency, the resilient ability to create a survivalist space.

However, because it tends to foreground the self-imposed rather than the structurally imposed nature of the ghetto, Park's model ultimately demeans the ghetto and its residents. Ghetto dwellers' survivalist agency is provisionally useful, but ultimately self-defeating. Though the ghetto might be initially meaningful and useful, it is a space that immigrants, or at least the competent among them, must and should ultimately leave: "the keener, the more energetic, and the more ambitious very soon emerge from their ghettos and immigrant colonies. . . . More and more, as the ties of race, of language, and of culture are weakened, successful individuals move out and eventually find their places in business and in the professions, among the older population group which has ceased to be identified with any language or group" (*On Social Control* 60–61).

Here, Park sketches a version of his "race relations cycle," which breaks down urban racial experience to stages of "contact, competition, accommodation, and eventual assimilation" (*Race and Culture* 150). Immigrants' "contact" with a racial-culturally foreign and hostile host country causes their ghettoization, because of discriminatory laws and attitudes, as well as immigrants' efforts to find a haven from this hostility. However, this haven is a space of socioeconomic disenfranchisement, offering only low-wage jobs that fill the basic needs of ghetto co-ethnics, or marginal, socially stigmatized work that serves the larger society. Thus the "keener" and "more energetic" begin to "compete" for better socioeconomic opportunities outside the ghetto. The larger society's recognition of or need for these immigrants' skills carves out a space for them to be "accommodated" and eventually assimilated into the mainstream. This cycle, which Park describes as "progressive and irreversible" and as "tend[ing] everywhere to repeat itself" (*Race and Culture* 150), is a teleology of space, class, and culture. It is a teleology of space and class, from the marginal economy and underclass of the segregated ghetto to "places in business and the professions" outside of it, to better-paying, more respectable jobs with paths for advancement in the larger society. It is also a cultural teleology in that the cultural assimilation to Anglo linguistic and cultural norms of the "older population group which has ceased to be identified with any language or group" accompanies ghetto dwellers' spatialized class mobility ("More and more, as the ties of race, of language, and of culture are weakened, successful individuals move out").

This model of ghettoization is a sanguine one in that it forecasts the eventual end of ghettoization. However, it has been heavily criticized for its pairing of cultural assimilation with class mobility. Park's ghetto model implies a causal link between the two. It postulates that "successful individuals move out" of the ghetto because of their weakening racial, linguistic, and cultural ties with their co-ethnics ("More and more, as . . ."). Immigrants cease to be ghettoized, to be part of a segregated underclass, only as they assimilate, as they cease to be culturally different. This degrades ghetto dwellers' culture. If assimilation is a driving force of, or at least a necessary companion to, class mobility, cultural difference is pathologized as regressive and self-defeating, as that which mires ghetto dwellers in a spatially segregated underclass. The teleology of Park's model of ghettoization, or of extricating oneself from ghettoization, assumes and reproduces a hierarchy of culture and class in which racial-cultural difference is pathologized as having a negative class effect, with the prescription and cure being assimilation to the racial-cultural and linguistic norms of whiteness.

This formulation undermines the agency that Park's ghetto model ostensibly gives to ghettoized immigrants. If immigrants possess the agency to create a survivalist space, that space is a repository of cultural pathology that in the long term will impede their class mobility. It could be argued that Park's model gives ghettoized immigrants another form of agency—the power to escape the space and class entrapments of the ghetto by assimilating themselves out of it. But this only empowers ghettoized immigrants through culturally chauvinistic terms. Assimilation is the cultural, spatial, and class prize; ethnic difference is denigrated. Moreover, not all ghetto dwellers possess this assimilatory agency, only "the keener" and "the more energetic" of them. Park's ghetto model links assimilation to white norms not only to class mobility, but also to superior human ability. Racial-cultural difference, in turn, is linked to incompetence. The ghetto is an irredeemable space after all. Insofar as class mobility is obtained by spatial-cultural assimilation, the ghetto is the symbol and material site of cultural, class, and human failure, the failure of the weakest immigrants, who do not have the competence to assimilate.

If Park's model sounds like a discourse of natural selection, it is. Drawing from Danish scientist Eugenius Warmings's *Plantesamfund* [Plant Communities], Park likens the urban landscape to an ecological system in which "species" compete for resources and survival. Mapping Warmings's ecology of plant communities onto the urban landscape, that is, rendering the urban landscape as a form of natural ecology, Park argues that ghettos are the "natural associations" that immigrant "species" groups form in order to survive (Park and Burgess 175–76). These "natural associations" provide provisional but inferior sustenance, life conditions that are inferior to those available to the stronger "species" of mainstream, white society. In the same way that the strongest plant species secures its survival and thrives over others by taking root in the richest soils and most temperate climates, the strongest of the immigrant species (the "keen" and "energetic") adapts to the characteristics, takes on the soils as it were, of the stronger group in order to thrive. Those remaining in the ghetto languish and die, as befits a weaker species: "[T]he individuals lodged in unfavorable places and the weaklings are vanquished and exterminated" (Park and Burgess 178). The ghetto is not just irredeemable, but is scientifically so, its residents fated to be casualties of the inexorable processes of natural selection.[3]

Given this history of the concept of the ghetto, it is not surprising that contemporary studies would seek alternative models that recuperate the ghetto from being more than a holding pen of weaklings, who are weak because they do not hew to the race and culture of the white mainstream. The pluralist ethos that informs contemporary ethnic studies has shaped some of these alternatives, enabling the ghetto to be reimagined as a space that does not have to be cured by the chauvinistic prescription for spatial and cultural assimilation, but that cultivates positive class and cultural relations within its spatial and ethnic boundaries. This perspective is not absent in the Chicago school. For instance, Louis Wirth, a student of Park's, took his mentor's work in a different direction in *The Ghetto*, a study of Jewish ghettos in Chicago from the late nineteenth century to before World War II. Wirth brings to light the productive relations of nurture, reciprocity, and human capital resources among those who dwell in these ghettos. He argues that meaningful social relations are able to develop because of the ghetto's social and spatial isolation from mainstream society. In other words, Wirth shows how spatial and cultural separation from the Anglo mainstream is not categorically detrimental to immigrant lives.

Jan Lin sees contemporary studies of the ethnic ghetto as heirs to

Wirth's perspective—ethnicity need not be a handicap to be assimilated away, but has positive social effects (8). The pluralist framework of contemporary race studies gives traction to such a perspective, enabling the inversion of Park's estimation of immigrant culture as pathology. Specifically, it repositions culture and ethnicity as an asset to ghetto workers and residents. However, though these contemporary studies share the spirit of Wirth's *The Ghetto*, they insistently turn away from the term "ghetto" to make their point, choosing "ethnic enclave" instead. Studies of Asian American ghettos especially deploy this shift, using "ethnic enclave" to foreground the productive role of ethnicity or culture in ghetto life. Here, ethnicity or culture does not render ghettos as irredeemable, culturally pathological spaces, but rather as vibrant communities to be cultivated and claimed, in which its members have the agency to determine their lives productively.

Early studies of Asian American spatial and economic segregation follow the *Plantesamfund* model of the ghetto and its teleology of assimilation and natural selection, the "survival of the assimilated." Although they continue to use the term "ghetto," they also note some variations that unsettle the *Plantesamfund* model. Rose Hum Lee, Park's student and one of the first sociologists to offer a sustained, systematic study of American Chinatowns, describes Chinatowns in the 1940s as part of "the general problem of 'ghettos,' or segregated communities resulting from immigration into the United States" (422). Yet Lee observes that U.S. Chinatowns do not categorically fit into the teleology of Park's race-relations cycle. If this teleology is "progressive and irreversible" and "tends everywhere to repeat itself," immigrant ghettos would eventually disappear in the United States, as their competent residents assimilated out of them and their weaker members died off. However, Lee observes that while some Chinatowns were indeed disintegrating and their residents assimilating, other Chinatowns were maintaining themselves and even growing. The latter could have been the result of new immigration. Though the Chicago school's teleology of assimilation should ultimately result in the disintegration of ghettos, if immigration rates were constant or increasing, ghettos would be continuously present. Immigrants who have been in the country longer would move out, but newly landed immigrants would repopulate the ghetto. This does not contradict the Chicago school's teleology of ghetto disintegration, but rather captures the teleology from ghettoization to assimilation in different temporal phases for immigrant populations in different phases of assimilation. If ghettos are not observed to be disintegrating to extinction, they are assumed to be disintegrating *toward* extinction, even as their populations are continually refreshed. Yet this was not the case for Chinese immigrants, as the ban on most Chinese immigration that began with the 1882 Chinese Exclusion Act and continued through other laws until the mid-twentieth century resulted in the shrinking of the Chinese American population over those years. In addition, Lee observes that some Chinatowns were growing because they were receiving migrants from the Chinatowns that were disintegrating (430, 427).

Chinatown residents, then, were doing something other than marching progressively and irreversibly toward spatial, cultural, and economic assimilation. Lee notes that this could be the result of structural barriers to assimilation, such as the exclusion of Chinese immigrants from U.S. citizenship. However, echoing the premises of her mentor's ghetto model, she finds more compelling causes of the persisting ghettoization of Chinese Americans in Chinese culture, which she does not quite pathologize, but renders outmoded and unproductive. For instance, Lee suggests that one reason that Chinatowns were not being assimilated out of existence is that Chinese immigrants hew to a racial-cultural preference for endogamy, leading them to remain in the ghetto in search of suitable marriage partners. Lee argues that cultural practices like this will reveal themselves to be outmoded and impractical and will eventually be given up, leading to the expected disintegration of Chinatowns (for instance, second-generation Chinese Americans would become dissatisfied with the limitations on their marriage choices and assimilate spatially and culturally to widen their pool of mates). Reiterating Park's chauvinistic prescription for assimilation, Lee posits this disintegration as socially, economically, and spatially beneficial: "As Chinese-Americans become acculturated and strive for higher status ... their dispersion ... [will make them] an integral part of the American society" (422, 429–30, 432). The teleology toward assimilation is not entirely observed for Chinatown, but is prognosticated and recommended for it. Lee concludes: "All available evidence points to the fact that no new Chinatowns will be created" (432).

Contemporary life shows otherwise. Chinatowns have proliferated and grown across the nation, suggesting that they are not just inferior "species" formations that Chinese Americans would do best to escape before they meet certain and beneficial "extermination." On the contrary, contemporary sociologists argue that there is much to recommend about Chinatown life, which I will generalize for the moment to refer to Asian American ghettos more broadly. This is reflected in Jan Lin's study of Manhattan's Chinatown in the late twentieth century, *Reconstructing Chinatown: Ethnic Enclave, Global Change*. Against the denigration of Chinatown as an undesirable and limiting space destined for extinction, Lin reconstructs Chinatown as a productive community to be preserved and cultivated. Notable here, as reflected in the title of Lin's study, is that the "reconstruction" of the Asian American ghetto as such entails its redefinition as an "ethnic enclave." For Lin, a main reason why Chinatown is not a ghetto but an ethnic enclave is economic. Chinatown's economy is "robust, and the built environment is in constant use or in a process of upgrading; this situation is in contrast to the capital-scarce, deteriorated urban terrain of the 'barrio' or the 'ghetto'" (11). That Chinatown is economically "robust" is certainly the case under globalization, the context of Lin's study, as Chinatown has become a nexus of economic development under the global integration of the U.S. and Pacific Rim economies. But this alone does not disqualify Chinatown from being a ghetto. Its development under globalization is uneven, benefiting some at the cost of others, namely benefiting the class of wealthy Chinese diasporics who have access to transnational mobility, networks, and investments, at the cost of the larger body of common laborers who are often exploited as the cheap labor needed to build Chinatown up into a "robust" and "upgraded" economy. Globalization has made Chinatown a profitable spatial and financial opportunity for a class of privileged Asian transnationals, but the space remains a ghetto for the class of menial laborers. Lin is not unaware of this bifurcation; one of his main goals is to examine the class fractures and uneven rewards wrought by Chinatown's globalization. In fact, it is the response of those who continue to experience Chinatown as a ghetto that brings Lin to the more central element of Chinatown's reconstruction as an ethnic enclave, what can be described as "ethnic agency."

Ethnic agency can be defined as the power of ethnic subjects to determine and contest encroachments upon their economic, political, and social well-being. It is an ethnic form of agency not just because the subjects are ethnic, but also because they gather under the rubric of shared racial-cultural difference to mobilize their efforts. This is a use of ethnicity as a form of politics, but it is not a rehearsal of identity politics that puts forth the claiming of ethnic identity as an end in itself or that reproduces old essentialisms. Rather, it is a strategic use of the emotional investments in ethnicity as a rallying point for political protest, akin to Gayatri Spivak's "strategic essentialism." Ethnicity as such is not something that is already "there," a "status or attachment that [is] biological, primordial, or ancestral," but is a "situational product of evolving intergroup relations in a changing U.S. society" (Lin 10). Ethnicity is a constructed, contextualized, and flexible use of race and culture to respond to situational needs. This use of ethnicity enables subjects like Chinatown residents and workers to reappropriate their racial-cultural difference as a form of social empowerment, into ethnically organized agency. For Lin, ethnicity is a point of strategic, political solidarity that Chinatown residents and workers use to build an ethnic community whose members work together to protest the destructive, local effects of global capitalist development. For instance, Manhattan's Chinatown residents and workers have rallied co-ethnics to protest the razing of affordable housing by developers of high-rent office buildings and luxury condominiums, and against the illegalization of street vending by city ordinances seeking the "beautification" of the Chinatown landscape for visitors and investors (147–70).

Redefining Chinatown as a space of ethnic agency is a direct counterpoint to the *Plantesamfund* ghetto model. Chinatown is not a space of racial-cultural pathology whose inhabitants are stripped of agency and become casualties of natural selection if they do not assimilate. It is reconstructed as a productive, empowered space in which racial-cultural difference is not a liability, but an asset, the source of ethnically organized, social, and political self-determination. Chinatown is not an irredeemable space of an inferior "species" formation that will and should naturally fall away, but a vibrant, ethnically defined community to be claimed, protected, and cultivated. A prognostication like Rose Hum Lee's ("no new Chinatowns will be created"), which is not just a dispassionate observation of social science, but an assimilationist advisement (no new Chinatowns *should* be created), need not determine or recommend the fate of Chinatown and its inhabitants. Chinatowns will persevere and flourish as spaces of productive ethnic community relations like ethnic agency. Chinatown is not a ghetto, at least in the *Plantesamfund* sense, but an ethnic enclave, a term that encodes and highlights the productivity and empowerment of ethnic agency and ethnic community.

Some care needs to be taken in this reconstruction of Chinatown, and Asian Americans ghettos more generally, as ethnic enclaves. Despite the empowerments of ethnic agency, it should not be lost that the development of ethnic agency is a response to ongoing class inequity. It is important to be vigilant about overfocusing on ethnic agency to the extent that the class inequities that it responds to recede from view. For instance, though the inhabitants of Manhattan's Chinatown have staved off gentrification and preserved street vendors' right to work in public space, these gains do not fully address their ghettoization. Chinatown inhabitants are fighting against gentrification because poverty, discriminatory laws, and unwelcoming social attitudes continue to restrict their housing choices; and though street vending is an important means of income with a respected history in Chinatown, it is still a marginal, difficult occupation that returns meager profits. Another pitfall of recasting the ghetto into an ethnic enclave is that ethnic agency and ethnic community can become fetishized so that cultivating ethnicity, even in its situational forms, becomes a misguided and politically defanged end in itself. The focus of the ethnic enclave model on productive ethnic relations, discussed by Lin as referring to ethnic political relations, but also referring more generally to building ethnic communities, risks turning ethnic community into a palliative or symbolic compensation for class inequity. The symbolic value of belonging to an ethnic community, important as it is and often useful in numbing the sting of ghettoization, is ultimately poor compensation for class inequity and risks making class inequity seem less severe or even tolerable. This is not to say that Chinatown inhabitants are blind to the symbolic seductions of ethnic community or to the economic ghettoization that remains even after successful uses of ethnic agency. But it is to say that reconstructing the Asian American ghetto into an ethnic enclave has its pitfalls and can also backfire, diverting attention from the class inequity that persists despite ethnic agency and ethnic community, and even as such class inequity animates such uses of ethnicity in the first place.

I contend, then, that some utility remains in retaining the vocabulary of "ghetto" in describing Chinatown and other racially segregated spaces of Asian American class inequity. I do not suggest a return to the ghetto model espoused by the Chicago school, in which ethnicity is pathologized, residents stripped of nonassimilatory agency, and the productiveness of community relations ignored. Rather, I retain the language of "ghetto" in order to recognize that even in the face of ethnic agency and productive ethnic community, spaces like Chinatown continue to be formed under structurally imposed class inequities, imposed by formal laws and public policies as well as hardened social attitudes.[4] The model and language of "ghetto" that needs to be retained foreground the *structural imposition of class inequity*, the spatial, social, political, and economic discriminations of race and class that, effected in systematic ways through legislation and public policy, and more diffusely but no less tangibly in entrenched social practices, create an Asian

American underclass. This is not to strip ghettoized Asian Americans of agency, ethnic or otherwise, or to deny that meaningful, productive, community relations are cultivated in the ghetto. But it is to foreground, first and foremost, the impositions of structural class inequity that these communities seek to battle. The ethnic enclave model, for all its productive redefinitions of ethnicity, risks diverting attention to these ongoing ghettoizations. Reconstructing spaces like Chinatown into ethnic enclaves in order to recuperate them from being one kind of ghetto (the irredeemable, pathological ethnic spaces of the Chicago school) can, paradoxically, diminish attention to the fact that they remain another kind of ghetto, spaces of imposed, structural class inequity that straiten Asian Americans lives.

An example of this can be found in the "ethnic enclave economy theory." The model of the ethnic enclave that I extracted from Lin's work is consolidated and codified in this theory. Like Lin's work, this theory reconstructs the Chinatown ghetto into an ethnic enclave by conceptualizing it as an ethnic community structured by ethnic agency. As its name indicates, the ethnic enclave economy theory focuses on an economic form of ethnic agency and ethnic community relations. This focus suggests that structural economic and class relations are at the forefront of this ethnic enclave model, that structurally imposed ghettoizations will not recede from view. Indeed, the ethnic economic agency of this theory is put forth as a means to redress structural ghettoization. However, the configuration of economic agency through ethnicity paradoxically diverts attention from as well as naturalizes the Asian American ghettoization that the ethnic enclave economy model seeks to redress.

Developed by Kenneth Wilson and Alejandro Portes in their research on Cuban communities in Miami, and applied to New York's Chinatown by Min Zhou, the ethnic enclave economy theory constructs the ethnic enclave as an affirmative, thriving, economic space comprised of co-ethnic small businesses and labor pools. It is a welcome alternative for racialized immigrants, who are often excluded from the mainstream labor market's primary sector or relegated to its dead-end secondary sector.[5] The ethnic enclave gives immigrants wage advantages over the secondary labor market; returns greater financial rewards on human capital, such as education and labor market experience; and increases access to skills acquisition, which leads to promotions and raises (Wilson and Portes 301–2).

The ethnic enclave economy theory is the source of much contention in sociological scholarship. Of concern is enclave theorists' definition of the enclave as a place of work versus a place or residence, or as a place of both (the economic profile of enclave subjects are positively or negatively skewed depending on which definition is chosen); the lack of differentiation between the advantages the enclave offers to small business owners versus to their employees; and the focus on wages as a measure of upward mobility, when nonmonetary labor market rewards, like health-care and retirement benefits, are less available in the enclave (Sanders and Nee, "Problems"; Sanders and Nee, "Limits"; Gilbertson and Gurak).

These contentions make the "ethnic enclave" unstable as an idea and physical space. I examine them closely, in order to underscore the instability of "ethnic enclave," indeed to argue that such an idea is self-defeating and such a place does not exist (my argument, after all is that the spaces in question are not ethnic enclaves). However, I give this term provisional stability, insofar as I position "ethnic enclave" as a counterpoint to "ghetto." As discussed in the introduction, this opposition stems from the suggestion that spaces described as ethnic enclaves are cultural communities, which suggests voluntary segregation instead of the structurally imposed segregation indicated by "ghetto." This is not to conflate "ethnic enclave" with "cultural community" in every instance, but it is intended to illustrate that such a conflation is produced by the ethnic enclave economy theory's core operational concept—"co-ethnic cooperation." Co-ethnic cooperation refers to trust and goodwill between co-ethnic small-business owners and employees animated by the bonds of shared race and culture. It is what produces the putative enclave-based labor market advantages described above. Co-ethnic cooperation makes spaces like Chinatown not economically and socially blighted ghettos, but positive cultural and economic spaces. It makes them economically advantaged cultural communities—economically advantaged *because* they are cultural communities. Cultural community is thereby constitutive of the concept of the ethnic enclave, at least in the ethnic enclave economy model as well as Lin's political model from which I derive my concept of ethnic enclave. Whether co-ethnic cooperation is operational to the extent that it is claimed to be is at the core of reconfiguring Asian American ghettos into ethnic enclaves and, constitutively, cultural communities.

Co-ethnic cooperation is an economic form of ethnic agency, which is said to benefit both employees and employers. The ethnic enclave economy thrives because co-ethnic employers and employees are said to use their racial-cultural bonds, their sense of connectedness and responsibility to each other because of shared race and culture, to aid each other's economic interests. For instance, Chinatown workers benefit by finding employment easily and readily with Chinese American business owners who, because of co-ethnic trust and goodwill, hire them without résumés or formal references, or generously extend other favors, like allowing children in the workplace so that workers can save money on daycare, or arranging flexible schedules to accommodate shifts at other jobs. Employers, in turn, can count on a stable workforce, on employees who, because of loyalty and gratitude to their compatriot bosses, are less likely to quit or complain. Employers and employees alike get an economic boost; business owners get their ventures more quickly off the ground, and new immigrants and unskilled workers find jobs more readily. Co-ethnic cooperation thereby gives Chinatown employers and employees alike ready and accessible paths to upward mobility. Business owners establish their financial well-being quickly and efficiently with the help of loyal co-ethnic workers. The benefit to workers, according to the theory, is that their employers do not see them as mere laborers, but as kinsman apprentices to whom they impart the skills and training of running a business so that they can one day ascend the class ladder from laborer to small business owner (Zhou 4–5, 137–51).

The ethnic enclave economy model reconstructs Chinatown as not only not a ghetto, but also as a site of economic opportunity that will lift its inhabitants out of economic ghettoization. It subverts the effects of structural ghettoization—structurally imposed, racial-economic segregation is redefined as providing the conditions for economic advancement. Chinatown becomes an alternate site of upward mobility, alternative because upwardly mobility within the confines of the enclave contravenes the Chicago school's premise that ghettoized immigrants need to assimilate spatially and culturally in order to advance economically. Economic opportunity is to be found within Chinatown itself. Cultural assimilation is also not required. On the contrary, retaining one's racial-cultural difference is the means to upward mobility. Zhou describes this as "assimilation without acculturation," assimilation into the middle class in terms of income without the need for or obedience to an imperative of spatial and cultural assimilation (5). The ethnic enclave economy model reverses the Chicago school's claims: ethnicity is not a pathological class liability, nor is ethnic community just a provisional means of survival or an inferior mode of life that will be extinguished by natural selection. Rather, both are literal economic assets that jump-start racialized immigrants' class mobility. Given its economic focus, the enclave economy model seems to address some of the pitfalls of recasting the ghetto into an ethnic enclave. In structuring the enclave through the economic ethnic agency of co-ethnic cooperation, this model appears not to forget about structural ghettoization, but rather puts forth economic ethnic agency as a response and means to redress it. In addition, the benefits of ethnic community appear not to be merely symbolic, but to have the direct economic reward of jump-starting class mobility.

As much as the ethnic enclave economy model gainsays the Chicago school model of ghettoization and seems to focus on, or at least responds to, structural ghettoization, it ultimately allows structural ghettoization in Chinatown to recede from view and even legitimates it. In fact, this model necessitates structural ghettoization in Chinatown even as it claims that Chinatown is not a ghetto, but a space of economic opportunity. This is evident through a closer look at the co-ethnic cooperation that is said to drive enclave economic opportunity. If co-ethnic cooperation reaps economic rewards, these rewards are unevenly distributed, heavily weighted toward Chinatown small business owners.[6] For instance, if employees are less likely to complain or quit because of co-ethnic loyalty, this is indeed a boon to their employers. However, workers are loyal and tractable not just because they share ethnicity with their bosses, but also because they are racially and spatially excluded from the mainstream labor market. This is why they are concentrated in the enclave in the first place, as the enclave economy theory notes. The enclave's ethnic labor force is a captive labor force, giving employers the leverage to depress wages and otherwise exploit their employees. This gives us another perspective on the co-ethnic "favors" that employers extend. Hiring workers without résumés or references might indeed be a favor and advantage for inexperienced co-ethnic workers, but it also enables employers to pay lower wages and cut corners on workplace conditions, health insurance, and the like, given that employees have few better options. Informal schedules might help those working several jobs, but it also enables employers to cut hours or enact seasonal layoffs at whim. Any number of abuses, like unpaid wages or unpaid overtime, can proliferate and promises to make good can be endlessly deferred under "trust me" assurances. Workers might be hesitant to protest these abuses under the perception that they have been given these jobs and so-called accommodations as co-ethnic favors but, at any rate, they must suffer them for lack of better options. Co-ethnic cooperation easily slips into co-ethnic exploitation. Exploitation and labor abuses abound under the banner of co-ethnic trust.

What we see is that Chinatown as an ethnic enclave economy is structured not just by co-ethnic cooperation, but by a co-ethnic class divide, between relatively better-off business owners and their easily exploited laborers.[7] The ethnic enclave economy's model of class mobility necessitates and instantiates this class divide—business owners are poised to advance economically, but they are so because their workers remain ghettoized, structurally excluded from better economic and spatial opportunities, and therefore tolerate co-ethnic exploitation. The ethnic enclave economy theory does not deny that co-ethnic exploitation occurs, but palliates it. Workers may be exploited, but it is "willing self-exploitation," offset by gratitude for having been given employment as a co-ethnic favor (Zhou 12, 118). Here we see ethnicity, for all the attention the enclave economy model gives to the class and economic functions of ethnicity, treading into the territory of being symbolic rather than material compensation for exploited workers. "[W]illing self-exploitation" is also claimed to be rewarding in the long-term. Workers' employment, however exploitative, is said to jump-start their upward mobility, specifically, by giving them training in how to one day become small business owners themselves (Zhou 12, 118). This legitimates co-ethnic exploitation by reconfiguring it as a kind of apprenticeship, an unfortunate but eventually economically advantageous fact of enclave life. Even if all workers cycled through this hierarchy, the ethnic enclave economy model necessitates that a stratum of workers remains ghettoized for this cycle to offer upward mobility. While the ethnic enclave economy theory is centrally concerned with redressing economic ghettoization, it paradoxically justifies a degree of it, making the ghettoization of some Chinatown workers, now perpetuated by co-ethnics, a structural necessity to propel the upward mobility of others. The attention to structural ghettoization that animates the enclave economy model is attenuated as ethnicity, in the form of co-ethnic cooperation, becomes an alibi for the ongoing ghettoization of a class of Chinatown workers.

Recasting the Asian American ghetto into an ethnic enclave has its drawbacks. Though this recasting can empower ghetto dwellers and gives productive value to ethnic communities, ghettoization persists. Ghettoization is also legitimated, as seen in the ethnic enclave economy model. Though this recasting is a useful corrective to ghetto models that do not give credit to productive uses of ethnicity and ethnic community, it is premature and obfuscating to take leave of the vocabulary of "ghetto," insofar as this vocabulary refers to the imposed, structural ghettoization that remains in ethnic communities, and might in fact be required and perpetuated in order for some community members to advance socioeconomically. Understanding spaces like Chinatown as ghettos is still necessary, inasmuch as attention still needs to be paid to the ghettoization that remains in these spaces despite—and sometimes because—of the productive uses of ethnicity that lead them to be recast as ethnic enclaves.

It is of course possible to see racially segregated spaces of Asian American class inequity as some combination of an ethnic enclave and ghetto, to recognize Asian Americans' productive uses of ethnicity as well as their ongoing structural ghettoization. However, I suggest a more insistent move toward the vocabulary of ghetto not only because of the pitfalls of the ethnic enclave model discussed above, but also to counter a broader problem that the ethnic enclave model can feed—the culturalization of class. The culturalization of class suggests that Asian Americans do not experience structural class inequity, either because they are said to be culturally immune to it or because class inequity is denied as being structural, naturalized instead as an expression of Asian culture. The following section examines how the recasting of the ghetto into an ethnic enclave feeds the culturalization of class. I will continue to focus on the ethnic enclave economy model as it overtly puts culture and ethnicity in relation to economic relations and class. Culture or ethnicity becomes, from my standpoint, a vehicle of epistemological damage with empirical effects, of denying or naturalizing Asian American ghettoization, in contrast to the ethnic enclave model's use of culture as a form of ethnic agency, and in contrast to the similar use of culture in the broader, pluralistic American and ethnic studies discourse from which the idea of ethnic agency emerges. I begin with an account of a few concepts of culture and how its use as a form of ethnic agency paradoxically undermines the empowerment that it seeks to engender.

Culture as Politics, Culture as Class

The reconstruction of the ghetto into an ethnic enclave relies on a pluralist and democratized idea of "culture." It also relies on a political form of culture that means to empower Asian Americans against social inequity. Of concern here is their empowerment against class inequity. But the ethnic enclave model's use of culture, as politics and ethnic agency, paradoxically obscures and legitimates Asian Americans' experiences of structural ghettoization. We can see this by tracing the construction of ethnic agency vis-à-vis various definitions of culture. First, there is the anthropological conception of culture, in which "culture" refers to the everyday social practices and behaviors of a distinguishable group, demarcated for instance by nation, geography, or, as is relevant here, by racial difference. Culture as such means to describe without judgment various "ways of life," in Raymond Williams's phrase, to describe social existence as a collection of cultural pluralities, without the suggestion that any culture is inferior or superior to another (*Keywords* 90). However, this understanding of culture is not entirely value-neutral, because it is intertwined with other senses of the term. Williams notes that culture as a way of life is intertwined with the use of culture to refer to "imaginative and intellectual" activity, in which culture refers to a body of art, philosophical knowledge, or other forms of expression that convey human experience beyond mere sensory reflexes. Culture in this sense is encoded with and encodes a hierarchy. Imaginative and intellectual activity connotes imaginative and intellectual *capability*, the ability of a society to produce what is deemed good, important, sophisticated, and superior, for instance, in the aesthetic domain of literature or visual art. This leads to societies being described as cultur*ed* and, of course, uncultured (*The Sociology* 298). The sense of culture as a way of life intersects with its sense as, say, aesthetic production, to continue this example, in that the former is often judged by the latter. Different cultures, different ways of life, produce different forms of art, and those ways of life are judged along the hierarchy encoded in the latter: cultures as ways of life are deemed sophisticated and refined, or not, by virtue of their sophisticated or unsophisticated aesthetic cultures. Culture, as a way of life, is not a neutral description of pluralities, but carries a hierarchy. If culture as imaginative and intellectual activity shows that humans live beyond sensory reflexes, that they are more than primates, its intertwining with culture as a way of life shows that this term can suggest that some ways of life are more primitive.

In our pluralist milieu, in which a main goal is to value all ways of life equally and to recuperate the cultures of racial groups that have been denigrated by Eurocentric measures of worth, a means to flatten the hierarchal assessment of cultures (as ways of life) is the use of culture as a form of politics and oppositional discourse, to use the very thing that has been denigrated to contest its denigration. The use of culture as politics means to democratize the field of culture as a way of life. One way that it does so is by democratizing the field of culture as aesthetic production that informs how culture as a way of life is evaluated. This is one of the central premises of American and ethnic studies, to recover or call attention to aesthetic productions of racial groups that have been marginalized by white, Anglocentric artistic canons, to showcase the inherent aesthetic value and innovation of these works, as well as to contest the Anglocentric aesthetic criteria that marginalize them. In Asian American studies, this is most evident in the pronouncements of the editors of *Aiiieeeee!*, one of the first anthologies of Asian American literature, originally published in 1973. Gathering unknown, or at least unread, Asian American texts, the editors assail the "pushers of white American [aesthetic] culture," the Anglocentric gatekeepers of the American literary canon, whether they be publishers, readers, or even Asian American writers themselves who neglect or dismiss what the editors define as a unique and valuable Asian American aesthetic. This aesthetic centers around what the editors describe as Asian American "sensibility," defined as a keen knowledge of Asian American history, especially of the racial injustices that structure Asian experiences in America, and the desire to express and contest those injustices through literary expression (Chan et al. xii, xiii). The *Aiiieeeee!* editors put forth Asian American literature as structured by an aesthetics of contestation that contest the politics of American literary canon formation and its sanctification of aesthetic value. Indeed, the editors call out that canon formation is a political project in which Anglocentric gatekeepers have had the strongest lobby. Asian American literary aesthetics are a form of politics, an intervention into the politics of aesthetic sanctification that seeks to democratize the terrain of aesthetic culture by demanding that Asian American literature be given its due.

Demanding that due value be given to Asian American aesthetic culture is a way to demand the same for Asian American culture as a way of life. This is evident in that the *Aiiieeeee!* editors' vision of an Asian American aesthetic is keyed to Asian American history, the places of Asian-raced people in the polity, both as targets of racism and as contributors to American society with their unique and valuable ways of life. The recognition demanded for Asian American ways of life is not a demand for greater recognition of Asian cultural practices and customs per se. As the editors note, Asian cultural practices are hardly unrecognized by American society, but are overrecognized through primitivizing Orientalist stereotypes. Rather, the Asian American culture that the *Aiiieeeee!* editors champion is a culture born of the dialectic between anti-Asian racism (which derives from Anglocentric hierarchies of racial-cultural worth and is expressed, for instance, in the caricaturing of Asian Americans as primitive Orientals) and Asian Americans' challenges to it. If Asian American literature is a form of politics, an aesthetics of political protest, Asian American culture, as a way of life, is also a form of politics, an ethics of sociopolitical protest that is embodied in the battle cry "Aiiieeeee!" (xxxii, xxii). This form of Asian American culture is constitutively structured to democratize the terrain of culture as a way of life. Structured as a culture of political protest, Asian American culture can, for instance, protest the Orientalist primitivization of Asian American ways of life and recuperate its proper value. As a culture of political protest against racism and its underwriting cultural hierarchies, it embodies the democratizing drive of pluralism's aim to flatten Anglocentric hierarchies of cultural worth.

The construction of Asian American culture (as a way of life) as a form of politics puts forth Asian American culture as a form of ethnic agency that, as in the ethnic enclave model, is a situationally produced form of culture that empowers racialized subjects. Asian American aesthetics are likewise a form of ethnic agency, in that they are constructed as Asian Americans' intervention into the politics of aesthetic sanctification. Though many aspects of the *Aiiieeeee!* editors' claims have been highly criticized, their view of culture as a form of ethnic agency has a firm hold in Asian Americanist scholarship. This is evident in the influential work of Lisa Lowe, which emphasizes the use of culture to protest economic injustice. Noting that American government cannot be relied upon to redress economic injustice because it is the very source of it, having historically prioritized capitalist development and the wealth stratification necessary to maximize capitalist profit, Lowe writes: "it is only through culture that we conceive and enact new subjects and practices in antagonism." Lowe refers here to culture both as a way of life and as aesthetic production. Asian Americans' experiences of economic justice give rise to social practices that contest economic injustice, with Asian American aesthetic production being one form of those social practices (22, 44). Asian American culture is the product of the confrontation between experiences of economic injustice wrought by capitalism's routine of exploiting racialized subjects, and aesthetic projects that seek to define and claim ways of life that contest those injustices (Lowe and Lloyd 1–2). Culture is posited as a form of economic ethnic agency, a vehicle of economic redress that is assigned the power not only to level the cultural terrain in order to fulfill the pluralist ideal of making all cultures equally valuable, but also to level the economic terrain by empowering racialized subjects with a contestatory culture through which they can advocate for economic and class parity.

The recasting of the ghetto into an ethnic enclave relies on a like-minded use of culture as politics and economic ethnic agency, as we saw in the ethnic enclave economy theory. The problem with using culture in this way is that, though it seeks to prevent the swallowing up of racialized lives by economic and class injustice, it can backfire by enabling the swallowing up of questions of economic and class injustice into questions of culture. Constructing culture as ethnic economic agency, that is, as an intervention in the field of economics and class, risks deflecting the problems of economics and class onto the terrain of culture. This deflection can suggest that culture is a driving force behind economic relations and class, diverting attention from the structural factors behind, as is of concern here, Asian American ghettoization. We already saw a version of this in the *Plantesamfund* model of immigrant communities, in its claim that the driving force behind immigrants' ghettoization is their pathological culture. Culture as the cause of ghettoization is not the primary issue at hand, as the recasting of the ghetto into an ethnic enclave seeks to reverse this valuation of immigrant culture from an economic liability to an economic asset. However, the use of culture as a positive economic resource in the ethnic enclave model, and in the ethnic enclave economy model in particular, posits culture as the *solution* to ghettoization, as if culture is responsible, if not for causing ghettoization, then for remediating it. This feeds an epistemology by which economic and class problems are privatized, as George Yudice notes, cast onto the private cultural terrain of, especially, racialized groups (7). States, corporations, and other institutions that shape economic structures and relations become less visible, and less responsible, for both causing and redressing structural economic inequity.

That culture as ethnic economic agency can privatize economic injustice is evident in the kinds of institutions that have enthusiastically embraced this use of culture. Yudice calls our attention to a 1999 convention held in Florence, Italy, entitled "Culture Counts: Financing, Resources, and the Economics of Culture in Sustainable Development." On the eve of the millennium, international development banks gathered to craft strategies that would draw upon culture to boost economic development in the Third World. The keynote address was given by James Wolfensohn, then president of the World Bank, who urged a "'holistic view of development' that focuses on community empowerment of the poor so that they may hold onto—sustain—those assets [culture] that enable them to cope with 'trauma and loss,' stave off 'social disconnectedness,' 'maintain self-esteem,' and also provide material resources" (Yudice 13;

Wolfensohn qtd. in Yudice 13). Culture is both salve and solution to economic distress. It is to soothe the Third World poor by helping to "cope
with 'trauma and loss'" and "maintain self-esteem," implicitly against
the deracination of their social structures under imperatives of capitalist
development. As the solution to economic distress, culture is to provide
"material resources" for, or more precisely, resources *from,* the poor under the World Bank's suggested "holistic view of development," which
includes culture in its portfolio. Wolfensohn elaborates: "There are de-
velopmental dimensions of culture. Physical and expressive culture is
an undervalued resource in developing countries. It can earn income,
through tourism, crafts and other cultural enterprises. . . . Heritage gives
value. Part of our joint challenge is to analyze the local and national
returns on investments which restore and draw value from cultural heritage" (qtd. in Yudice 13).

Culture is to be a tool of economic development. As both aesthetic
expression and a way of life, it "can earn income," for instance, through
the selling of tourism crafts that reflect local Third World groups' aesthetic sensibilities and underlying social sensibilities. Culture as a tool
of economic development is a form of economic ethnic agency. It enables racialized Third World cultures to improve their economic situations through the value of their culture or ethnicity. Culture has double
value here; this is why it is also an "investment." It "restore[s]" the human
value and dignity of local cultural groups and their nations who find
their culture deracinated by capitalist development, but it also "draw[s]
value," that is, tangible economic returns. Investment in culture brings
tangible economic returns not only for local cultural groups, as seen in
the tourism crafts example, but also for the World Bank and its peer
institutions, which can better ply their development programs to Third
World nations given that these programs are now attuned to respecting
the preservation of native cultures. This appears to be a win-win situation: as global development institutions seek to bring Third World nations up to capitalist speed, this need not have a destructive effect on
local cultures, but on the contrary can help them preserve their ways of
life and aesthetic forms. In turn, cultural groups need not be adversaries of capitalist development, but can use their unique ways of life and
aesthetic products to profit from it.

"Culture counts"—the pun of this phrase is telling. It appeals to a
humanistic respect of all cultures' inherent social value, but only inasmuch as this respect extracts a literal, economic accounting from culture. Though this might bestow economic agency to cultural groups,

that agency depends on forms of cultural exploitation, for instance, on the commodification of culture. More precisely, this use of culture turns culture into an economic *resource*—this is Yudice's main point: culture becomes something to be mined and invested in as a tool for local and global economic development (1). This confronts us with an epistemological problem. Culture as an economic resource is the "lynchpin of a new epistemic framework in which . . . economic or ecological rationality . . . [depends on the] management, conversation, access, distribution, and investment . . . in 'culture' and the outcomes thereof" (Yudice 1). Culture as economic agency, or its use as an economic agent, reflects an attitude in which culture is the foot solider of economic development, as seen in the World Bank's "holistic view of development."

If culture is the foot soldier of economic development, this suggests that structural problems of political economy can and should be resolved in the private sphere of culture. A UNESCO representative complains (somewhat ironically and perhaps existentially, given UNESCO's mission), "culture is invoked to solve problems that previously were the province of economics and politics" (Yudice 7). This understanding and use of culture relieves states, corporations, and development institutions from having to think through more equitable forms of capitalist development, which would not deracinate local cultures in the first place and require the cultural preservation remedies that these institutions now heroically suggest, or which would not merely preserve culture by fashioning it to serve capitalist rationality. Moreover, this turn to culture as an economic development resource legitimates a pluralist, neoliberal ideology. If culture is a resource for economic development, those who suffer under capitalist development can now be expected to develop their own cultural solutions, to be tested in and resolved by the free market. Economic justice becomes privatized, dissociated from the systemic injustices of global capitalism and deflected onto the private terrain of culture (Yudice 1).

In the American race and class landscape, the privatization of economic justice finds its expression in the recasting of the Asian American ghetto into an ethnic enclave. We recall that this recasting hinges upon the use of culture as form of politics, as ethnic agency, and in the ethnic enclave economy model, as a form of economic ethnic agency. However, by positing culture as a form of economic ethnic agency, the ethnic enclave economy model also turns culture into an economic resource and thereby privatizes economic justice. Vis-à-vis co-ethnic cooperation, Chinatown workers and business owners' shared culture is posited as the

economic resource that will lift them out of ghettoization. Culture becomes the solution to Asian American ghettoization, much as it is to be a
solution, according to development institutions like the World Bank, to
the impoverishment of the Third World poor. The ethnic enclave economy model thereby participates in and perpetuates the "epistemic framework" that deploys culture as a tool of "economic rationality," privatizing
economic inequity, as if the solution to Asian Americans' ghettoization
is to be found in the private sphere of their cultural behaviors.

A more specific way to describe the ethnic enclave model's privatization of ghettoization is to say that its use of culture as an economic resource culturalizes class. The culturalization of class, which I defined as
the reconfiguration of the structurally produced inequities of class into
internally produced expressions of culture, privatizes class, positing culture as the driving force behind racialized subjects' class situations. Class
is being culturalized in the Chicago school's claim that immigrants'
pathological culture is the cause of their ghettoization. Class is also culturalized in the ethnic enclave economy model in its claim that culture
is the solution to Asian Americans' ghettoization; now, upward mobility
instead of ghettoization is constructed as being caused by culture. The
ethnic enclave economy model ironically shares the premise and problem of the Chicago school model that it seeks to gainsay. By positioning
culture as an economic resource that improves rather than damages immigrants' class possibilities, the ethnic enclave economy model merely
inverts the Chicago school's estimation of immigrant culture while
maintaining the attribution of class to culture. Whether as pathology or
virtue, whether to be assimilated away or to be pluralistically harvested,
culture is positioned as determining class—class is turned into culture.

The culturalization of class is not limited to Asian Americans. For
instance, Park's ghetto model is meant to apply universally to ethnic immigrants. African American ghettoization is also culturalized, notably
through the neoconservative rhetoric of the "culture of poverty." However, what is unique about Asian Americans' class culturalizations is that
they obscure Asian American ghettoization, by either denying that it is
structurally imposed or by denying that it exists at all. This is not the
same effect that class culturalizations have for other racial groups. For
instance, the "culture of poverty" rhetoric denies that African American
ghettoization is structurally imposed, but it does not obscure the fact of
black ghettoization. Rather, this culturalization makes black ghettoization hypervisible. The rhetoric of the "culture of poverty" deflects the
problem of African American ghettoization onto the terrain of black

culture, attributing blacks' poverty to a pathological culture of vice, laziness, and lack of family values, but does not let that poverty recede from view. On the contrary, it has drawn much attention to African American class inequity, to the extent that African Americans are axiomatically taken as experiencing high rates of ghettoization, even if that ghettoization is denied as structural. At times, a similar dynamic is at work for Asian Americans, for instance, when the ghetto conditions of Chinatown are recognized, but are attributed to a "Chinese mode of living." However, it is also the case that the culturalization of Asian American class experiences has the opposite effect, of claiming that Asian American ghettoization does not exist at all. This is most evident in the model minority myth, which claims that Asian cultural values of hard work, self-sacrifice, commitment to education, and so forth, make Asian Americans a racial group that does not experience, or is even culturally immune to, poverty and ghettoization. The culturalization of black poverty does not deny black ghettoization, indeed, it is an exercised explanation for it, but for Asian Americans, the culturalization of class is weighted in the opposite direction, of making them the prototype of a racial group for whom class inequity does not exist.

One reason for the opposite effects of class culturalizations for African Americans versus Asian Americans is a difference in the assessment of culture. The former's culture is said to be pathological, while the latter's is said to be richly productive. We might also say that African American class culturalizations are not actually culturalizations, but a presumption that African Americans are evacuated of culture. The claim that African Americans are steeped in a "culture of poverty" is a claim that their culture is impoverished, that they have no culture, or at least no productive culture that can obviate ghettoization. In contrast, Asian Americans as model minorities are seen as having a superlatively productive culture in relation to class. This cultural overdetermination, lending itself to the denial of Asian American ghettoization, turns Asian Americans into the object lesson through which the national myths of classlessness and color-blind meritocracy are vindicated. However, there are times when national ideologies find it necessary to recognize Asian American ghettoization. In this case, Asian Americans' class culturalizations are akin to those of African Americans. They call attention to ghettoization in order to deny that it is structural. Asian Americans' class culturalizations work along these two strains. They recognize ghettoization, but deny that it is structural; as well as deny that ghettoization exists at all.

Unique to Asian Americans or not, these culturalizations are keen and pronounced for them. They are keen and pronounced because culturalizations more generally have heavily imprinted the understanding of Asian American experience and subjectivity. For example, the discourse of Orientalism stubbornly dominates the ways that Asian Americans are fathomed. As has been well discussed, Orientalism culturalizes. It uses Asian culture, in primitive and reductive forms, as a Rosetta stone to decode and determine Asian American experiences, turning external, social dynamics into internal expressions of cultural ontology and proclivity. As a result, Asian Americans as a racial group have been primarily understood as a culturalized group. Returning to Stuart Hall's vocabulary that I invoked in the introduction, we can say that culture is the modality of race through which Asian American subjectivity and experience are articulated.

At the core of America's brand of Orientalism is a culturalizing class discourse. American Orientalism shares the basic principles of Edward Said's original concept. It consolidates the primitivization of Asian cultures into a "style of thought" that engenders and legitimates practices in law and custom that racially manages and disciplines Asian subjects. Asians have been managed and disciplined in this way so that they could be used as objects against and through which Western nations have materially and symbolically funded their social, political, and economic power (2). Colleen Lye discusses how Orientalism in America served this purpose as the United States sought over the twentieth century to become a modern, that is, rationally capitalist nation. However, Lye points out that an important difference in American Orientalism is that it "signifie[s] an exceptional, rather than paradigmatic, Other." While Said's Orientalism assisted European colonial ambitions by homogenizing colonialized subjects into essentialist embodiments of social, political, and economic pathology, American Orientalism aided and aids U.S. capitalist development with an essentialism that *distinguishes* Asian Americans from the white mainstream polity as well as from other racial groups.

Lye notes that this is a bifurcated distinction that constructs Asian Americans along two prominent nodes; the "yellow peril" labor coolie of the late nineteenth and early twentieth centuries, and the modern-day model minority. Gary Okihiro has previously noted this bifurcation, arguing that rather than being antipodes, the yellow peril and model minority are two sides of the same coin. Okihiro notes that the flip side of "diligent" is "slavish," of "assimilation" is "mongrelization," and of "integration" is "infiltration": "the model minority blunts the threat of the yellow peril, but the former, if taken too far, becomes the yellow peril" (142, xiii).[8] For Lye, what the yellow peril and model minority share is that both, through their contrasting Orientalist depictions, have materially and symbolically aided the nation in its march toward capitalist modernity. Asian Americans as the yellow peril are more typically Orientalized, essentialized as racial-cultural primitives, as a teeming swarm of crude, inassimilable, foreign workhorses with a primitive racial-cultural proclivity for mindless drudge and toil. Yet this racial-cultural primitivism paradoxically made the yellow peril an instrumental labor force for America's development into a modern capitalist nation across the turn into the twentieth century.[9] In contrast, the model minority position renders Asian Americans as *modern* Orientals. Asian Americans as model minorities are also essentialized as having a racial-cultural capacity for hard work, but in a way that dovetails with modern capitalist values of economic rationality (Lye 2–3). For instance, Asian Americans as model minorities are constructed as culturally embodying free-market rationality. As we know, the model minority thesis, first articulated during the civil rights movement, is as an attack against African Americans who, as stated in a 1966 *U.S. News & World Report* piece, were causing the nation to be "awash in worry over the plight of racial minorities." Asian Americans, in contrast, win "wealth . . . [by] depend[ing] on their own efforts—not a welfare check," that is, by depending on their cultural values of hard work and self-reliance (Peterson 73). Rather than lobby for a welfare check, thereby appealing to and expecting government to be the engine of an economically irrational welfare state, Asian Americans bootstrap their way to upward mobility and middle-class integration by plying their "own efforts" in the free market.[10]

Lye's insight is to call attention to the ambivalence of American Orientalism, the simultaneous disgust and love for Asian Americans in the material and ideological march toward capitalist modernity. This Orientalist scheme also makes visible that at the heart of American Orientalism is a culturalizing class scheme. Both the yellow peril and model minority are Orientalist essentializations that construct Asian American ontologies as determined by reductive notions of Asian culture. These essentialist reductions notably create two class nodes, the yellow peril, coolie underclass on the one hand, and the middle class or upwardly mobile, model minority on the other. These are culturalized class nodes: it is the yellow peril's primitive cultural ontology that naturally limits Asian Americans as such to a coolie underclass of mindless, grunting laborers; likewise, it is the model minority's modernized, Oriental cultural ontology that naturally makes Asian Americans upwardly mobile or economically middle class.

Insofar as culturalization has been a dominant epistemology through which Asian American subjectivity and experience have been understood, as exemplified by Orientalism, and insofar as there is a culturalizing class scheme at the core of American Orientalism, the culturalization of class is a central way that Asian Americans have been apprehended in the national imagination. Instrumental to the nation's material and symbolic efforts to become a modern capitalist state, these class culturalizations feed a corollary logic of economic rationality—of privatization—here, the privatization of class inequity, both in terms of causes and solutions. Class inequity ceases to be structural; it is denied or naturalized, but in both cases it becomes a matter of the private sphere of culture, as well as of the privatization ethos of capitalist rationality (that government is not to intrude in the market). Asian Americans are made to be either part of a yellow peril underclass that naturally ghettoizes itself, or they are model minorities who show that government is not necessary to create economic parity because their cultural virtues of self-reliance and hard work have proved to be amply rewarded in the free market. If culture is the modality of race through which Asian American subjectivity and experiences are articulated, it is also the modality through which the structural dimensions of Asian American class experiences are privatized.

A concluding note on the ethnic enclave economy model: as mentioned, the recasting of the ghetto into an ethnic enclave rehearses and reinforces a privatizing epistemology that culturalizes class by constructing culture as an economic resource that will remediate Asian American ghettoization. In addition, this model rehearses and enriches the particular culturalizations of Orientalism, namely by echoing American Orientalism's class scheme in which Asian Americans are naturalized as either a laboring underclass or an upwardly mobile, model minority class. This is evident in the ethnic enclave economy's basic class structure, of small business owners and their co-ethnic employees. The small business owners function as a model minority class in that they productively draw upon Asian culture to become upwardly mobile (co-ethnic bonds). However, enclave business owners' use of Asian culture as a class resource is a bit different than is typically described by the model minority myth. Asian culture propels their upward mobility not because it equips them with ethics of hard work and so forth (though this is implied), but by establishing relationships of co-ethnic cooperation with their employ- ees. Business owners use Asian culture to extract the hard work, not to mention the exploitation, of others. As discussed, the upward mobility of the enclave economy's business owners/model minorities thereby struc- turally relies upon the existence of a class of menial co-ethnic laborers who purportedly willingly "self-exploit" in exchange for the co-ethnic "favors" extended to them by their employers. These laborers, then, func- tion as the ethnic enclave's necessary coolie underclass. Their underclass position is not attributed to cultural primitivism as in American Orien- talism's scheme, but they are nonetheless claimed to suffer this position because of the inclinations of their culture, here because of their cultural inclination to be loyal to their co-ethnic bosses. As in American Orien- talism's estimation of yellow peril coolies, Asian American ghettoization becomes part of a natural, racial-cultural order. It should also be noted that while American Orientalism's class scheme spans a historical pe- riod from the late nineteenth century through the present day, in which the coolie underclass construction emerges first and is then transformed into the model minority in order to suit a change in national ideological and material needs, the ethnic enclave economy model enables, indeed requires, these class positions to coexist in time and space. The ethnic enclave economy model is a more efficient vehicle of American Orien- talism. It collapses time and space to revive a historical form of class culturalization and to place it alongside a more modern one.

Ghetto and Genre

The recasting of the ghetto into an ethnic enclave is a form of author- ship. It seeks to enable Asian Americans to write themselves into the polity, to draw upon their ethnicity as a form of agency that empowers them to determine their social places and demand visibility. Less figura- tive Asian American writers also seek self-determined and empowered social legibility; doing so has been a central project of Asian American literature. It could be argued that much of Asian American literature confronts the question of class, if only in a broad, implicit sense of con- fronting social hierarchies that demean Asian American lives. Other texts more directly engage themes of class, of socioeconomic stratifica- tion and lives restricted to the Asian American ghetto. In any case, Asian American writers confront a literary body that has already spoken for and about them, that has consolidated their subjectivity and experience into a few reductive stock images. For instance, in popular American literature, the Asian American ghetto has been reduced to cultural spectacle, to a space of dense, mysterious, and consumable culture, emblematized by the touristic imagination of Chinatown as an ethnic amusement park. This line of representation culturalizes the Asian American ghetto, unmooring it from the structural pressures of race and class that condition its formation. In other words, the Asian American ghetto has been recast into an ethnic enclave in the literary realm too, filtered through a privatizing epistemology that culturalizes class and thereby obscures and naturalizes Asian American ghettoization. Market pressures and available social vocabularies have encouraged Asian American writers to take up this privatizing, culturalizing epistemology themselves. In the literary realm, the adoption of this epistemology is compelled by what I describe as the "ethnographic imperative," implicit and explicit pressures on Asian American writers and texts to hew to a genre that hyperculturalizes Asian American life, particularly its class dimensions. The ethnographic imperative has had a shaping influence on Asian American literary production. Its history is a genealogy of how Asian American class inequity has been represented in Asian American literature, how Asian American textual bodies make visible and invisible the structural ghettoization of their social bodies.

Asian American ghettos are not absent in American literature and other aesthetic forms. It might even seem as if they are hypervisible. For instance, there is an abundance of popular film and fiction that uses Chinatown as its backdrop, such as Roman Polanski's *Chinatown* and John Carpenter's *Big Trouble in Little China* to name a couple, as well as a wealth of gritty crime fiction in which Chinatown is a staple landscape. These works comprise a genre that can be described as "Chinatown Confidential," in that they purport to lift the veil over a seedy underworld of racial mystery and intrigue. The set pieces of this genre are familiar; Chinatown is represented as a brooding warren of poverty, vice, gangs, tenements, and sweatshops. Chinatown as such most certainly looks like a ghetto.

These stock images of Chinatown as a ghetto, however, do not depict it as a structurally created class landscape. They might rely on typical symbols of ghettoization, but Chinatown is ultimately put forth as a sensationalized space of cultural pathology. This is evident in Michael Cimino and Oliver Stone's film *The Year of the Dragon*, which stars Mickey Rourke as a New York City police detective, Stanley White, who is assigned to the Chinatown beat. White fashions himself as the maverick who will heroically reign in the Chinatown netherworld, where his predecessors have failed, especially after the recent murder of a high-profile tong leader. White learns that the police department cannot control Chinatown because they are unwilling to try. The police department has given up on Chinatown, partly because it has a "gentleman's agreement" with a powerful tong to leave the governance of Chinatown to the tong, but also because it claims that Chinatown's crime, poverty, and other ghetto conditions result from "one thousand years" of Chinese culture that a twentieth-century American police department is powerless to rehabilitate. White is incensed by his colleagues' policy of benign neglect and bursts into a meeting shouting: "[I'm] tired of all the Chinese this, Chinese that. . . . All this thousand-year-old stuff is shit to me. This is America and it's two hundred years old so you better get your clocks fixed."

Here, Chinatown is depicted as a ghetto, but only insofar as it is a collection of stock images of crime and lawlessness. We also see White squirming, psychologically and physically, at and through tableaux of tenements, sweatshops, and gambling dens in the course of his quest to reform Chinatown. But this depiction does not represent Chinatown as a structurally created ghetto. Absent from the picture is an account of the structural discriminations of race, space, and class that have created these ghetto conditions. Instead, the problem of Chinatown as a ghetto is presented as a problem of culture, the "thousand-year-old stuff." Chinese culture ostensibly creates Chinatown as a racially segregated space of vice and poverty. The Year of the Dragon represents Chinatown as a Chicago school–type ghetto, an irredeemable space of racial-cultural difference in which that difference is the pathology that produces ghettoization. It cannot be fixed by an American police department with little power over or entry into this ancient, degenerate culture. White disagrees, but his contention is actually consonant with his colleagues' logic. Though he believes that Chinatown's ghetto conditions can be reformed, his solution is to discard the "Chinese this, Chinese that" and to get the police department's "clocks fixed," that is, to make the department see Chinatown as part of America modernity. This solution implies that Chinatown needs to fix its clocks too. Chinatown needs to be brought up to speed to American ways of life ("This is America"), to take leave of their pathological culture and assimilate into the law-abiding ways of modern American life. White is a kind of Chicago school sociologist. He prescribes assimilation as the means to relieve Chinatown residents of the ills of ghetto life. Though White seems to be at odds with his colleagues, he actually shares their attribution of Chinatown's fate to culture. While his colleagues claim that Chinatown cannot be fixed because of culture (Chinese culture), White prescribes that it will in fact be fixed through culture, by American culture, by assimilation, showing that he agrees that Chinatown's ghetto conditions are created by Chinese Americans' pathological racial-cultural difference.

The maverick and his naysayers share a culturalizing logic. Whether they think Chinatown is an irredeemable ghetto or can be assimilated out of being one, ghettoization is represented as having little to do with structural discriminations, understood instead as driven by culture, in terms of both causes and solutions. These culturalizations turn the Chinatown in *The Year of the Dragon* into a kind of ethnic enclave. Proponents of the ethnic enclave model would certainly disagree, given that this Chinatown is hardly represented as a space of ethnic agency, but as one that needs to be "saved" by a police officer, tellingly named "White." But it wends toward the ethnic enclave model in that it is screened through an epistemology that culturalizes class and obscures structural ghettoization. Poverty and vice are privatized, attributed to and made a problem of Chinese culture.[11]

Notably, White's entry into Chinatown is textual—he prepares for his mission by reading a book called *Things Chinese*. This book is an apt choice as it models a literary version of the privatizing, culturalizing epistemology through which White and his colleagues understand the Chinatown ghetto. *Things Chinese*, by Rita Aero, is a compendium of Chinese "things," as it were, textually collected to serve as a primer on Chinese culture. It is an ethnography, an explication of Chinese ways of life for a non-Chinese audience to examine and behold. This type of ethnography is not innocent but, as has been well discussed, derives from and reinforces an imbalance of racial-cultural power, in this case, between white subjects, emblematized by "White," who seek knowledge of a racial-cultural other; and Chinese objects, who are written up as passive vessels and embodiments of the racial-cultural difference being gazed at and probed. Such ethnographies indeed become compendia of "things," of entertaining cultural curiosities offered up for consumption, for the pleasure of touring a world of racial-cultural difference. For Asian Americans, this kind of ethnography reduces them and their culture to Orientalist exotica and spaces like Chinatown to ethnic amusement parks (incidentally, the author of *Things Chinese* also wrote a guidebook to Walt Disney World). Frank Chin describes this ethnographic genre's conventions: "the same cunning 'Confucius says' joke . . . memories of Mother in the kitchen slicing meat paper thin with a cleaver. Mumbo jumbo about spices and steaming. The secret of Chinatown rice" (3).

By caricaturing Asian American life as Orientalist "mumbo jumbo," this ethnographic genre obscures and culturalizes Asian American experiences of class inequity. If this genre reveals the "secret of Chinatown rice," what it does not disclose are the discriminations of law and custom that have ghettoized Asian Americans to spaces like Chinatown. The high focus on exoticized culture displaces attention to such ghettoization. The ethnographic genre represents Chinatown as a space that is rich with dragon dances and hacked ducks, but that floats ahistorically and synchronically, unmoored from the structural contexts that have made it a ghetto. If ghettoization is recognized, if along the cultural exotica there are tenements and sweatshops, as we see in *The Year of the Dragon*, these images of ghettoization are culturalized. They are attributed to the "thousand-year-old stuff," as if Chinatown's poverty and squalor were cultural exotica too. The ethnographic genre turns the Chinatown ghetto into something of an ethnic enclave, not the more nuanced but flawed kind discussed above, but a caricatured ethnic enclave, in that it privatizes the Asian American ghetto as a space that is primarily, and ahistorically, organized and driven by culture.

That works like *Things Chinese* and *The Year of the Dragon* participate in the genre of Orientalist ethnography might not be surprising, given that they are produced by a white author and white filmmakers who command a privileged position in the ethnographic coupling. However, the objects of ethnography have also become its perpetrators—Asian Americans in their own literature participate in the ethnographic genre, serving as native informants. They purport to offer a more intimate and authentic ethnography, an "insider's view" of Asian culture, but they also reduce Asian American life into ahistorical, consumable spectacle. Chin maligns these Asian American ethnographic texts as "Chinatown book[s]." Rife with Orientalist fantasies and stereotypes, they serve as guidebooks on how to consume Asian culture. This is exemplified in a convention that Chin calls "food pornography," the spectacularization of Asian food as a metonym of an exotic and consumable Asian culture (3). Chin and the cohort of writers with whom he edited *Aiiieeeee!* point out that early and mid-twentieth-century Asian American texts like Leong Gor Yun's *Chinatown Inside and Out* (1936), Yutang Lin's *Chinatown Family* (1948), and Calvin Lee's *Chinatown, U.S.A* (1965) provide standard fare exotica, literally so, often dedicating pages to step-by-step recipes and other titillating, readily consumed how-tos of Asian culture (Chan et al. xvi–xviii). "Part exposé, part cookbook" (Chan et al. xviii), Chinatown books provide a guided ethnographic tour of Chinatown as a synchronically cultural space abstracted from its historical and, as is of concern here, its class contexts.

Chin and the *Aiiieeeee!* editors argue that Asian American writers who work in the genre of the Chinatown book are "yellow white suprema[cists]" who are steeped in racial self-contempt (Chan et al. xvi, xii). This accusation neglects to examine the conditions under which Asian American literature is produced. The Chinatown book is not a spontaneous creation of individual, racially self-loathing authors, but reflects the conditions of production that mediate the writing, publishing, distribution and reception of Asian American literature. The Chinatown book is symptomatic of a broader ethnographic genealogy of Asian American literature. Elaine Kim points out that early Asian American literature was produced in response to publishers' solicitations and social tastes for informative, entertaining literature about the increasingly visible Asian American population. The object of curiosity was Asian immigrants' intriguing culture. Promising firsthand accounts of this culture's mysteries and mores, works like Etsuko Sugimoto's *Daughter of a Samurai* (1925), Yutang Lin's *My Country and My People* (1935), and Jade Snow Wong's *Fifth Chinese Daughter* (1950) enjoyed high praise and multiple print runs for their quaint ethnographies of Asian ways of life (E. Kim, *Asian American* 24–29, 66–72). To put it another way, Asian Americans writers have been beholden to an "ethnographic imperative," explicit directives from publishers as well as implicit ones from mainstream reading audiences for fanciful, nonthreatening ethnographic portraits. The fancifulness of these ethnographies is what makes them nonthreatening. They caricaturize and decontextualize Asian culture, omitting attention to the historical contexts that created that culture, both in Asia and America, as well as to historical contexts more generally, especially of the racial discrimination and social inequity that immigrants experienced in the United States. It is for these omissions that ethnographic texts are praised, not to mention published and widely read. Kim points out that Sugimoto's popular *Daughter of a Samurai* was published just a year after the 1924 ban on Japanese immigration, but it makes no mention of this or other tensions between Japan and the United States, or of more general discriminations against Japanese Americans. Instead, it is comprised of recollections of Japanese customs, legends, and fairy tales, for which it was lauded in the *New York Times* for "plead[ing] no causes, and ask[ing] no vexing questions" (*Asian American* 27). Asian Americans were to be mere ethnographic scribes, native informants who channel raw cultural "data" denuded of "vexing questions," that is, of expressions of social critique. These unvexing cultural portraits are what gained praise and purchase. It was a main genre through which Asian American authors could have their voices heard. The ethnographic imperative ghettoizes Asian American literature to the genre of the Chinatown book.

The ethnographic imperative has class effects. It engenders texts that culturalize class and privatize economic inequity. This is evident in Huie Kin's *Reminiscences* (1932), which describes some of the social and economic discriminations experienced by Chinese immigrants but, as Elaine Kim points out, ultimately blames Chinese culture. *Reminiscences* claims that immigrants self-ghettoize through their clannishness and unwillingness to assimilate, echoing the culturalizations of early twentieth-century studies that attribute the squalid tenement and street conditions of San Francisco's Chinatown to a "Chinese mode of living," to Chinese immigrants who "apparently delight to exist in . . . dense conditions of nastiness" (E. Kim, *Asian American* 31; Loo 44; Farwell 4). Lee Phan You's *When I Was a Boy in China* (1887) takes the opposite opinion of Chinese culture. Although it does not blame Chinese culture for social ills like ghettoization, it nonetheless subscribes to a culturalizing logic by positing culture as the solution to structural discrimination against Chinese immigrants. Written during the height of the Chinese Exclusion Era, the text seeks to educate readers about the ignored virtues of Chinese culture as a way to improve public opinion and policies affecting Chinese immigrants (E. Kim, *Asian American* 25). Under the ethnographic imperative, Asian culture is alternatively vice and virtue, drawn upon to naturalize as well as rectify structural class inequities. Structural class inequities are rendered absent or epiphenomenal in a self-feeding loop of cultural attribution and resolution.

This is not to say that Asian American writers are unthinking scribes who mindlessly comply with the ethnographic imperative, nor are they "yellow white supremacists" or, in milder terms, "sell-outs." Rather, it is to say that the ethnographic imperative is a powerful pressure that permeates Asian American literary production and heavily modulates this literary body. Even when authors reject the ethnographic imperative, they are subject to its modulation. Take, for example, a comparison of the work of Edith and Winnifred Eaton, Chinese-English sisters who lived and published in North America in the late nineteenth and early twentieth centuries. The Eaton sisters are not the first authors of Asian ancestry writing in English, but they are often positioned as inaugural figures of Asian North American literature because of the contrasting ethical positions that are assigned to their work and that have deeply shaped the critical disposition of Asian American studies. Edith, taking on the Chinese pseudonym Sui Sin Far and claiming a mixed-race identity, spoke out in her work against racial discrimination against Chinese and Eurasians in the United States and Canada. Winnifred, in contrast, took on the Japanese pseudonym and flowery persona of Onoto Watanna to write formulaic, Orientalist pulp romances that served quite predictably as reductive, cultural ethnographies of the Japanese culture she claimed to embody. Viet Nguyen and Tomo Hattori observe that critics deem Sui Sin Far the "good sister" and her work "good literature." Claiming an oppositional, antiracist voice, Sui Sin Far is hailed as the foremother of Asian American literature, a model of the articulation of antiracism that is the central practice of Asian American studies, as well as ethnic studies more generally. Watanna is the "bad sister" whose literature is devalued because it perpetuates the reduction of Asian American experience to Orientalist caricature. Watanna is thereby either dismissed as insignificant or as a sell-out, or retooled as subversive so that her work is better aligned with the oppositional ethics of Asian American studies as exemplified by her sister (Nguyen 34; Hattori 229). Nguyen and Hattori detail the fallacy of judging aesthetic value along this ethical dichotomy, showing how this judgment reflects the political interests of critics rather than a careful, if discomfiting, account of the history of Asian American literary production, in which ethical uniformity cannot be taken for granted. What is more, even when authors adopt the favored, oppositional ethics, that position can be modulated by surrounding discourses. A case in point is the ethnographic imperative's effect on Sui Sin Far's oppositional voice. This effect is emblematic of the modulating power of the ethnographic imperative on Asian American authorship.

While Watanna's Orientalist tales of Japan quite faithfully abide by the ethnographic imperative, Sui Sin Far's antiracist critiques often thematize an explicit rejection to its pressure. The pressure of the ethnographic imperative manifests in the literal form of both sisters' literary bodies, that is, in the physical form of their books. Both sisters' books were published in a notable physical style. In Watanna's Orientalist tales, the text is arranged in centered blocks that are overlaid on sketches of Japanese curios and geisha figures. Most of her many books were published in this fashion. Likewise, the text in Sui Sin Far's *Mrs. Spring Fragrance*, a collection of short stories and the author's only existing monograph, is overlaid on the generic Orientalia of flower blossoms, pensive birds, and Chinese characters.

The material form of Watanna's books dovetails with the ethnographic

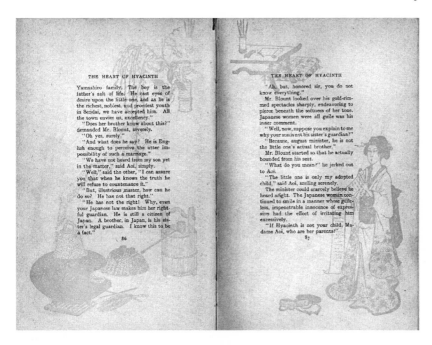

FIGURE 1. Onoto Watanna, *The Heart of Hyacinth* (New York: Harper Brothers, 1903).

decontextualizations of their content, enhancing their tales of an exoticized East, usually embodied in an Asian female figure, meeting an analeptic West, usually embodied in a chivalrous Western male figure, with ethnographic tidbits about Japan offered along the way. The text, as written word, becomes a design element itself, its arrangement and repetition in stylized blocks rendering it another picturesque object nestled in the Japonica. As physical monographs, these books collect Orientalist objects within their pages, as well as themselves become part of the collection. As compendia of Orientalist content that takes on a physical, Orientalist design, Watanna's books are not only vessels of cultural ethnography, but they are also its material artifacts.

This was a highly successful marketing strategy for Watanna. For an author abiding by the ethnographic imperative, this mode of physical, textual expression enhanced her ethnographic project. However, the same packaging of *Mrs. Spring Fragrance* jars against Sui Sin Far's antiracist narratives. If *Mrs. Spring Fragrance* offers ethnographic portraits, they are not

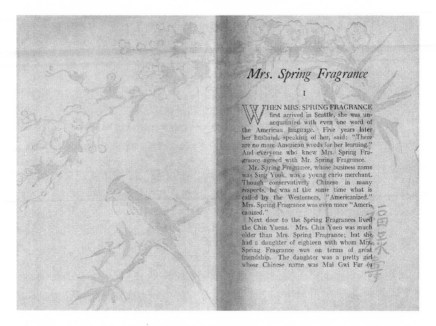

FIGURE 2. Sui Sin Far, *Mrs. Spring Fragrance* (Chicago: A. C. McClurg, 1912).

the kind that the design of her book suggests. Rather, this work offers an "insider's view" of the brutality and despondency of Chinese American life, including stories about a Chinese man who is murdered for marrying a white woman and the cruel separation of an infant from his parents by immigration officials.[12] Several of the stories are also angry critiques of the ethnographic probing of Chinese American life. "Its Wavering Image" tells the story of Pan, a Eurasian woman who is bitterly betrayed by a white American journalist who seduces her in order to obtain inside information for a piece he is writing about the mysteries of Chinatown. "The Inferior Woman" takes a lighter tone, but nonetheless critiques the reduction of Chinese Americans to ethnographic caricatures. Here, the title character, Mrs. Spring Fragrance, announces that she will write a book about white Americans, ironically quipping: "'The American[s] write[] books about the Chinese. Why not a Chinese woman write books about the Americans? [*sic*]," "The American people [are] so interesting and mysterious" (Sui Sin Far, Ling and White-Parks edition 39, 28).

Sui Sin Far's work is extruded through an ethnographic apparatus even as its spirit and content explicitly speak against ethnographic reductions.

This testifies to the powerful, shaping influence of the ethnographic imperative on Asian American literary production. Asian American literature is willed into an ethnographic form, here physically so, even as its content indicts it. How would Sui Sin Far's readership reconcile *Mrs. Spring Fragrance*'s Orientalized physical form with the text's antiracist, anti-ethnographic critiques? How would the author herself reconcile this disjunction? Perhaps the Orientalized mode of production was simply imposed on her. Or, given Sui Sin Far's modest notice in her lifetime (she published short pieces in serials and local newspapers, but did not enjoy the widespread acclaim of her sister), she might have conceded to the Orientalist production of her book in order to gain a foothold in the literary market. Perhaps she conceded strategically, to exploit the book's visual-tactile promise of reductionist Orientalia in order to draw in a mainstream readership whose gaze she could then redirect to her "insider's view" of anti-Chinese violence and racism. We can only surmise the cause, but the observable effect of *Mrs. Spring Fragrance*'s Orientalized material form is a modulation of the text's antiracist critique, the muting of its anti-ethnographic voice with the physical apparatus of its circulation. Nestled in the Orientalist design, the harsh edges of Sui Sin Far's raw and ironic accusations against racism and ethnography (indeed, against racist expectations for ethnography) are softened, and perhaps defanged, by the physical framing of the book with ethnographic design elements. Ralph Ellison famously defended his own modulated literary style, in response to critics who did not find his antiracism strident or programmatic enough because he drew too heavily from white, canonical authors for their taste. Ellison defends that he is at liberty to choose his own literary heritage (140). Sui Sin Far presents us with a similar problem of the modulation or muting of antiracist critique. However, the issue of choice is clouded here since we have no clear opinion from the author about the material form of her book. Nonetheless, whether Sui Sin Far agreed with, conceded to, or actively contested the physical form of *Mrs. Spring Fragrance*, her options were constrained by an ethnographic aesthetic that heavily imprinted—here quite literally so—the generic parameters of Asian American literature. Whether Sui Sin Far willfully chose to comply with the ethnographic imperative or not, her literary heritage appears to have been chosen for her, or at least heavily constrained in its options.

In contemporary Asian American literature, the ethnographic imperative is no longer as baldly imposed, nor is it totalizing. However, its continuing influence is evident in the texts that win widespread distribution and acclaim. Amy Tan notably sustains the ethnographic genealogy of Asian American literature with an oeuvre that Sau-Ling Wong characterizes as producing an "Oriental effect." This gives "low resolution" to unpalatable elements of Asian American experience, such as ghettoization, preferring to offer entertaining, but grossly decontextualized, bite-sized, anthropological lessons about Asian culture ("Sugar Sisterhood" 187, 184). Even when contemporary authors seek to write outside of the ethnographic genre, ethnographic desires are imprinted on their texts, as they were for Sui Sin Far. Chang-rae Lee, who routinely rejects categorization as an Asian American writer and whose work does not always focus on Asian American characters, finds his success rooted in the reading of his texts as ethnographic autobiography.[13]

Chang-rae Lee's quandary is predated and exemplified by the canonical reaction to one of the most canonical texts of Asian American literature, Maxine Hong Kingston's *The Woman Warrior*. Kingston's text returns us to the central issue at hand—how the cultural reductions and decontextualizations produced under the ethnographic imperative obfuscate Asian American experiences of ghettoization and class inequity. An account of the author's childhood in Oakland, California's Chinatown, *The Woman Warrior* explicitly rejects the ethnographic pressure on Asian American literature. This rejection is embodied in a clarion call found in the early pages of the text: "Chinese-Americans, when you try to understand what things in you are Chinese, how do you separate what is peculiar to childhood, to poverty, insanities, one family, your mother who marked your growing with stories, from what is Chinese? What is Chinese tradition and what is the movies?" (5–6). Here, Kingston challenges the assumption that Asian American texts are vehicles of cultural revelation, are mere "Chinatown books" comprised of ethnographic portraits that are to inform and entertain non-Chinese audiences trolling for Asian culture to consume. Yet Kingston has been accused of feeding the ethnographic genre, for instance with her exotic Chinese ghost stories and the "food pornography" ostensibly found in the detailed accounts of her mother's grotesque food choices. But the quote above ("how do you separate what is peculiar to childhood, to poverty, to insanities . . . from what is Chinese?") demands that we read differently. Kingston's mother cooks pigeons, skunks, and weeds scavenged in the city alleyways not because they are exotically grotesque, Chinese delicacies, but because this food is available, and free, in the urban landscape for the immigrants who live there. Kingston's family eats this grotesque food because they are poor, not because they are Chinese (90–91). Likewise, her mother tells Chinese ghost stories not because she is a native informant who imparts fantastical cultural stories to her children, and readers, but to distract Kingston and her siblings from the heat in the family laundry business where they are recruited to work to help make ends meet. The ghost stories are to "get some good chills up [their] backs" as they "changed from pressing to sorting" (87). Notwithstanding, most reviews read *The Woman Warrior* under clichéd notions of the narrator's negotiation and revelation of the mysteries of her Chinese cultural heritage. The reviews that notice Kingston's poverty still manage to sneak in words about yin/yang and dim sum, or transform it into an instrument of culture, for instance, marveling at Kingston's ability to turn the "grim reality of poverty" into "fabulous [cultural] stories" (Smith 6; Dezell 49; Loke 28). With reviews like this, the more elusive ghost of Kingston's "Memoirs of a Girlhood among Ghosts" is the Oakland Chinatown ghetto and the structural pressures of race and class that configure it.[14]

These are some of the ways that the ethnographic imperative has influenced Asian American literary production and resulted in the obfuscation of Asian Americans' experiences of structural class inequity. The following chapters detail how specific texts about ghettoization negotiate this aesthetic genealogy, sometimes by being complicit with it and other times by contesting it. In the latter case, as with Sui Sin Far and Kingston's texts, Asian American literature is nonetheless unable to make ghettoization fully visible from within the trappings of the ethnographic imperative. That is, Asian American literature remains strongly inscribed in an ethnographic genealogy, even when authors write against it. Given that the impetus of this project is to make Asian American ghettoization visible, a more expected approach might be to focus on texts that do successfully contest the ethnographic imperative or show how complicit texts actually subvert it. Bringing socially oppositional discourse and subversion to light is, after all, a main thrust of Asian American and ethnic studies. It would also be simpler to discount or ignore texts that are too beholden to the ethnographic imperative, in favor of focusing on ones that readily articulate class critique. Why call for the legibility of Asian American ghettoization by examining texts that make it, or are made to make it, illegible? Why not dismiss these texts and focus on those that solve, rather than perpetuate, the problem?

My approach partly stems from a resistance to parsing Asian American literature into a binary of "accommodation and resistance," in Nguyen's terms, to hegemonic discourse. This binary is the central scheme through which Asian American literature has been evaluated, with "resistance" being fetishized. Critics clamor over texts that are antiracist and otherwise oppose structures of power, while discounting or ignoring texts that accommodate or are complicit with them. Or, they retool accommodationist texts as subversive so that these can also hew to the ethos of resistance. Nguyen argues that this methodology falsely assumes and creates the illusion of ethical uniformity in Asian American literature and sensibility. This approach fails to offer a full, because discomfiting, picture of Asian American literary production, a picture in which there are texts that are complicit with structures of power, and that are, for better or worse, part of the Asian American corpus too (3–24, 35). In addition, I move away from the binary of accommodation and resistance because, as I have started to show, this binary does not hold. Asian American writers who abide by the ethnographic imperative can be dismissed as "yellow white supremacists" or "sell-outs," but it could be argued that they abide by it strategically. For instance, salient in the work of authors like Tan, as well as of Winnifred Eaton before her, is the issue of cultural commodification. These authors might be exploiting the social tastes for reductive portraits of Asian culture, exploiting the "symbolic stock of minority culture," in Hattori's phrase (245), in order to gain recognition in a multiculturalist literary market, or to slip in subversive messages within a palatable ethnographic frame. At the same, reading subversion into complicit texts may be too facile an approach. As mentioned, doing so serves the ethical interests of critics, but glosses over the issue of complicity and what that tells us about how Asian Americans live and write. Moreover, texts that readily fall into the category of "resistance" can be shaded with complicity. The examples of Sui Sin Far and Kingston show that explicitly anti-ethnographic texts can perpetuate and bear, or be made to bear, the ethnographic genealogy of Asian American literature, and their oppositional discourse defanged. Asian American literature has a complex, difficult-to-fix relationship with the ethnographic imperative. Asian American literature is apparently complicit, vocally oppositional, oppositional but reabsorbed, subversive by being complicit, confounded, and ambivalent, as well as a mixture of several of these positions in shifting combinations.

The following chapters trace this arc of articulation, of Asian American writing under the shadow of the ethnographic imperative, the ghettoization of Asian American literature to the genre of the Chinatown book. As mentioned, this literary ghettoization legitimates Asian Americans' literal ghettoization, obfuscating and naturalizing their experiences of class inequity. Though my point is that Asian Americans' literal ghettoization is structural, that is, externally imposed, their literary ghettoization, while for the most part is also imposed, can be abided by and agreed to by Asian American authors voluntarily. My goal, however, is not to conclude simply that Asian American literature is a heterogeneous corpus in which obfuscations of class need to be resigned to or merely acknowledged. Rather, if Asian American ghettoization has been especially silenced, as I argued in the introduction, I seek to understand the shape of that silence, so that we can better understand what and how it is that we need to speak. We would do well to understand how that silence is perpetuated by Asian Americans writers, to attend to a fuller range of Asian American voices, so that the goal to make class inequity visible is more complexly contextualized within the silences that Asian Americans create themselves. To put it another way, though I do not seek to rehearse a limited ethics of inquiry, of focusing primarily or exclusively on resistance and oppositional discourse, there is an ethical dimension to this project, which is to mitigate the illegibility of Asian American ghettoization. By looking at how Asian American writers struggle to do so (or decline to do so), we can better understand the vocabularies that are available and that also need to be created in order to enable Asian Americans to author their positions in the polity, the strategies by which they make their ghettoization legible, or not.

3 / The Japanese American Internment: Master Narratives and Class Critique

If Monica Sone's *Nisei Daughter* is an internment critique, it is a curious one. In the preface to the 1979 edition, Sone states that her autobiography means to "attend to unfinished business with the [U.S.] government" regarding the [World War II] internment of 120,000 Japanese Americans, half of whom were American citizens. Her autobiography is to tell of her personal experience of internment so that the internment "story will not be forgotten and lost to future generations," the story of how Japanese Americans "became prisoners of their own government, without charges, without trials" because of their race (xvi). Yet for a text that claims to indict a racist, unconstitutional imprisonment, its critique is tempered. Sone routinely leavens the hardships and psychical damage caused by her family's evacuation from Seattle and incarceration in Camp Minidoka with lighthearted anecdotes, for instance, about fussing over a bad haircut on evacuation day, and her future sister-in-law's comical search for a wedding dress in the provincial Idaho town where Minidoka was located. Likewise, though Sone remarks upon the racist assumptions and hypocrisy of a government that proclaims but does not practice democracy, she tends toward conciliation and patriotism. This attitude is emblematized by statements like: "When [the government] failed me, I [initially] felt bitter and sullen. Now I know I'm just as responsible as the men in Washington for its actions. Somehow it all makes me feel much more at home in America" (237). In other words, the overall tone of *Nisei Daughter* is of "smiling courage."[1] The injustices of the internment are recognized, yet they are palliated and, at times, legitimated and condoned. The text's internment critique is further tempered by the framing of the autobiography as the coming-of-age story of Kazuko Itoi (Sone's Japanese-language first name and her birth surname), which centers around Kazuko's racial-cultural identity crisis, her struggle as a Japanese-raced person to find a place in American society. The internment is an important context for this identity crisis, but the identity narrative takes precedence. At times, Sone's autobiography reads less like an internment narrative, whether critical or conciliatory, and more like a survey of Kazuko's identity formation in which the internment is an incidental occurrence. This survey begins with Kazuko's childhood in Nihonmachi, the Japanese American section of Seattle's Skidrow slum in which Kazuko's parents run the Carrollton Hotel, a seedy, sixty-room, port lodging house; and then moves through nearby locales as the Itois attempt to move out of Seattle's Japanese American ghetto. By the end of the text, several years after the internment, Kazuko's identity crisis is resolved and its teleology fulfilled. Kazuko declares: "The Japanese and American parts of me were now blended into one" (238).

From this brief sketch, we see that *Nisei Daughter* is structured by several "master narratives," familiar scripts that derive from and reproduce normalizing social ideologies and their common wisdom. These master narratives are about race, culture, the internment—and they are also about class. First, *Nisei Daughter* is structured as a teleological, racial-cultural identity crisis story, a familiar genre of immigrant literature that progressively moves through incidents of racial alienation and culture clash to resolve in the foreign subject's reconciliation with her social estrangement. In the pre-pluralist World War II setting of *Nisei Daughter* and in the 1950s when the autobiography was first published, the normative resolution is that of Americanization and assimilation, which Sone's text fulfills through its closing pronouncement of Kazuko's "blending." The language of "blending" might reflect a proto-multiculturalist discourse in which Kazuko's Japanese and American identities are well mixed, but despite this language, Kazuko's narrative drives hard toward assimilation, the denuding of Japanese identity and culture from her subjectivity.

Second, *Nisei Daughter* abides by the master narrative of internment, the U.S. government's claim that the internment was justified as a wartime necessity. As such, the internment was said to be serving Japanese Americans' best interests. For instance, the War Relocation Authority (WRA), the federal agency established by President Franklin Roosevelt in March 1942 to create and manage the internment camps, claimed that

Japanese Americans' confinement in military-guarded camps was to protect them from the general public's heightening wartime racism (Lye 161–62). The internment was not an expression of racism, but a defense against it. More striking is the WRA's claim that the internment served Japanese Americans' class interests. In evacuating Japanese Americans from the West Coast, the internment removed them from their "Little Tokyos" or Nihonmachi ghettos in which most of the Japanese American population was segregated before the war. Through the WRA's "relocation program," which transferred internees from the camps into "resettlement communities" across the nation, the internment opened up previously unavailable opportunities for upward mobility. Kazuko's experience is exemplary: the relocation program sends her to middle-class communities in Chicago and southern Indiana, where she has access to educational and professional opportunities unknown and unavailable to her as a child of the Japanese American ghetto. This was a master narrative of the internment—that the internment was a socioeconomic opportunity.

Nisei Daughter lends truth to a third master narrative, the narrative that class is symptomatic of culture. The culturalization of class has been used to fathom and naturalize racialized ghettoization. For instance, as discussed in chapter 2, the Chicago school posits assimilation to American cultural norms as the engine of upward mobility, suggesting in turn that ghettoization is caused by foreign culture. Both ghettoization and upward mobility are privatized, unmoored from structural conditions of racialized economic inequity that are not simply caused or cured by culture. *Nisei Daughter* rehearses the culturalization of class through the first master narrative, Kazuko's teleology toward assimilation, described above. As Kazuko progressively Americanizes, her family simultaneously—and spontaneously—moves out of the Nihonmachi ghetto, as if cultural assimilation alone propels upward mobility and as if Japanese cultural difference caused their ghettoization. Sone's text also perpetuates the culturalization of class through its support of the second master narrative, the claim that the internment was a socioeconomic opportunity. The culturalization of class was the linchpin of the WRA's efforts to turn the internment, materially and discursively, into a socioeconomic assistance project. The WRA's economic assistance came in the form of cultural assistance; the agency sought to assimilate internees as a prerequisite for their participation in the relocation program, through which they gained access to upward mobility. The WRA thereby concretized culturalist assumptions about class. It gave institutional form to the idea that culture drives upward mobility. If the Chicago school codified culturalist assumptions about class, the WRA federally administrated it.

The culturalization of class is iterated in another master narrative that structures *Nisei Daughter*, the denial of Asian American ghettoization in the literary domain through adherence to the ethnographic imperative. The ethnographic imperative strongly shapes Sone's coming-of-age autobiography. As a telling of Kazuko's personal development, it is also a telling of the Japanese culture that influences it. In explicating Japanese culture, *Nisei Daughter* falls into the genre of Frank Chin's "Chinatown book." It provides reductive cultural portraits of Asian American life, which turn the Japanese American ghetto where Kazuko grows up into a caricatured cultural community. By abiding by the ethnographic imperative, *Nisei Daughter* perpetuates the master narrative that the Asian American ghetto is not a ghetto, but an ethnic enclave or voluntarily formed cultural community.

These overlapping and interwoven master narratives mute and neutralize internment critique. They directly extenuate the internment, or do so indirectly via their culturalization of class. Yet *Nisei Daughter* has a secure place in the Asian American literary canon, which selects for politically oppositional texts, as described in chapter 2. Even the *Aiiieeeee!* editors, strident proponents of a politically oppositional aesthetic, include Sone's text in their pantheon as a compelling expression of antiracist, anti-internment protest (Chan et al. xxi). The contradiction here—that Sone's text supports several master narratives yet has been canonized as politically oppositional—has a simple resolution. If *Nisei Daughter* iterates master narratives, it can also be read as subverting them. This is the standard approach to the text. Internment critique is not necessarily absent or compromised in *Nisei Daughter*; it is just buried within, but recoverable through a subversive, anti-internment subtext. This perhaps makes Sone's internment critique all the more plangent and literarily interesting. Rather than being a document of transparent political protest, *Nisei Daughter* skillfully weaves internment protest through the scaffolding of silencing master narratives.

We might, however, pause to consider this project of recovery. Is *Nisei Daughter*'s internment critique worth recovering? The importance of internment critique is not to be denied, as the internment stands as an instance writ large of how racism has historically constituted federal policy. The internment's continuing relevance to contemporary life is evident in the exhortations to round up Muslim Americans after the September 11, 2001 attacks on the World Trade Center. I ask this question, however,

to forbear the assumption that all internment critique is productive critique—to make visible that internment critique can itself function as a
master narrative. Internment critique can reproduce reigning social ideologies and mute alternate voices. For instance, Elaine Kim notes that
internment critique, with its focus on figures like the male heterosexual
nisei solider, can be inattentive to gender and sexuality. Kim urges Asian
American writers and critics to go "beyond the internment," to move
forward to different topics, or at least different hermeneutics, that are
inclusive of a wider range of voices ("Beyond" 11–19). Yet Kim's exhorta-
tion also gives the internment increased viability as a topic of inquiry.
Because internment critique is omissive, because there is much left to
discuss, going "beyond the internment" does not have to empty the event
of its significance, but can be an opportunity to create nuance, to give
the internment fresh relevance. What, by master narratives of internment critique, has been omitted or buried? Responding to this question
through *Nisei Daughter* poses an additional challenge. Given that the
text often extenuates the internment, if there is an internment critique in
the text, that critique is itself buried. How do we go "beyond the internment" through *Nisei Daughter*, to recover a buried internment critique
that does not have a master narrative, burying effect itself, but that brings
to light unaddressed or neglected aspects of the institutionalized racism
against Japanese Americans during World War II?

I do so here by examining *Nisei Daughter*'s attention to the class dimensions of the internment, which have been unaddressed or effaced
under master narratives of both the internment and internment critique.
Class deeply inflected the evacuation, imprisonment, and resettlement
of Japanese Americans. The internment's conditioning by and impact on
class are not merely by-products or shadow symptoms of wartime policy.
Nisei Daughter shows the reverse—World War II provided an occasion
to formalize and institutionalize a national desire to manage, contain,
and exploit Asian American class situations. The internment, as a historical narrative of Japanese American experience during World War II,
provides a historiography of Japanese American ghettoization and class
mobility. At the heart of the internment story is a class narrative.

Like the general anti-internment critique ascribed to *Nisei Daughter*,
the class critique I identify also requires reading for subversion. For one,
if there is a class critique in Sone's autobiography, it must speak against
the text's apparent support of the WRA's claim that the internment was
a socioeconomic opportunity. But subversion-searching comes with a
caveat. To see Sone's text as only subversive entails a willful blindness, a

refusal to see the energy and care that *Nisei Daughter* invests in articulating the master narratives that structure it. Moreover, the subversion attributed to the text can be a reflection of contemporary critics' desires rather than a carefully historicized reading. Viet Nguyen points out that the politically oppositional ethics that drive mainstream Asian American studies has led to the anachronistic assignation of oppositional discourse to texts that might not have had the interest, available vocabularies, or market freedom to express political opposition (3–24). Nonetheless, my point is that *Nisei Daughter* is subversive. However, this is not because Sone's text can be assumed to have subversive aims, but because of quite the opposite—because it appears that it did not.[2]

Specifically, *Nisei Daughter*'s class critique emerges as a subversion of master narratives of internment because the text so faithfully abides by them. This contrasts with the conventional mode of subversion in which master narratives are not abided by, but pointedly rejected. For instance, Theresa Hak Kyung Cha's *Dictée* is routinely recognized as exemplifying conventional subversion. Lisa Lowe characterizes *Dictée*'s literary strategy as an "aesthetics of infidelity" that subverts discursive and social domination by being "unfaithful to the original," by responding to master narratives with disobedience and error (130). Anne Cheng sees a more counterintuitive means of subversion in the text. *Dictée* is subversive not because it is unfaithful to master narratives, but because it is *too* faithful to them. Whereas most critics read the dictation exercises that form the core of the text as opportunities for recalcitrance, Cheng notes instances where *Dictée* is exceedingly obedient to the exercises. By faithfully and droningly reproducing the exercises used to shape the Korean woman into a Europhilic subject, the narrator turns them into parodies and imitations of themselves, emptied of their significance, signification, and authority (159). Subversion "insists as much on the principle of sameness as on the principle of difference": "The narrator of *Dictée* makes a poor scribe by being, in fact, too literal, too faithful" (160, 159).

Nisei Daughter's faithfulness-as-subversion unsettles master narratives not by emptying them of meaning, but by overfilling them with meaning. Faithfulness is subversion not because the text's master narratives become vitiated shadows of themselves, but because they are filled and refilled to the extent that they become magnified, bloated, and ruptured by their internal contradictions. These contradictions show the master narratives to be crafted fictions, not dispassionate reflections of social truths. From these narrative dynamics, *Nisei Daughter*'s class critique emerges. Sone is a "poor scribe" who enables her text to generate subversive meanings because she is an excellent scribe, whose diligent adherence to master narratives prevents her from seeing when she should disobey.

Nihonmachi and Imponderable Ethnography

Before World War II, Japanese Americans comprised the largest non-white group in Seattle. Most lived and worked in the urban core, within a few blocks around Main and Jackson streets in the Skidrow slum area. This cluster of Japanese American residences and businesses was referred to as "Nihonmachi," literally "Japanese Street." Here, in the booming, pre-Depression years, the frontier economy of Seattle provided niche opportunities for Japanese immigrants. Many found opportunities in the hospitality trade, managing dilapidated hotels and boardinghouses to capitalize on the housing demand from the stream of multiracial transient port workers, developing Japanese families, and newly arriving immigrants. Other Japanese Americans opened restaurants, cafés, laundries, and fruit stands to serve co-ethnics, laying the foundation for the prewar Nihonmachi.

Nihonmachi provided rich community life and social support networks, but it can be characterized as a ghetto in that it was a racially segregated site formed and sustained, not exclusively but heavily, by structural, that is, legislated and socially encoded racism. For instance, employment opportunities for the foreign-born issei (first-generation Japanese Americans) were limited to racially segregated Nihonmachis or "Little Tokyos" because a wide range of professional fields in the mainstream labor market, like law, architecture, accounting, dentistry, medicine, and teaching, required citizenship, from which the issei were barred (WRA, *People* 33). Likewise, residential choices were limited by structural racism. "Caucasian only" real estate covenants limited Japanese Americans to undesirable urban districts like Seattle's Skidrow slum (Taylor 115–16). Second-generation Japanese Americans, or nisei, most of whom were American-born and citizens *jus solis*, sought opportunities outside Nihonmachi, but racist policies and attitudes returned them there. A Seattle employer's "whites only" policy exemplifies the discrimination against Japanese Americans (and others) in the mainstream labor market. The employer explains: "[I]t just [wasn't] in the picture to hire Japanese or Negroes" (qtd. in Taylor 107). In *Nisei Daughter*, Kazuko recounts how her spatial and professional possibilities are determined by structural racism. She wants to attend the University of Washington, but her father urges her to go to secretarial school instead, knowing that a college degree is of little use in a racist job market. Even so, she is accepted into Washington State Vocational School on the condition that she will seek employment "among [her] own people" (133).

Simply put, as Roger Daniels notes, in the decades before World War II, "all but a very few of the second-generation adults were confined, economically and socially, within Japanese America" (qtd. in Lye 155). Characterizing Seattle's pre–World War II Nihonmachi as a ghetto is not to devalue the rich community life developed there, but to foreground the structural imposition of spatial and socioeconomic racial ghettoization that formed and maintained Nihonmachi. Nihonmachis and Little Tokyos were, in Colleen Lye's words, "product[s] of the Jim Crow order" (155).

Kazuko depicts Nihonmachi as a ghetto, insofar as it is characterized by urban grit and poverty. It is a landscape of brothels, run-down taverns, "shoddy stores, decayed buildings, and shriveled old men" (16, 8). Childhood recreation consists of scavenging "dingy allies" for discarded candy, and of games like "climbing the laundry," in which the Itoi children race each other to the top of the "ill-smelling mountain of soiled sheets, pillowcases, and damp towels" that their parents gather and wash as managers of the Hotel Carrollton (13–15). These markers of ghettoization, however, are not quite linked to structurally imposed racism. Rather, Kazuko puts a cheerful spin on ghetto life, characterizing it as a picaresque adventure that makes her childhood an "exciting world" and games like climbing soiled laundry "a wonderful treat" (15, 14).

Another way that Kazuko puts a cheerful spin on the ghetto conditions of Nihonmachi is by highlighting the cultural aspects of her family's racial-economic segregation. She represents Nihonmachi as a culturally driven community and in doing so recasts the Nihonmachi ghetto into an ethnic enclave. It is rendered less as a site of structurally imposed ghettoization and more as a voluntarily formed cultural community in which structural ghettoization is obscured or naturalized as emanations of culture. These obfuscations are most evident in the first half of *Nisei Daughter*, which hews to the genre of the "Chinatown book." Obedient to the ethnographic imperative, this portion of the text is filled with explications of Japanese traditions, turning the Nihonmachi ghetto into a delightful microcosm of Japanese culture. For instance, the chapter entitled "The Japanese Touch" is an ethnographic catalogue of Japanese cultural customs. These include New Year's rituals; Tenchosetsu, the celebration of the Japanese emperor's birthday; and *undo-kai*, an annual picnic. The text's surface glimmers with italicized words describing and defining Japanese culture for the titillation of non-Japanese, implicitly white, audiences, rehearsing the conventions of Frank Chin's reviled "food pornography" (3).

Parts of the text are literally concerned with food, filled with descriptions of *maki-zushi, nishime, otsukemono,* and *botamochi* that teach and entertain readers with the deliciousness of Japanese culture. The text even provides step-by-step recipes, for instance, in Kazuko's description of the preparations for *undo-kai*:

> Mother said the rice must be exactly right that day. She washed the rice over and over again until the water in the pot was clear and fresh. She placed her hand, palm down, into the pot to measure the water, and added enough to cover her hand completely. The pot of rice was set aside for twenty minutes to soak, then placed over a high flame to boil. . . . "Now to steam it until it sprouts." . . . Mother spread the cooked rice on crisp squares of toasted seaweeds. She sprinkled chopped red ginger, eel meat, cooked cold spinach, and carrots down the center of the rice. With a bamboo mat she rolled the seaweed into a cylinder shape, like a jelly roll, and sliced it into one-inch thickness. *Maki-zushi* not only looked colorful, it was a gourmet's favorite. (71–72)

This lesson in Japanese cooking is for young Kazuko's benefit as she solicitously helps her mother boil, chop, and roll, but the reader also gets a peek into the enchanting ways of the Oriental kitchen. Mrs. Itoi instructs her neophyte daughter as well as a readership hungry for exoticized cultural caricatures: "No, no. It's still too coarse. Japanese food is supposed to be dainty as well as flavorsome" (72). "Dainty" and "flavorsome" food metonymizes Japanese culture, which is represented as sets of fixed practices that do not change over time or geography. For instance, at *undo-kai* the Nihonmachi women behave along synchronic, gendered cultural stereotypes. They are either self-effacing, self-sacrificing, submissive women, who degrade their culinary offerings while busily serving others despite their own hunger; or they are delicate models of Oriental femininity, who languish under "pretty silk Japanese parasols" while fanning themselves with "moon-shaped paper fans" (76–78).

Sau-Ling Wong notes that representing Asian American culture as synchronic Asian culture depicts Asian Americans as "direct transplants from Asia or as custodians of an esoteric subculture" (*Reading* 9). The Nihonmachi residents and workers appear to have been plucked from Japan and dropped into the American landscape, where their cultural practices proceed apace without any modifications caused by time, space—and class. Frank Miyamoto supports this view in his 1939 study of the Nihonmachi where Kazuko grows up, asserting that migration, temporality, and situational contexts did not alter the Japanese culture that immigrants brought with them to Seattle ("Social" 59).[3] He quotes a colleague: "If one wants to study the Japan of thirty years ago, he could not do better than to investigate some of the Japanese communities existent in America today" (62 n. 11). The culture of these communities is a pre-Meiji feudalistic culture, the values of which are so "sacred," time-honored, and "deeply rooted" that "none may now question it." Anyone who "fails to live in accordance with [this culture] sins as deeply as the religious heretic who denies a god" (Miyamoto 61–62).

This assessment of Japanese American communities culturalizes them, representing the Nihonmachi ghetto as voluntarily, or at least reflexively and even imperatively, organized by culture. Nihonmachi is also an inevitably formed cultural community, as Miyamoto identifies a primary cultural characteristic of Japanese-raced people as a rigid, self-feeding adherence to Japanese culture:

> It is not possible for the Japanese to make their world as they go along, as the Western individualists, relatively speaking, do. The Japanese live, rather, in expectation that their world will be patterned after the traditional Japanese mode of behavior, and they find themselves at loss when those expectations are not met. The judgments of the past constitute the authority which compels the Japanese to create a highly integrated community, and they have no alternative, for these people have no knowledge of other ways. (123)

Attributing Nihonmachi formation to a "Japanese mode of behavior" recalls the attribution of the formation of San Francisco's Chinatown in the late nineteenth and early twentieth centuries to a "Chinese mode of living" (Loo 44). Though the latter means to pathologize Chinese culture, and Miyamoto's "Japanese mode of behavior" means to recognize the productiveness of Japanese culture,[4] the effect is the same—ghetto formation is taken out of its structural class contexts and rerouted to the terrain of culture. Class is absent as an organizing rubric through which to understand Japanese American ghettoization. In fact, Miyamoto argues that because of culture, class is not a concern of, or even a concept intelligible to, Nihonmachi residents. He notes that a Nihonmachi resident was perplexed when asked about the ghetto's class structure.

The resident had "difficulty in understanding what I [Miyamoto] meant" (71). Miyamoto concludes: "[O]ne feels the absence of class consciousness at least on the basis of wealth" in Seattle's Nihonmachi. Instead, the space is organized by a "single class-interest" (71). This class is not an economic class, formed by structural, economic relations and hierarchies, but a cultural class, in which Japanese culture is the "*a priori* premise[] to all [Nihonmachi residents'] social interpretations" (60). The concept of class is stripped of its economic meanings, making ghettoization illegible to the ghettoized Nihonmachi residents themselves.[5]

This assessment of Nihonmachi is the sociological counterpart of literature written under the ethnographic imperative. Like the analysis above, the ethnographic imperative extrudes Asian American subjectivity and experience through the filter of culture, effacing class as an organizing social rubric. Class inequity does not exist in *Nisei Daughter*'s "food pornography" and other synchronic ethnographies. For example, the Nihonmachi women live and work in a slum, yet there is no room for this fact in their depiction at *undo-kai* as caricatures of Japanese cultural femininity. This cultural behavior might be a respite from or antidote to the women's ghettoization, but this is not the suggestion. Class inequity is simply effaced in these cultural representations.

Class inequity is also effaced as a part of culture. If the depiction of Nihonmachi's women excises class inequity, it also confers class privilege. Languishing under silk parasols denotes the class privilege of ease and leisure, but this practice is offered as generically cultural, as if Japanese culture, in Japan, America, or elsewhere, is untouched or uninflected by experiences of ghettoization. This implication is iterated in Kazuko's ethnography of Tenchosetsu, the ceremonial celebration of the Japanese emperor's birthday:

> [O]ne white-gloved man walked gravely to the stage center in measured strides. He made a stiff quarter turn toward the cabinet, his back to the audience, and took three steps forward. Then he bent forward, sliding his hands slowly down his legs, in a deep, formal bow called the *sai-kei-rei*. He remained thus for a sacred half minute, then straightened up slowly, sliding his hands up his legs. He stepped forward again, and reverently opened the cabinet doors. There, to our humble eyes, the photograph of Emperor Hirohito himself was revealed. Only once a year was the Emperor's likeness unveiled to the public. It was a sacred moment. (67)

As with the recipe for *maki-zushi*, the rituals of Tenchosetsu are explicated in fastidious detail. The process of ethnographic revelation is encoded in the explication itself: the ceremony attendants' anticipation of a sacred glimpse of the emperor's portrait tropes the readers' ethnographic anticipation, which is incrementally satisfied as the description of the practice gradually and meticulously unfolds. But is this solemn and sacred ceremony suitable for staging in the Nihonmachi ghetto? Would it even be performed in the ghettos of Japan? In Japan, Tenchosetsu is performed in the Imperial Palace in the presence of the reigning royal family. Though all Japanese might have opportunities to attend, the ceremony is performed and commanded by class-privileged dignitaries. Yet in *Nisei Daughter*, Tenchosetsu is ethnographized as if were a generic cultural practice. It is represented as the natural province of the Nihonmachi residents, even though ghettoized Japanese, whether in America or Japan, would hardly be staging Tenchosetsu.[6] Japanese culture ceases to be classed, that is, inflected by class inequity. As is the case for Miyamoto's interviewees, who putatively have no conception of the idea of economic class, class inequity is illegible for and in the cultural community of Kazuko's Nihonmachi.[7]

So far, I have described the faithfulness of Kazuko's narration to the ethnographic imperative. It dutifully records Japanese culture to create synchronic ethnographies that suggest that Nihonmachi is a culturally driven community denuded of class inequity. Yet Kazuko is not blind to her ghettoization; we recall that she introduced Nihonmachi as a gritty, impoverished space. So there is an inherent tension in Kazuko's narration. It articulates markers of ghettoization, but bends toward the class-effacing terrain of culture. This tension is not necessarily a contradiction, but rather is a consistency that results from being too faithful to the ethnographic imperative. As discussed in chapter 2, the ethnographic imperative commands Asian American writers to be mere scribes, siphons of raw cultural "data." The imperative is a command for dispassionate documentation, for authors to be, as Chang-rae Lee writes in *Native Speaker*, "sentient machine[s] of transcription" (203). Yet this is a disingenuous command. The ethnographic imperative does not seek disinterested documentation, but depoliticized cultural portraits denuded of "vexing questions" (E. Kim, *Asian American* 27). The ethnographic imperative is a command to edit and filter, to excise socially and politically unsettling information, while masking as a mechanism of dispassionate cultural documentation.

The contradiction of Kazuko's narration results from a consistent faithfulness to the ethnographic imperative's *ostensible* command. Kazuko responds with such alacrity to the imperative's documenting directive that she fails to filter out the "vexing questions" that antagonize its actual demand for editing and excision. In an ethnographic vocabulary, Kazuko's documentation of Japanese culture does not filter out the *imponderabilia*, James Clifford's term for the detritus of the ethnographer's cultural data, the information that cannot be assimilated into a unified synchronic portrait of cultural difference, but that nonetheless presents itself as part of the ethnographic objects' lives (104). Specifically, Kazuko includes class-related *imponderabilia*, making visible that class inequities structure Nihonmachi life. Kazuko is too compliant to the ethnographic imperative, too much of a "sentient machine of transcription" that she records too much. The tension of her narrative is thereby subversive in that it produces class critique. But this is not because the tension is an oppositional strategy to generate critique, but because it results from Kazuko's faithfulness to a master narrative, her documentary obedience to the ethnographic imperative's ostensible directive.

Imponderabilia emerge in an extended section on class that qualifies Nihonmachi's staging of Tenchosetsu. Though Kazuko initially describes the ceremony as a generic cultural convention denuded of the effects of ghettoization, she recalls one year's staging of the event in which class inequity has an emphatic presence:

> [T]he year Mr. Sakaguchi [presided over Tenchosetsu] we thought the occasion lost some of its solemnity and dignity.
>
> Mr. Sakaguchi was a hotel proprietor like Father. . . . Father and his friends felt a little embarrassment whenever Mr. Sakaguchi came around. It was well known that Mr. Sakaguchi's one great desire in life was to be elected president of the Japanese Chamber of Commerce. Mr. Sakaguchi poured every ounce of his oily personality into the gears and wheels of the nominating mechanism so that he might one day roll into office with ball-bearing ease. . . . That year he found himself on the platform at Nippon Kan Hall on Tenchosetsu, ill at ease in formal clothes. He looked as if he had encountered a morning frock for the first time in his life and he had come out second best. The coat sleeve plunged down to his knuckles. The narrow shoulders pulled his bulging, fat arms back and the split coattail dangled behind him. (68)

The Nihonmachi staging of Tenchosetsu is inflected by class inequity vis-à-vis its officiation by Mr. Sakaguchi, an "oily" slum businessman.

Having been confined to life and work in a ghetto, Mr. Sakaguchi is not rehearsed in the niceties of formal dress and shows himself to be literally ill-suited to preside over the ceremony. He is socially ill-suited to do so because he does not have inherent or learned knowledge of this cultural practice of the elite. He fumbles the proceedings, stuttering the words of the ritual recitations and grasping for the appropriate intonation (68–69). The gap between the knowledge available to Mr. Sakaguchi as a member of Nihonmachi ghetto's class community and the expertise needed to perform Tenchosetsu, to which membership in an elite class would provide access, makes the ceremony suffer. This gap also makes Japanese culture lose its ethnographic decontextualization. Nihonmachi's Tenchosetsu is not a generic, disembodied practice of Japanese culture, but a version of that culture as it is inflected by living and working in a Japanese American ghetto.

The class contextualization of Tenchosetsu might suggest that *Nisei Daughter* is invested in the oppositional discourse of class critique and that Kazuko disobeys the ethnographic imperative. However, given the reductive, ethnographic frame that dominates the first half of the book, we must account for the accommodationist pull of the text as well. We cannot simply dismiss the accommodationist pull or reinvent its ethics. If the class contextualization of Tenchosetsu subverts the ethnographic imperative, it is not because Kazuko rejects the imperative, but because she so faithfully abides by its documentary command. The class information is not a refutation of the text's ethnographic frame, but a perpetuation of it. The class information is the *imponderabilia* that Kazuko records in her *over*obedience to the ethnographic imperative. This overobedience, however, derails the ethnographic imperative because the imperative's demand for dispassionate documentation is disingenuous. This derailment is encoded within the ethnography of Tenchosetsu. In the same way that Mr. Sakaguchi's body strains against and spills out of his ill-fitting suit, the class markers of the Nihonmachi ghetto's social body presses against and escapes from the seams of a crafted, class-effacing culturalist ethnography.[8]

The lack of filtering of the class *imponderabilia* from Kazuko's cultural documentation shows that the ethnographic imperative's master narrative, that the ghetto is a cultural community and not a class formation, requires filtering, that it produces and is produced by a selective social vision, an engineering of social truth. Another social fiction that *Nisei Daughter* unmasks is that the internment served Japanese Americans' best interests, namely their class interests, as espoused by the WRA's narrative that the internment was a socioeconomic opportunity. As with the ethnographic imperative, Kazuko unsettles this fiction, making it visible as a manufactured social truth with her faithful reproduction of it. How was the narrative of internment-as-socioeconomic-opportunity manufactured in the first place? This narrative is built on the astonishing claim that Japanese Americans were never interned at all.

Internment: Manufactured Narratives and Manufactured Class Mobility

It is true that the internment gave Japanese Americans a substantial socioeconomic boost. First, the evacuation of Japanese Americans from the West Coast under Executive Order 9066 removed them en masse from their Little Tokyo and Nihonmachi ghettos. Second, the WRA's relocation program enabled many Japanese Americans to enter the spatial and social mainstream as well as the professional middle class. The relocation program moved internees out of the camps into resettlement communities across the nation, where the WRA had presecured jobs and educational opportunities, such as college admission. The WRA worked hard to find employment and opportunities commensurate with the internees' skills, education, and aspirations. This especially transformed the socioeconomic futures of the U.S.-educated, professionally skilled nisei, who had the same qualifications as their white peers but, before the war, not the same professional opportunities. In *Nisei Daughter*, a Nihonmachi resident complains: "How many sons of ours with a beautiful bachelor's degree are accepted into American life? Name me one young man who is now working in an American firm on equal terms with his white colleagues. Our Nisei engineers push lawn mowers" (121).[9]

That the WRA, the federal agency formed to create and manage the internment camps, applied itself to improving Japanese Americans' socioeconomic situations is both curious and logical. Relocation was a logical goal because the WRA could not be Japanese Americans' custodians indefinitely, and because it was a practical way to "liquidate" the camps toward the end of the war. However, relocation was curious not only because it extended a counterintuitive benevolence to "enemy aliens," but also because it was pursued *during* the war. The WRA took pains to document that relocation procedures were in place as early as May 1942, just six months after the bombing of Pearl Harbor and three months after the issue of Executive Order 9066. Why would the WRA release Japanese Americans into mainstream American communities just after they were imprisoned for being too dangerous to live within them? What were the relocation program's mechanics and effects? How was the relocation used to turn the internment into a socioeconomic opportunity, and what had to be suppressed in order to peddle this narrative as social truth?

If relocation efforts began as early as May 1942, they were ineffective. By July 1942, the WRA had relocated only eleven evacuees. The agency attributed this poor relocation rate to policy growing pains. By October 1942, the WRA implemented a more stable and effective relocation policy, and by the end of 1944, approximately thirty-five thousand internees had been relocated, mostly in resettlement sites in midwestern and Mountain states. These states were considered the friendliest to Japanese Americans, who could not return to the West Coast until early 1945 (WRA, *Human* 35–40, 143).

Because a barrier to relocation was the internees' lack of contacts in and familiarity with areas identified for resettlement, the most expeditious way to move internees out of the camps was to prearrange transportation, housing, and jobs. The WRA set up field offices in cities like Salt Lake City, Denver, Chicago, and Kansas City, where agency staff worked with local employers and community leaders to ensure that internees would arrive safely, be sheltered, and be employed. The field offices were also public relations agencies. Another barrier to relocation was hostility against internees, the sentiment that "if these people were too dangerous to be permitted on the west coast, aren't they dangerous here [in resettlement communities]?" (WRA, *People* 7). A main job of the field offices was therefore to create "favorable community acceptance," to be achieved through campaigns that sought to convince employers and local residents that Japanese Americans were loyal Americans (below I discuss the paradox that the agency charged to incarcerate "enemy aliens" lobbied on behalf of their patriotism). These campaigns were successful, eliciting sympathy for the internees' plight, which, coupled with the need for wartime labor, resulted in the waning of suspicion against potential relocatees. Soon, job offers came in more quickly than they could be filled, to the extent that employers became resentful when they were deprived of Japanese American workers (WRA, *Relocation Program* 21–22; WRA, *Human* 38).

Beyond securing an abundant quantity of jobs, the relocation program improved their quality. Vouched for by the federal government, educated and skilled Japanese Americans began to be accepted in professional fields. A 1941 Los Angeles survey records just less than 5 percent of Japanese Americans categorized as working in professional and semi-professional occupations, but in 1947, of Chicago relocatees from Los Angeles, that number more than doubled to 12 percent (Broom and Riemer 40). The WRA cites numerous examples of Japanese American professionalization enabled by the relocation program: scientists and scholars becoming faculty at prestigious universities; artists gaining national and international prominence; journalists hired by major newspapers, including previously anti-Japanese publications; and engineers who were actually working as engineers instead of "push[ing] lawnmowers," as bemoaned by Kazuko's Nihonmachi neighbor (*People* 162–65; Sone 121). The relocation program appeared to have put Japanese Americans on more equal footing with their white peers. Sometimes, it even enabled them to supersede whites. The WRA notes the astounding phenomenon that Japanese Americans in "positions requiring supervision of Caucasian crews, an arrangement practically unknown before the war, have not been infrequent" (*People* 23). The agency pronounced: through relocation "the level of [Japanese American] white-collar employment . . . has been raised to a degree never experienced before the war" (*People* 147).

Those who did not have professional qualifications were helped to gain them, particularly through facilitated access to higher education. Since many of the nisei were around college age or had had their studies interrupted by the evacuation, their placement in universities was a quick route to resettlement. Collaborating with the National Japanese American Student Relocation Council, the WRA persuaded universities to accept evacuee students. Between 1942 and 1945, more than four thousand internees were placed in nearly seven hundred institutions (Nisei Student). Nonprofessionals also fared better socioeconomically due to relocation. For instance, the relocation enfranchised Japanese American laborers. Persuading unions to ease racial restrictions on membership, the WRA gave laborers access to better-paying and better-protected jobs. For the first time, Japanese Americans were able to join prominent, influential organizations like the United Auto Workers, the Teamsters Union, and the International Ladies' Garment Workers Union (WRA, *People* 28–30). That organized labor was now accepting Japanese Americans was a marked contrast to the virulent anti-Asian nativism that dominated the labor movement from the late nineteenth century to the early twentieth. Under the auspices of the relocation program, Japanese Americans were no longer the despised "yellow peril," but were compatriots in the labor movement (*People* 30).

The portrait of the internment here is not of racial injustice, but of racial uplift, of the internment as a federally programmed means to un-precedented upward mobility for Japanese Americans. Because of the internment, "Americans of Japanese descent have gained a degree of economic acceptance hitherto unknown in the United States" (WRA, *People* 165). Some internees heartily agreed. In Ann Hayashi's oral his-tory of her family's internment experiences, her father deems the intern-ment a blessing because it enabled him to become a prominent profes-sor of medicine: "*How else* would I have become a Professor Chairman of a department? [The internment] completely turned . . . my career around. . . . [I]t opened up new vistas that *never* would have opened up if I stayed in California. *I'm sure of this*" (152, emphasis in original). From "pushing lawn mowers" to "Professor Chairman"—the internment charted Japanese Americans paths to upward mobility.

This narrative that the internment was a socioeconomic opportunity is compelling and validated by the statistics, case studies, and testimonies above. However, this narrative is held together by a selective vision that minimizes and suppresses counternarratives that unsettle it. For one, the representation of the internment as a socioeconomic-opportunity glosses over the limited scope and uneven quality of internment-related upward mobility. Upward mobility through relocation was pronounced, but not expansive. The thirty-five thousand internees who left the camps through 1944 represent only a third of the total internees. Within this minority, an even smaller percentage was successfully professionalized. For instance, though the number of Japanese American professionals more than doubled in the 1941 Los Angeles and 1947 Chicago compari-son, the 12 percent in this category represent a small minority of the total Japanese American population in Chicago. Gender also influenced pro-fessionalization, with men dominating the relocatee professional class.[10]

The narrative of internment-as-a-socioeconomic-opportunity also re-quires forgetting those who did not benefit socioeconomically from the internment, but who were more deeply disenfranchised by it. If upward mobility through relocation was unevenly distributed by gender, it was also unevenly distributed by generation. Most of the nisei were young adults still exploring their career and educational futures, making them more inclined and better-suited to participate in relocation. Of internees who were relocated by the end of 1944, 83 percent were nisei (Thomas, *Salvage* 616).[11] The aging issei generation, in contrast, had fewer ambi-tions to start anew and also strongly desired to return to the homes and businesses on the West Coast that they had spend their immigrant lives establishing (WRA, *Human* 192; *People* 13). Even issei with the best

resettlement prospects, such as those with professional skills and training, relocated at far lower rates than their nisei counterparts.[12] Of the
35,000 internees relocated by the end of 1944, only about 6,100 were issei
(Thomas, *Salvage* 616).

The majority of the issei was therefore confined to the camps during
the war, making the internment not a route to upward mobility, but a
form of programmatic, federally mandated downward mobility.[13] Confinement in the camps was confinement to a condition of institutionalized poverty. The standard pay for camp jobs was twelve to nineteen
dollars a month, hardly a living wage (WRA, *Relocation Program* 5). It
could be argued that prisoners did not need personal income since they
were fed and housed by the government, but it should not be lost that
they were prisoners; the internment was no luxurious welfare program
and the unrefusable trade-off was the loss of the means and right to self-
sustenance. In other words, the internment did not improve the class
conditions of the majority of the internees (who did not relocate) and
especially of the majority of the issei (who comprised the largest unrelo-
cated population within the camps), but exacerbated them to the extent
that Japanese Americans became wholly dependent on state welfare. By
the WRA's own admission, the camp prisoners became "maladjusted"
"wards of the Government" lacking in "initiative and self-reliance" (*Human* 184).

The internment might be forgiven as only a temporary economic disenfranchisement if those who did not relocate resumed their livelihoods
on the West Coast after the excision of Executive Order 9066. However,
Japanese Americans who returned to their West Coast homes were not
able to reestablish economic activity to prewar levels, especially in fields
like agriculture and small business ownership in which they had been
heavily concentrated. Only 25 percent of the acreage tended by Japanese
American farmers was recovered, and Japanese American participation
in small business likewise shrank (WRA, *People* 57–61; *Evacuated* 69–
70).[14] Aggregate measures depict a similar picture of internment-induced
socioeconomic loss. Internment-related property and asset losses are
estimated in the range of $77 million to $400 million (the range is so
wide because financial records were lost in the haste and confusion of
the evacuation).[15] Even at the conservative figure of $77 million, internee
losses were severe. Claims paid through the 1948 Evacuation Claims Act
equaled only $37 million, showing that more than half of evacuee losses
went uncompensated (Commission 118–19). These losses affected both
nisei and issei, but were weighted toward the issei, who held more assets

and business interests than the younger generation (WRA, *Evacuated* 70).

The uneven class benefits of the internment, skewed by gender and generation, the limitation of their scope to a minority of the internees, and the internment's worsening of the socioeconomic conditions for the majority of Japanese Americans qualify the view of the internment as a socioeconomic opportunity. It is only so through obfuscating synecdoche, in which the class gains of a few stand in for and obscure the losses of the whole. This is not to say that the WRA categorically denied that the internment had negative economic effects. The agency provides a detailed record of internee financial losses, as reflected in the citations above.[16] In fact, for the WRA, these losses represented the nation's singular failing in regard to the Japanese people: "The loss of hundreds of property leases and the disappearance of a number of equities in land and buildings which had been built up over the major portion of a lifetime were among the most regrettable and least justifiable of all the many costs of wartime evacuation" (*Human* 162). The agency's clear recognition and repudiation of the internment's negative economic effects suggest that its narrative of internment-enabled upward mobility is not ham-fisted, that it admits loss as well as gain. However, even in the face of its own contravening evidence, the WRA remained devoted to the claim that the internment was a socioeconomic opportunity. It did so by asserting that if the internment did not always manifestly produce socioeconomic opportunities, those opportunities were present in purpose. The agency recognized that the internment had negative economic *effects*, but hewed to the claim that the internment had a beneficial economic *intention*. This claim produced and was produced by the assertion that, contrary to simple observation, Japanese Americans were not incarcerated during World War II. That is, another denial required to shore up the narrative that the internment was a socioeconomic opportunity is the claim that Japanese Americans were never interned.

The actuality of internment was denied through the WRA's careful parsing of its role. It describes its raison d'être: "The job of this agency, briefly, is to assist in the relocation of any persons who may be required by the Army to move from their homes in the interest of military security" (*Relocation of* 1). The WRA makes an important distinction here between itself and the army. The army desired and was responsible for ordering Japanese Americans to "move from their homes" in the Western Defense Command area, a process that the WRA punctiliously refers to as "evacuation." In contrast, the WRA was a civilian agency that was responsible for what followed—the "relocation of any persons." The agency's job was to address the by-product of military evacuation, to help Japanese Americans relocate after their mass displacement.

"Relocation" is key the word here, as is the WRA's definition of it. The obvious destination of relocation was the internment camps, which the WRA created and managed. However, the WRA painstakingly defines "relocation" as the movement of Japanese Americans not into, but *out of* the camps, to the dispersed areas across the nation that became internee resettlement sites. The agency specifies: one of its primary objectives was to aid and expedite Japanese Americans' "reabsorption into private employment and normal American life" (*Relocation of* 2). In other words, "relocation" was defined as liberation from the camps. Since relocation was the WRA's mandate, liberation, not imprisonment, was the agency's self-claimed goal.

If imprisoning Japanese Americans was not the WRA's goal, how do we account for the reality that Japanese Americans were held behind barbed wire in military-guarded camps? The WRA's answer was that involuntary confinement was an unfortunate symptom of executing a relocation project of such overwhelming scale. The camps were holding grounds where evacuees could be safely and efficiently gathered while the agency secured resettlement opportunities. They were "dispersion points from which evacuees could relocate" (*Relocation Program* 5). The internment camps were not the destinations of the relocation, but instruments of it. The camps were not prisons, but "way stations" en route to resettlement (*Relocation Program* 5).

The WRA took pains to make clear that it was not in the business of incarcerating Japanese Americans. It was the War *Relocation* Agency, not a military or police force, with "relocation" defined as liberation from, not confinement in, internment camps, which were not prisons. Internment camps were not even internment camps. The WRA acknowledges that internment camps were indeed prisons; they were a handful of sites operated by the Department of Justice to detain "aliens of enemy nationality" who were identified as having acted or intending to act against U.S. security. In contrast, the ten camps that the WRA operated and that we commonly know as internment camps, were and are misnamed as such—they were not internment camps, but "relocation centers." They held most of the 120,000 evacuated Japanese Americans who were acknowledged, in the main, to be innocent, loyal Americans who, caught up in wartime maneuvering, found themselves in need of new places to live (*Relocation of* 5–6). The WRA defends: "The relocation centers . . . are NOT and never were intended to be internment camps or places of confinement" (*Relocation of* 2, emphasis in original).

"Internment camps" versus "relocation centers," the nomenclature is important. Regardless of the term, it is undeniable that these sites were "places of confinement." Yet, as with the socioeconomic damage caused by the internment, if the WRA could not deny empirical fact, it could deny intent. Reasons offered for the fact of confinement were inefficient relocation procedures; Japanese Americans' inability or unwillingness to "self-relocate" after evacuation; and internees' own resistance to leaving the camps, for instance, because they feared racism in unfamiliar resettlement sites (*Human* 37, 141; *Relocation of* 1). Japanese Americans were only de facto prisoners, subjected to a "very technical and temporary sort of detention" because of unfortunate eventualities, not intentional policy (*Human* 184). This is how the WRA denied that Japanese Americans were interned, or at least intentionally interned. There was no internment, just a slow and imperfect process of relocation that led to the unintended confinement of Japanese Americans in "relocation centers."

Internment-as-relocation was the platform for the narrative that the internment was a socioeconomic opportunity. Since relocation was the route to upward mobility, if the internment was actually a relocation program, what we usually call the internment was a socioeconomic assistance program. Equating upward mobility with the relocation program's spatial dispersal of Japanese Americans, Dillon Myer, Milton Eisenhower's successor as the director of the WRA, proclaims: "[The] dispersal [of the evacuees] is not an excuse for the evacuation, but it is a direct by-product of the evacuation and the relocation program. And that dispersal is healthy for the nation and for [Japanese Americans]. . . . It is demonstrably true that the engineering graduate moved from the produce bench in California to a relocation center in Arkansas to a drafting table in Boston" (qtd. in WRA, *People* 31).

Myer's statement indicates that the WRA was not insensitive to the ill effects of de facto imprisonment and the reprehensible evacuation that led to it. Often overlooked is that the WRA vocally decried the internment as "xenophobic," "undemocratic behavior," a "stain on our national record" (but this criticism is careful to assign the injustice to the army's evacuation phase of the internment) (*Human* 190). These outrages, however, were offset by the WRA's provision of compensation and redemption. If the internment was a racial injustice, at least there were socioeconomic indemnifications. These class compensations were, of course, administered by the WRA. This narrative of compensation is also a narrative of redemption. If the internment was a racist "stain on our national record," the WRA redeemed the nation by offering upward mobility as compensation to a wronged people, while pricking the national conscience to resume its commitment to American ideals of "fair-mindedness," "racial tolerance," and the "realization of democratic values" (*Human* 193). The WRA was also Japanese Americans' redeemer. Furnishing them with socioeconomic prospects superior to those available to them before the war, the WRA was Japanese Americans' socioeconomic deliverer.

The WRA was neither armed nor adversarial. It did not seek to surveil and defeat an enemy under unsubstantiated charges of treason, but had a much more peaceable, sociophilic mission. It was to provide shelter and sustenance for a displaced population, and in doing so significantly improved Japanese Americans' class prospects. Colleen Lye makes the striking argument that the WRA was a New Deal agency (141–203). Here, we see that the WRA's rhetoric and definition of relocation transformed Japanese Americans' incarceration into a public works project, specifically, a socioeconomic assistance project. We might also say that the WRA transformed the internment into a kind of GI Bill, enacted during, not after, the war, and not for soldiers on America's side, but for ostensible adversaries from the other.[17] The internment was not an internment, but a federally sponsored program for socioeconomic uplift.

The internment-as-socioeconomic-opportunity renders World War II strangely peripheral, as if the removal of Japanese Americans from the Western Defense Command area was not motivated by wartime security needs, but was a public works project for which the war happened to provide an occasion. In fact, as Lye points out, the relocation was touted in itself as effecting a general "desirable redistribution of the Japanese American people," and as "one of the most rapid population readjustments in American history" (WRA qtd. in Lye 162). Whereas before the war Japanese Americans were spatially "congregated in a strip of land about two hundred miles along the western coast line," they now had a dispersed presence in every state except South Carolina (WRA, *Human* 192). This population redistribution was reflexively "desirable" because of the privileging of assimilation, spatial and cultural, by Anglocentric schemes of social value (Lye 155). In breaking up Japanese Americans' spatial-cultural segregation on the West Coast, where their employment and residence were limited to Little Tokyo and Nihonmachi ghettos, the internment also broke up their concomitant economic marginalization. Relief from economic marginalization through the relocation program benefited many Japanese Americans, but this does not disqualify the internment from being an internment. To deny that it was requires a finessing of vision, a distortion of perspective that overdraws the relocation aspect of the internment to blur the sight of Japanese Americans' racist imprisonment. This denial is one of the several denials, though the boldest, necessary to create the narrative that what most call the internment was merely a phase en route to upward mobility.

"Receding into the Background": Americanization and a Cultural Cure for Japanese American Ghettoization

Nisei Daughter makes visible the distortion in perspective that underwrites the WRA's denial of the internment and its reconfiguration as a socioeconomic assistance project. Sone's text does so through faithful iterations of the WRA's narrative, in the same way that the text unsettles the ethnographic imperative's erasure of class by being faithful to that imperative. Whereas Kazuko subverts the ethnographic imperative through an overly obedient lack of editing, she unsettles the WRA's narrative through zealous attention to narrative filtering. Kazuko so abides by the process of narrative filtering, that is, the process of omitting and obscuring counternarratives and contravening details—the *imponderabilia*—that she not only enacts, but also enunciates its mechanisms. Her narration narrativizes the stitching and seaming required to produce the claim that the internment was a socioeconomic assistance project, thereby making visible that this claim is a manufactured fiction. In this regard, Kazuko's unsettling of the WRA's claim is akin to her subversion of the ethnographic imperative. She remains so keen to documentation, to being a "sentient machine of transcription," that she records the mechanics of narrative elision.

The mechanics of narrative elision are narrativized by the phrase "receded into the background." Kazuko repeats this curious phrase three times throughout the text. Diegetically, it describes the mechanics of her spatial, cultural, and class journeys. These journeys are evolutionary trajectories that lead her to what is represented as better spatial-economic conditions and better cultural subjectivity. Of her former selves and landscapes, Kazuko declares that they "recede into the background," put aside as past and inferior ways of living and being. "Recede into the background" also describes Kazuko's narrative practice, her method of crafting the narratives that describe her journeys. The phrase denotes that her narratives are indeed crafted, produced through a filtering process that selects and foregrounds certain details while making unsettling or antagonistic information "recede into the background." Kazuko's personal relocation experience is testimony to the WRA's claim that the internment was a socioeconomic assistance project. But she enunciates the narrative "receding" necessary to make this claim, making visible that it is a manufactured social truth.

The narrative of internment-as-socioeconomic-opportunity is underwritten by the two remaining master narratives that structure *Nisei Daughter*: Kazuko's teleology of Americanization, in which cultural assimilation is the normative, desirable goal for racial subjects; and the culturalization of class, which construes upward mobility and ghettoization as driven by culture. Kazuko is faithful to these underwriting narratives, but also subverts them by documenting the mechanics of elision necessary to uphold them as social truths. By unsettling the truth of these underlying narratives, Kazuko unsettles the larger narrative that they uphold. The narrative of internment-as-socioeconomic-opportunity and its constituent claims are not boldly overturned, but are at least made visible as narrative manipulations.

Unfolding like a textbook case of internment-enabled upward mobility, Kazuko's resettlement experience is apparent testimony to the WRA's narrative of internment as socioeconomic assistance project. The relocation program frees Kazuko from Seattle's Nihonmachi, to which she was spatially and socioeconomically confined before the war, and integrates her into white, middle-class, midwestern communities. Her relocation sponsors arrange for her to attend "Wendell College" in Indiana, a watershed opportunity. We recall that before the war Kazuko was especially hampered in pursuing higher education, choosing secretarial school over college because of the racist job market. She eventually matriculates at the University of Washington, but remains keenly aware that her professional future will be circumscribed by race. She is too "intimidated by racial barriers" to explore her professional and intellectual interests freely. For instance, she is pessimistic about her hopes to become a teacher: "I knew this was a fancy . . . destined to wither" (229). The WRA's relocation program intervenes. If Kazuko's prewar educational-professional prospects are limited, her life in relocation is defined by a surfeit of them. Emboldened by the "refreshing attitude and naturalness" in her relocation sites, that is, by a racially tolerant atmosphere, Kazuko's intellectual "interests explode[] in a number of directions" (221, 229). This educational freedom lays the foundation for her class freedom, the liberty to study a professional field of her choosing with the confidence that she will find employment in that field. The relocation enables Kazuko to "embark[] on a life more normal and happier than [she] had dared hope for"—to join the professional middle class (229).

The "refreshing attitude and naturalness" in her resettlement communities are Kazuko's springboards into the mainstream middle class. But how did these communities come to be so purged of anti-Japanese racism? Kazuko places her departure from Camp Minidoka around early 1943, "scarcely a year after Evacuation Day" (216). Is it plausible that anti-Japanese racism had abated so dramatically by then? The most concrete explanation that *Nisei Daughter* offers is tied to Kazuko's Americanization. The relative lack of racism in her white, middle-class resettlement communities is not the result of their ceasing to see Kazuko's race (in fact, Kazuko notes that she is regularly singled out because she is Asian, but now with more positive results, with curious Orientalism [220]), but from their beginning to see Japanese Americans' culture.[18] In its efforts to persuade potential resettlement communities that Japanese Americans were not dangerous aliens, but loyal Americans, the WRA vouched for national allegiance through the proxy of culture. The agency distributed pamphlets, like *Uprooted Americans in Your Community*, that assured resettlement communities that an "outstanding characteristic . . . is the great extent to which they [the nisei] are assimilated to American ways" (8). In *Myths and Facts about the Japanese Americans*, the WRA excerpts scientific studies that conclude that Japanese Americans are "readily assimilated" at much greater rates than other ethnic groups (27–32). Japanese Americans were loyal Americans because they were cultural Americans.

The narrative of internment-as-socioeconomic-assistance-project is thereby underwritten by assimilation or cultural Americanization. Americanization was the relocatees' pass key into resettlement sites and the socioeconomic opportunities available there. This gives political and socioeconomic purpose to the coming-of-age story that frames *Nisei Daughter* and that normalizes Americanization. Kazuko's claim to cultural American-ness is a claim to national allegiance and thereby a means to upward mobility via relocation.

Another narrative that underwrites the claim that the internment was a socioeconomic assistance project is the culturalization of class. The link described above between assimilation and relocation, interwoven with the link between relocation and upward mobility, throws into relief the class dimensions of Americanization—Americanization is the driving force behind internment-related upward mobility. Kazuko's relocation-enabled upward mobility rehearses this culturalization of class. The linchpin of her upward mobility is her acceptance into her relocation community. This acceptance gives Kazuko the confidence to pursue her intellectual interests because it suggests that she will not be discriminated against in the professional job market, that she will be able to become part of the professional middle class. If upward mobility is enabled by social acceptance, and social acceptance is based on the belief that internees were Americanized, then Americanization is if not quite the cause, then the precursor to upward mobility.

The WRA concretized this association between culture and class. Not only did the agency vouch for internees' Americanization to gain them entry into resettlement sites, but it also sought to produce their Americanization so that they would qualify for entry in the first place. The WRA did the latter by making Americanization a formal and informal prerequisite for participation in the relocation program. Given that the relocation program was the means to upward mobility, this made Americanization the driving force behind the internees' upward mobility. The WRA turned sociological hypotheses into a federal program.

Americanization was a formal prerequisite for upward mobility via relocation through the camp school curriculum. The WRA's pamphlet *Education Program in War Relocation Centers* states that a central mission of the camp schools was to prepare young Japanese Americans for relocation. "[O]ne of the major educational aims was to prepare the pupils for reabsorption into normal community life," that is, movement out of the camps and into relocation sites. The preparation for "reabsorption" was cultural assimilation, the development and maintenance of "an understanding of American ideals, institutions and practices" (1). A measure and means of cultural assimilation was language fluency. English instruction began in nursery school, normalizing early on that English was the dominant social language. In elementary schools, "special drills" were given to students who were not fluent; and by high school, internees were assumed to be linguistically acculturated, prepped to embark on a curriculum that taught the fundamentals of "American social living" (9, 12, 15). The WRA also offered extensive postsecondary adult programs to improve English and provide "training in American customs and habits" (19). The WRA's acculturation programs were pervasive, extending through all levels of education. They began with the inculcation and development of linguistic-cultural assimilation in nursery and elementary school, continued with its refinement and maintenance in high school, and offered remediation at the postsecondary level.

Lane Ryo Hirabayashi characterizes the camp school curriculum as programs of "forced Americanization." Education was a cover for cultural imperialism (47, 49). As such, assimilation was not only explicitly imposed through formal policies, but also implicitly impelled through compliance to cultural hegemony. Hirabayashi writes that assimilation programs in camp schools, vis-à-vis the racial self-degradation caused by the fact of internment, turned internees into hyper-assimilationists who strove to become "110 percent American" (48). This was a compensatory response to the psychological traumas of racism, but also a rational aspiration within the reward structure of the camp educational system. Since the goal of the school curriculum was to prepare students for relocation, satisfying curricular requirements, by Americanizing, was an expeditious way to leave the camps.

Americanization was also a postrequisite for relocation. Before internees were released to resettlement sites, they had to undergo extensive exit interviews in which they were directed to maintain their cultural assimilation vigilantly. Ann Hayashi notes that relocation applicants were instructed "not to congregate with other Japanese Americans or display any 'Japanese-type' cultural behavior which might diminish acceptance in the white community" (42). Kazuko is given the same directive in *Nisei Daughter*: "Before I left Camp Minidoka, I had been warned over and over again that once I was outside, I must behave as inconspicuously as possible so as not to offend the sensitive public eye" (219). Kazuko obediently resolves to be "scarce and invisible" (219). She cannot efface her race, but she can assiduously assimilate, make herself culturally indistinguishable from white Americans.

The culturalization of class thereby subtends the claim that the internment was a socioeconomic assistance project. If the internment bestowed socioeconomic assistance, it did so through cultural assistance, through the facilitation (if not imposition) of Americanization. This suggests that assimilation drives, or at least qualifies one for, upward mobility. Kazuko's representation of her relocation experience faithfully reproduces the culturalization of class, as well as the teleology of Americanization that also underwrites the WRA's narrative of the internment. However, Kazuko's faithfulness to these narratives documents their manipulations, the omitting and obfuscation of counternarratives and antagonistic information that need to be "receded into the background" to uphold these claims as social truths. Through her Americanization narrative, Kazuko records the general mechanics of discursive "receding," providing a template of narrative elision. Through her culturalization of class, she documents how the structural pressures that configure class are "re-ceded" by the attribution of class to culture. The WRA's instantiation of cultural assistance as socioeconomic assistance privatizes Japanese Americans' prewar ghettoization, implying that it was caused by the personal failure to assimilate. Left out is that Japanese Americans' pre-war ghettoization was not cultural, but structural, caused by race-based economic discriminations that cannot be overcome by merely adjusting one's cultural bearing.

The first time Kazuko uses the phrase "recede into the background," she is describing the basic social mechanics of her Americanization nar-rative. This narrative models the general, discursive mechanisms of nar-rative elision. For Kazuko to claim an American cultural identity, the Japanese culture she ethnographizes in the first half of the book must ul-timately "recede into the background." This receding is enacted through several cultural conflicts. When her parents enroll her in Nihon Gakko, a Japanese language and culture school, Kazuko bristles, declaiming that she is a "Yankee" (22). On her first trip to Japan, she is irked by Japanese customs and yawns through history lessons; the country and its culture are alien to her. The ship journey back to the United States provides an-other occasion to assert her American cultural identity. Approaching Seattle, Kazuko is relieved: "Suddenly as if a heavy weight had slipped from my chest, I realized we were home again, and my visit to Japan *re-ceded into the background* like a sad, enchanted dream. We had explored the exotic land of the Japanese . . . but I had felt I was an alien among them. This was home to me, this lovely Puget Sound Harbor stretched out before us" (107–8, emphasis added). The nation of Japan "recedes" from Kazuko's memory and sightline to demonstrate her inhabitation of American-ness.[19]

The process of "receding" also structures the discursive mechanics of Kazuko's Americanization narrative. If being American means shedding other cultural-national subjectivities, the narratives that correspond to those subjectivities must also "recede into the background." That is, nar-ratives that suggest the development of alternate subjectivities must be suppressed, especially if they disrupt the privileged Americanization narrative's forward movement. This is demonstrated by a notable snag in Kazuko's trip to Japan. It turns out that Kenji, the youngest of the Itoi children, dies of dysentery during the visit. Kazuko imparts little about this startling event. She simply notes that Kenji caught a fever, and without much more explication, provides one perfunctory line to relate the tragedy: "I put my face down in Uncle Fujio's lap and wept long, bitter tears for Ken-chan, my little brother who had not wanted to come to Japan." The narrative then abruptly jumps into the Kazuko's encomium to America, inspired by the sight of the Washington coastline (106, 108).

The lack of a more sustained treatment of Kenji's death is conspicuous, inasmuch as the death of a family member warrants sustained treatment. That for Kazuko it does not, indicates that her narration adheres to a different value system—her Americanization narrative takes precedence. As a trauma that piques interest and concern, Kenji's death can take Kazuko's Americanization story off topic. It is therefore quickly dispatched so that Kazuko can return to narrating her Americanization. Because it is a story that could derail her Americanization narrative, it is filtered out and shed. Kenji's death is more specifically dispatched because it figures the derailment of the cultural assimilation that Kazuko's Americanization narrative describes. Kenji did not want to go to Japan because, like his sister, he fashions himself as inveterately American. Therefore, he is uninterested in, even, hostile to Japanese culture (87, 91–92). However, his death, the infiltration of his body with a disease originating from a site of foreign culture—perhaps infiltrated by the disease of foreign culture—figures how an Americanized subject can be encroached upon. Kenji's death in Japan figures how American subjectivity, exposed to other socialities, can be infiltrated, and in this case, destroyed. This episode must "recede into the background" so that the threat to his American subjectivity, and in turn the possibility of alternative ones, are suppressed.

The phrase "recede into the background" thereby takes on an extradiegetical meaning. It describes the narrative strategy that is necessary for Kazuko's Americanization narrative to proceed apace. In the same way that the imperative of cultural assimilation cannot admit alternative subjectivities, the narrative that reflects it must slough off discursive distractions. Kazuko participates in this narrative manipulation, but she is so faithful to this practice that she enunciates its mechanisms. Her statement that Japan "recedes into the background" as she returns to her proper home figures how narratives that might suggest the development of a Japanese subjectivity must also recede if Kazuko's Americanization narrative is to stay on track. Kazuko's enunciation of this process of narrative crafting makes visible that Americanization is neither an axiomatic nor inevitable endeavor, but a socially constructed value that requires narrative manipulation to look like a natural teleology.

Kenji's death also sets up the terms by which Kazuko documents how the culturalization of class also requires discursive "receding." Kenji's death disrupts Kazuko's Americanization narrative, but also advances it. His death maintains the Americanization narrative's cultural value system: Japanese culture is objectionable, while assimilation to American culture is the ethnic subject's aspiration. This binary is figured through the association of Japanese-ness and disease. To Kenji, a consummate American like Kazuko, Japan is a dangerous country. He expresses his fear through apprehensions about the country's famed earthquakes (87). That Japan is dangerous is confirmed when Kenji dies there of dysentery, turning Japan into a site of not only geological, but also biological danger—into a site of disease. Given the framework of cultural subjectivity that structures Kazuko's account of the Japan trip, the disease at hand is the disease of Japanese culture. Japanese culture is a dreaded pathogen that compromises the well-being, indeed, the viability, of Kenji's American subjectivity.

The advancement of Kazuko's Americanization narrative through the figuration of Japanese-ness as disease feeds the culturalization of class. We recall that the pathologization of foreign culture is a central tenet of the Chicago school. Foreign culture as pathology is class pathology; culture causes ghettoization. *Nisei Daughter*'s figuration of Japanese-ness as disease likewise renders Japanese culture as class pathology. If Japanese culture is disease, the Itois wisely return to Seattle soon after Kenji dies, to their home in America, which in the disease-culture scheme is a more healthful environment, biologically and culturally, for the surviving and certainly American children. But the Itois' American home is Nihonmachi, the Japanese American ghetto. Nihonmachi is a dense site of Japanese culture, according to Sone's ethnographic representations. Nihonmachi is thereby a site of cultural and class pathology. It is a dense site of Japanese-ness as well as a ghetto (in the Chicago school's formulation, it is ghetto because it is a site of Japanese culture). Accordingly, upon the family's return home, Sumiko shows signs of tuberculosis. Japanese culture, in its emanation in America, is causing sickness too.

The cure, then, for the disease of Japanese-ness should be to redouble the cultivation of Americanization. This is precisely the recommended treatment for Sumiko; the doctor suggests that she be moved out of Nihonmachi, ostensibly to get fresher air than is available in the congested ghetto, but in the disease-culture scheme, to move the American child to a more healthful, that is, culturally American site. The chosen site is Alki Beach, which is coded as a site of American culture insofar as it is a site of whiteness. Kazuko rudely learns the latter when her family cannot find a house there because the landlords "don't want any Japs around" (114).

So the Itois never move to Alki Beach, and it turns out that Sumiko does not have tuberculosis. But Kazuko's fantasy of the move links culture with disease, and extends both to class:

Sumiko and I dreamed about a little white cottage by the beach, planning in detail how we would spend our days. We would wake with the sun no matter how sleepy we might be, put on our bathing suits and dash out for an early morning dip. We would race back to our cottage, rout Mother and Father out of bed and have a wonderful big breakfast together. We would see Father off to work, help Mother with the house chores and prepare a lunch basket to spend the rest of the day on the beach. Every evening Father would join us at the beach and he would build a roaring bonfire for us. . . . Then we would walk slowly back to the cottage, deeply tired and content. A brisk shower to rinse off the sand, the seaweed and salt water, then to bed. (111–12)

Kazuko's fantasy is a dream of middle-class domestic normativity. The children and their mother are no longer unpaid labor at the family's slum hotel: Mrs. Itoi dedicates herself to housewifely chores; and instead of inventing games out of soiled hotel laundry, the children are engaged in normative play. Despite the reduction in staff, Mr. Itoi's work is transformed to that of a normative breadwinner, whose evenings are free to spend time with his family at the ocean hearth. Americanization, figured through the move to Alki Beach, is not only the recommended cure for Sumiko's Japanese-ness as disease, but is also a tonic for the entire family's socioeconomic well-being. Americanization engenders not only cultural health, but also class health. No mention is made of how the Itois will secure the financial means to transform their lives into a model of middle-class normativity. Rather, this transformation is set in motion by Sumiko's need for health/Americanization, as if upward mobility is the natural companion and consequence of cultural assimilation.

This culturalization of class obfuscates the structural contexts that cause ghettoization and enable or hinder upward mobility, contexts of discrimination that are hinted at and prevents the Itois from moving to Alki Beach ("we don't want any Japs around"). Kazuko does not develop this experience into a full critique, but her faithfulness in culturalizing class results in a documentation of "receding," here of the obfuscation of structural pressures of race and class necessary to attribute class to culture. This is demonstrated when Kazuko finds that she herself needs to be cured of Japanese culture.

If moving to Alki Beach is an unrealized dream, and Sumiko never had tuberculosis, that dream of middle-class normativity is fulfilled when Kazuko undeniably contracts the disease. She is sequestered at North Pines Sanitarium, where she makes a startling discovery—she is not as American as she thought she was. Kazuko is welcomed by the other patients at North Pines, all of whom, except for Kazuko and two others, are white and, implicitly, culturally American. However, she observes that she is "not quite in step with [her] companions" (139). In Nihonmachi she did not doubt her Americanization, but within this majority white community she is not American enough, often embarrassing herself and her white friends with what they take as Japanese behavior. Kazuko redoubles her Americanization. By the time she is discharged from the sanitarium, she feels thoroughly Americanized, so much so that she is apprehensive of returning home to Nihonmachi's Japanese American community (142–43). The apposition of culture and disease is iterated here. Kazuko is treated for tuberculosis as well as improves her Americanization at a medical institution, suggesting that Japanese culture is a disease. Her release from the sanitarium indicates that she is cured of both tuberculosis and Japanese-ness, made healthy and more sufficiently American.

Japanese-ness as cultural pathology is also class pathology. This is seen in that Kazuko, now cured of tuberculosis and Japanese-ness as disease, does not have to return to the Nihonmachi ghetto after all. Her father has a present for her; a new house on Beacon Hill. Beacon Hill was a multiracial working-class neighborhood just south of the central Jackson and Main Street area of Nihonmachi. It was one of the few areas outside of the Seattle Skidrow ghetto that did not have "whites only" real estate covenants, making it a migratory point for modestly upwardly mobile, racialized subjects (Taylor 115–16). Moving here materializes Kazuko's fantasy of middle-class normativity that was first provoked by Alki Beach:

> [Father] halted in front of a large brown and yellow two-story frame house. This was our new home. Father had moved the family when he had heard about my impending discharge. . . . I had never known such delirious joy. [My] family . . . rushed me up to the second floor where my bedroom awaited me, sunny and beautiful with fresh organdy curtains and deep blue rugs to match the bedspread. The house was plain but wonderfully huge with four bedrooms on the top floor, and on the ground floor a comfortable living room

and a dining room large enough to hold a banquet. . . . The family
was together at last, healthy and happy. (143, 144)

Sunny bedrooms, organdy curtains, and matching décor—these accouterments of middle-class comfort are Kazuko's homecoming present.
Yet, as in the plan to move to Alki Beach, no mention is made of how the
Itois secure the financial means to obtain this new home. In the economy
of this passage, Kazuko's "impending discharge" from the tuberculosis
sanitarium is all that is needed to enable her family to leave the Japanese
American ghetto. If Kazuko's release from the sanitarium signals her
Americanization, her healing from Japanese culture as disease, it also
marks a recovery from Japanese culture as class pathology, as the cause
of ghettoization—her release from the sanitarium/her Americanization
is represented as the engine of her family's upward mobility. Kazuko's
sequestration lasts nine months, suggesting that upon discharge she is
reborn as a more thorough American. Here, we see that her hospitaliza-
tion and the Americanization she undertakes during it gestate the cultural conditions that drive her family's upward mobility.

Nisei Daughter's disease-culture-class scheme and its rehearsal of the
culturalization of class give credence to the WRA's strategy of improving
socioeconomic conditions by improving cultural subjectivity (insofar
as assimilation is an improvement). The scheme shares the notion that
economic assistance comes in the form of cultural assistance, a helpful boost in assimilation, which the internees received in the camps and
Kazuko in a tuberculosis sanitarium.

Yet in the same way that Kazuko documents that her Americanization narrative requires a filter, the dispatching of disruptions, she narrativizes how the culturalization of class "recedes into the background" a
structural understanding of ghettoization. Kazuko sums up her sequestration at North Pines Sanitarium: "During my nine months' stay at the
sanitarium, I became so absorbed in people and finding out about myself, that the tragedy of having tuberculosis *receded into the background*"
(142, emphasis added). On the one hand, the "receding" formulation
here perpetuates the culturalization of class. "Finding out about myself"
refers to Kazuko's discovery that she is insufficiently assimilated and
to her ensuing quest to rectify this cultural shortcoming. Fittingly, the
"tragedy of having tuberculosis" is mitigated by this quest. If tuberculosis
is a figure of Japanese culture, Kazuko's ensuing quest for assimilation,
accompanied by and figured as medical treatment, necessarily makes
Japanese culture/tuberculosis "recede" from her subjectivity and health.

Ghettoization also recedes from view and experience. If Japanese culture as disease also figures class pathology, as the cause of ghettoization, Kazuko's assimilation and ensuing upward mobility cure it. If ghettoization is cured by culture, class is culturalized and the structural discriminations that cause ghettoization and hinder upward mobility, regardless of one's Americanization, "recede into the background."

On the other hand, Kazuko's use of this phrase makes visible that the culturalization of class is built on narrative elision. Even as tuberculosis figures Japanese class pathology, perpetuating the idea that ghettoization can be remedied through the class healing of Americanization, Kazuko's experience of the disease intimates that ghettoization is structural, not cultural. This is because her experience of tuberculosis engenders an opposing, structural portrait of ghettoization. Kazuko's illness instigates the regularized, socially constructed response of promptly sending her to a sanitarium. This response is neither arbitrary nor primordial, but one that has been developed over time into an accepted routine. As such, it constitutes a social *structure*, an apparatus of norms and codes that are not immanent and natural, yet are long-standing enough to be naturalized, but are externally imposed. The structural response to Kazuko's tuberculosis is a marginalizing one. It is to quarantine her with the similarly infected, to remove her as a threat and undesirable element of general society. Kazuko's sequestration at North Pines is thereby a kind of structural, social ghettoization, an externally imposed segregation of devalued social bodies. This segregation is not racial (as mentioned, most of the patients are white), but it shares the logic of racialization. The tuberculosis patients are segregated because of an internal defect, the tuberculosis bacteria that inhabit their bodies. This echoes the logic of racial essentialism, which likewise posits race as a bodily deficiency that warrants differential treatment and marginalization. Kazuko's segregation for tuberculosis is a form of structural ghettoization that follows the logic of racialization. It is an externally imposed marginalization of subjects who are understood to be carriers of bodily defects.

Kazuko's declaration that her Americanization makes "the tragedy of having tuberculosis recede[] into the background" thereby suggests that her Americanization and its related class rewards obfuscate the structural aspects of ghettoization. If Americanization takes precedence over the "tragedy of having tuberculosis," and insofar as the latter is a form of structural social ghettoization, Americanization takes precedence over a structural condition of social marginalization. Given that Americanization is a vehicle of class culturalization, in that it drives her family's class mobility, its precedence over Kazuko's experience of tuberculosis is an expression of how the culturalization of class obfuscates structural conditions of social ghettoization. *Nisei Daughter* participates in this obfuscation; after all, Kazuko creates the formulation in which Americanization makes tuberculosis "recede into the background." But as with her use of this phrase vis-à-vis her alienating visit to Japan, the phrase takes on an extradiegetical meaning. It is a narrativization of Kazuko's discursive strategy, her making visible that for culturalizations to hold, structural discriminations must be obfuscated, even as she participates in their obfuscation.

The third and final time that Kazuko says "recede into the background," she feeds the claim that the internment did not happen at all, while laying bare the discursive manipulations necessary to make such a claim. We recall that Kazuko represents her internment experience as a cheery one. There are tears, dust storms, and indignation, but the hardships of internment are routinely leavened with humor and "smiling courage." This palliation of the internment is reflected in the single chapter dedicated to the Itois' incarceration (and in that there is only a single chapter in *Nisei Daughter* dedicated to the Itois' imprisonment at Minidoka). This chapter, titled "Henry's Wedding and a Most Curious Tea Party," focuses on the comical mishaps of Kazuko's brother's wedding ceremony and reception. As in the two other incidents of "receding," attention is diverted from alternate narratives by Kazuko's Americanization. In this case, the alternate narrative is that the internment was a racist imprisonment, not a paternalistic welfare project.

Henry's "curious tea party," his wedding reception, is a vehicle for Kazuko to express her Americanization. The reception is "curious" because of the culture clash it provokes between the issei guests and the nisei hosts. Kazuko, Sumiko, and the sisters of Henry's wife, Minnie, transform the bare, dingy space of Minidoka's recreation barracks for the party:

> Sunday afternoon, the stage was finally set for a formal hat-and-gloves reception. The silver tea set, the coffee urn, china cups and saucers, gleaming silverware, silver trays of nuts and mints, all borrowed, were set in their proper places. . . . I [Kazuko] anticipated a delightful afternoon with people drifting in and out for the next two hours to chat . . . [as well as] a blend of laughter, the polite tinkle of silver against teacups, and soft bouncy music. (211)

Despite this careful planning, the tea party flops. Guests arrive late and do not mill about sociably while chit-chatting. Instead, they congregate mutely in a corner of the room, letting the refreshments on the center serving table grow stale. Kazuko attributes the issei guests' lack of festivity to culture. According to her, Japanese find it rude to arrive at a party on time; forbearing chit-chat is also a gesture of politeness; and serving themselves, as the guests are expected to do from the refreshment table, gives the impression of greediness (212–14). Embarrassed, yet amused, Kazuko concludes: "In our runaway enthusiasm for a genuine tea party with all the trimmings, we had forgotten that the Issei were accustomed only to Japanese tea parties. We had planned an American one" (211).

Kazuko's declaration that the tea party, held in an internment camp barracks, is genuinely American has important connotations. The mistake of throwing an American tea party critiques the mistake of internment. That Kazuko and her nisei peers erred in organizing an American tea party is a claim that they are reflexively American. What other kind of tea party would they have thrown? Why, then, did the government intern them? But the tea party/Americanization narrative is only partially oppositional. It is also complicit with the WRA's denial of the internment. The wedding reception boasts one success. It takes Kazuko's mind off the internment: "Confronted with this polished glamour, the ugly bare rafters and the two by four planks crisscrossing the walls *receded hastily in the background*" (211, emphasis added). This final use of the motif phrase counterposes the elegant accouterments of the tea party with the unsightly camp barracks where the wedding reception must be held. The diversionary effect of the tea party is a form of solace, but it is the solace of denial; the internment is made to disappear in the imagination vis-à-vis the present festivities. Kazuko thereby models the WRA's logic in a general sense. She makes the internment disappear; she "recedes" it in her imagination through one of its physical emblems, the barracks, like the WRA tried to recede or deny it in the social imagination.

There is a class dimension to Kazuko's "receding" of the internment. The emblem of internment is made to disappear by emblems of Americanization, the polished tea set, delicate finger foods, and other elegant accessories of the reception. The tea party is not a generic American party, but planned to be a "hat-and-gloves reception," a formal affair that connotes social sophistication and the implicitly concomitant social and economic privilege (211). That the American-ness of the tea party is fused with class privilege implies a link between Americanization and upward mobility. Therefore, it is not only the nisei's American-ness, but also the association of American-ness with class privilege that makes the experience of internment "recede into the background." This is a distillation of the WRA's formula for denying the internment. Kazuko makes the internment disappear, at least momentarily, through the distraction of the American tea party, which signifies class privilege. The WRA made the internment disappear as a racist imprisonment by reconfiguring it as a socioeconomic assistance project through the distraction of the upward mobility that the Americanizing relocation program enabled.

As in the other instances of narrative "receding," even as Kazuko engages in this practice, she announces that a narrative manipulation is at work. She announces that the "ugly bare rafters" of the camp barracks, emblems of the fact and experience of internment, must be made to disappear, in imagination and discourse, to construe her present incarceration as an incubator of Americanization as well as upward mobility.

The opposing movement of Kazuko's narration, its subversion of the process of narrative fitting and dressing, even as it participates in that process, is captured by a literal instance of fitting and dressing, the attempt to find a wedding gown for Minnie. When Kazuko, Sumiko, Mrs. Itoi, Minnie, and Minnie's mother foray into a nearby town to shop for Minnie's dress, they cannot find one in her size. The stores cater to white American women, whose bodies Kazuko typifies as characterized by "full-blown Brünnhilde bosom and hips," making the dresses too big for Minnie's petite Japanese frame (204). Minnie's quandary allegorizes the racism at the root of the internment. American normativity is figured here as gendered bodily normativity. Deviance cannot be admitted. One saleswoman sniffs: "'My dear, everything we have here is size sixteen'" (204). Like the engineers of the internment, the saleswoman is not interested in adjusting her conception of who qualifies as an American. She refuses the possibility that nonwhite female bodies and nonwhite races can be American, choosing instead to ply Minnie with ill-fitting dresses, in the same way that supporters of the internment decided that Japanese Americans were ill-suited for the nation.

Yet the saleswoman ultimately makes adjustments so that an American dress fits Minnie's Japanese body:

> The saleslady cast the billowing satin over Minnie's head like a fisherman with his net, drowning Minnie's feeble protest. In an instant she was swarming over Minnie with a pincushion, and soon the gown was a perfect fit. The woman had deftly tucked the dress with straight pins up and down Minnie's back so that it resembled a dinosaur's spine. The sleeves were folded back six inches and the

waistline, which had dangled at Minnie's knees, was doubled and hoisted over the abdomen so that it resembled the silken pouch of a kangaroo.

"It's delicious, delectable!" the saleswoman said. . . . "I just love the neckline," she added, trying to lift our gaze above this wanton surgery. . . .

Sumi and I were too fascinated by the glittering row of straight pins down Minnie's back to say anything. Mrs. Yokoyama and Mother, ever polite and noncommittal, smiled and nodded at no one in particular. (205)

The saleswoman's modification of the dress might suggest that she has adjusted her idea of American subjectivity, insofar as she has adapted the dress, the mold that an American should fit, to accommodate Minnie's Japanese body. Yet despite the saleswoman's rapturous self-approval, the fit is not right. The dress's transformation does not signify a more capacious understanding of American subjectivity; rather, the dress is turned into a grotesque, ungainly apparatus that cannot for all the saleswoman's disingenuousness be accepted as properly fitting. The dress is akin to the WRA's narrative of the internment, which relies on an apparatus of discursive pins and tucks to make its claim that the internment was a socioeconomic assistance project, a claim that does not fit empirical reality. Kazuko's narration has been complicit with this discursive manipulation. In the same way that Mrs. Yokoyama and Mrs. Itoi smile and nod at the distorted dress, Kazuko for the most part assents to the WRA's master narratives of internment. But notwithstanding her narrative's polite smiles and nods, Kazuko calls attention to the discursive manipulations necessary for such agreeability. Through the tension between Kazuko's participation in narrative "receding" and her subversion of it, *Nisei Daughter* shows that the WRA's version of the internment is a distortion that is created by subjecting narratives to "wanton surgery."

Way Stations and "Residues"

The inherent tensions and contradictions within the master narratives that structure *Nisei Daughter* engender subversion, but a form that is counterintuitively generated by Kazuko's faithful reproduction of those master narratives. What emerges is a class critique, a portrait of the internment in which class is visible as a central concern in the imagination. That the WRA, the entity created to manage and administer the internment, brought class into the foreground paradoxically contributes to Asian American critique. The agency's archive allows Asian Americanists to go "beyond the internment," to address neglected aspects of the internment, like class. This is possible even though the WRA's attention to class, the upward mobility enabled by resettlement, is meant to deny the internment, and suggest that its reincarnation as the "relocation program" was a solution to Japanese American ghettoization. Despite these effacements, the WRA's master narratives can make Japanese Americans' ghettoization visible.

We recall that the agency renames the internment camps as "way stations," as temporary holding centers rather than prisons (*Relocation Program* 5). We also recall that the idea of the "way station" is central to the Chicago school model of ghettoization. Ghettos are way stations, gathering points for racialized and ethnic immigrants, from which "the keener, the more energetic, and the more ambitious very soon emerge" to assimilate into mainstream society and take up the attendant upward mobility (Park, *On Social Control* 60).

The WRA's use of the term "way station" thereby invokes the idea of ghettoization. This invocation suggests that the internment camps, even if they were not prisons, were a form of ghetto. This is implied in the Itois' spatial trajectory on evacuation day. They leave Beacon Hill, pass through Chinatown, and return to Nihonmachi to await their assignment to the evacuation buses (169). Kazuko documents this trajectory as a matter of course. There is scant explicit class critique here; the journey is merely a documentation of how the evacuation procedure works. But we see that this journey is a regressive physical movement that codes a regressive socioeconomic movement. The Itois travel backward from their house in the working-class suburb and back to the Japanese American ghetto.

But Nihonmachi is not the last stop. The Itois' destination is Camp Minidoka, preceded by a stay at the Puyallup Assembly Center. As the last stops in the Itois' spatial journey, the internment sites are implicated in the concomitant, regressive socioeconomic journey. They are its endpoints, suggesting that the internment sites are forms of ghettos. Indeed, if a ghetto is characterized by structurally imposed economic disenfranchisement and racial segregation, the internment camps comport. In the camps, Japanese Americans lived in institutionalized poverty and forced racial segregation. The WRA's reconstruction of the internment camps into relocation "way stations" enable an understanding of the camps not just as a tool for upward mobility, but as the opposite, as a site of reiterated ghettoization.

Sone's autobiography ends with Kazuko returning to Camp Minidoka to visit her parents, who remain incarcerated long after their daughter has been relocated. Mr. and Mrs. Itoi are part of the population who were unable or unwilling to relocate, in their case, because they hope to return to their Seattle home. Dorothy Thomas, an ethnographer of the internment camps, describes this population as the "residue" (*Spoilage* xiii). They were, in her scheme, neither part of the "spoilage," issei who returned to Japan and nisei who rejected their American citizenship; nor were they part of the "salvage," the internees who successfully relocated (*Spoilage* xii). They could not be integrated into the binary scheme of traitor versus loyalist, or traitor versus economic beneficiary. The "residue" is the internment's *imponderabilia*, bodies that neither fit into Thomas's scheme nor into the WRA's narrative of internment-as-socioeconomic-assistance-project. *Nisei Daughter*, by documenting the residue of narratology, of the disruptive discursive bits and the apparatus of narrative manufacture, while not offering outright critique, enables critique to emerge, impelling a pondering of the imponderable in master narratives of internment and class.

4 / Chinese Suicide: Political Desire and Queer Exogamy

Last summer, as I was having dinner in Washington, D.C.'s Chinatown, two tourists hesitantly stepped into the restaurant. A waiter summoned them to a table, but they were disoriented and cautious, mumbling briefly together before asking: "Is this Chinatown?" I laughed—not because they were standing in the shadow of a sixty-foot gate, all gilt and dragons and pagodalike peaks, the unmistakable sign that they were smack in the middle of Chinatown. Rather, I laughed because the tourists' skepticism bespoke an observant irony—not much about this Chinatown is very Chinese. Beyond the gate, one block north and barely two blocks to its east and west, is the entirety of D.C.'s Chinatown, its thin arrangement of restaurants, a few souvenir shops, and not many Chinese people on the streets. The most eye-catching sights are hardly Chinese at all, the blazing marquee of the Verizon Center and the gleaming storefronts of mega-retail stores and chain restaurants that were built in the 1980s ostensibly to renew the neighborhood. The bilingual signs of these shops are ornamental contrivances, shallow significations of an ethnic aura, "Starbucks" and "Subway" translated into phonetic but semantically nonsensical Chinese. But all was not lost for the disappointed tourists. The waiter reassured them, settling them at a table as he chatted them up with a history of the better days, when there were more Chinese people, more dragon dances, flapping fish in sidewalk buckets, and venerated elders officiating over the urban village in high Confucian style. Now I was the one who was disappointed, in hearing the waiter reiterate a familiar, denuded Orientalist script. I expected him to tell a different story, of the communities and histories razed by gentrification and corporatized renewal, or perhaps of the labor market discrimination and structural ghettoizations that led him to scavenge for tips in a dying Chinatown. In other words, I had a fantasy of Chinatown too. If Chinatown was not Chinese enough for the tourists by failing to live up to their fantasy of racial-cultural difference, it failed to be Chinese enough for me in terms of racial-political sensibility. I had expected that the waiter, as someone who might have experienced the racist laws, public policies, and social attitudes that named him as Chinese, would evince more interest in protesting and critiquing his racializations. I was mapping a political position onto a Chinese person's racial position. Like the tourists, I wanted Chinatown to be more Chinese.

Fae Myenne Ng's *Bone* tells a story about a Chinatown that is not very Chinese. Ng's novel rethinks Chinatown as an idea and a place that, paradoxically, cannot be captured through the lens of race, specifically though the racial categories of Chinese-ness described above; as a tourist's dream of racial-cultural exotica and as an idealized embodiment of racial-political solidarity. *Bone*'s Chinatown resists the recognizable essentialisms of racial-cultural difference, but it also confronts the less willingly recognized essentialisms of racial-political desire. The latter refers to what Viet Nguyen calls the "disavowed essentialism of racial identity"—a *racial-political* essentialism that essentializes racialized subjects as politicized subjects who protest and critique their racializations (145). Asian American studies is arguably structured and animated by racial-political essentialism. Its methodologies assume that Asian American voices are politically oppositional, readily contesting the material and discursive disciplines of race. Notable progenitors of this practice are the *Aiiieeeee!* editors, for whom being racialized as Asian American is to have a "sensibility" that is necessarily, even inherently, politicized (Chan et al. xxvi). The *Aiiieeeee!* editors are routinely excoriated for their overwrought prescriptions, but Asian Americanist practice continues to carry the editors' spirit. Sau-Ling Wong offers a cogent and tempered distillation of the literary field's goal: to build a coalition of texts and social formations that "acknowledge and resist" the discriminations shared by Asian-raced groups, a coalition that does not essentially, but "voluntarily adopt[s]" politicization (6). Yet the texts that volunteer themselves, or that we allow to volunteer, hew to oppositional discourse, resulting in our current canon, which is characterized by antiracist discourse. Race-based politicization, however voluntary, is nonetheless selected for, potentially naturalizing race-based politicization as, if not an innate, then the proper Asian American aesthetic.

Racial-political essentialism has produced important and necessary insights, but it presumes that racialization predictably produces or even inherently embodies political desire. Asian American studies has extensively and convincingly de-essentialized race, yet racial-political essentialism risks retrenching that work by reinforcing the logic of racial embodiment, though admittedly in a less injurious form, that the field works so hard against. Also of concern is the ever-changing character of our contemporary globalized and diasporic sociality, as well as the cross-hatching of race with class, gender, and sexuality, which make allegiances difficult to catalogue into clear-cut racial-political schemes. This is not to suggest an abandonment of politics. Though racial-political essentialism might not hold, political critique need not be evacuated from the heart of Asian Americanist practice. In fact, the fallacy of racial-political essentialism does not suggest a need for less oppositional discourse, but for more of it, given a paradox of race: race still centrally straitens Asian American lives, yet is an unreliable rubric through which to contest that discipline. *Bone* enables us to imagine an alternative politics, specifically one that takes class and sexuality more fully into account. Class and sexuality, in turn, impel a reimagination of what constitutes the political. Like race, these vectors of social experience can engender political essentialisms, but I look at the potential that class, overlaid with gender and the queer, has to unsettle them.

Read primarily through racial-political essentialist frameworks, *Bone* has been canonized as a politically oppositional, antiracist text, specifically as a critique of the racialized class inequities that structure San Francisco's late twentieth-century Chinatown. Of note are Lisa Lowe and Juliana Chang's works, which show that the novel's antichronological, anti-bildungsroman structure contests the denial of the racialized, gendered labor exploitation necessary for the national march toward modernity and capitalist maximization. *Bone*'s assembly of Chinatown's racialized working class, working poor, and underemployed is attendantly read as desiring to rise against its exploitations. Indeed, the novel's portrait of the Leong family, beaten down by unrelenting poverty and labor exploitation, as well as by the suicide of Ona, the middle daughter, indicts the structural race, class, and gender inequities that materially and affectively aggrieve Chinatown life.

Rather than unequivocally espousing the kind of racial-political "sensibility" sanctified by the *Aiiieeeee!* editors, how might *Bone*'s antinovelistic form critique the assumed link between race and political desire? The standard reading of the text is important and necessary, but *Bone* also confronts this standard's limits. The novel presents a more intractable Chinatown than it is given credit for, where racialized subjects' political desires are not so easily assigned. As a canonical text of racial-political protest, *Bone* unsettles the orthodoxies of the relationship between racialization and politics, impelling a recalibration of that canon's assumptions and parameters.

The vagaries of political desire in *Bone*'s Chinatown map the insufficiency of race as a political category. The novel's faltering narrative does not unequivocally express a racial group's political critique, but reflects the failure of its full articulation. This failure is mapped through Ona's suicide, which remains unresolved throughout the text. Narrativizing the inability to ascertain, that is, to create a narrative about, why Ona killed herself, the novel is a narrativization of narrative failure. This narrative failure tropes and enacts the failure of constructing a unified articulation of racial-political protest, the failure to find a solidarity of Chinatown workers and residents' political desires. I frame the forestalling of racial-political critique through the intersection of the two essentialisms described above. *Bone* stages an attempt to articulate racial-political critique by contesting Chinatown's racial-cultural essentializations. These racial-cultural essentializations rely on a culturalizing logic that naturalizes racialized class inequities as voluntary expressions of Chinese culture. *Bone* voices its racial-political critique by critiquing the ethnographic imperative, a culturalizing pressure that the narrator explicitly rejects as she tells her story about Chinatown and Ona's suicide. However, the novel shows how the articulation of racial-political critique, which is meant to empower the Chinatown community, is impeded by Chinatown residents and workers themselves. They reproduce the obfuscating culturalizations of their life and labor, showing that racialization is not a reliable, or inherent, index of political oppositionality. *Bone* stages a contest of contestation, how the attempt to critique one insufficient racial epistemology (racial-cultural) is confronted with the limits of another racial epistemology, the racial-political essentialisms that we use to speak differently.

That class-effacing culturalizations are perpetuated by Chinatown residents and workers is not a matter of false consciousness or ideological determinism. *Bone*'s Chinatown underclass wields culture purposefully, as a means of self-subjectification and agency, just not always toward the goal of racial-political protest. The heterogeneity, or absence, of racial-political desire does not evacuate the possibility of a political future for racialized subjects. But it does impel an examination of how failure, of race-based politics and narrative, can generate alternative, though provisional and imperfect, politicized epistemologies and practices. The first half of this chapter shows the need for racial-political desire, sketching how systems of class inequity structure the family life of the Leongs in *Bone*'s Chinatown, but are privatized under culturalizations. This makes the need for racial-political protest all the more acute, but *Bone* depicts the absence of a uniform racial-political desire. The second part of the chapter turns toward the queer for an alternative to race-based politics. The queer is not a cure-all, but it is an effective way of reimagining Asian American politics, as well as a necessary one. It is necessary not just generally, because race is encoded with sexuality and sexuality with race, but also because the queer is constitutive of Asian American sociality. In turn, Asian American race and class formations are necessary in the imagination of the queer. From these cross-hatchings, the queer emerges as a productive channel through which to envision Asian American political practice and imagination.

Chinatown Stories: "Spidery Writing" and the Ethnographic Imperative

The Leongs are a broken family. Their heartache stems from an entanglement of emotional and economic privation: the drudgery of Mah's life as a sweatshop seamstress; the racial discriminations that preclude Leon from being a steady breadwinner, husband, and father; and the reluctant fealty of the three daughters, Leila, Ona, and Nina, to their parents and the burdens of Chinatown life. The family's distress is brought to an unmanageable crisis when Ona kills herself. The novel's loosely backward, antichronological temporality shrouds Ona's suicide in an uncertainty of time and reason, offering scant resolution of narrative or sorrow.

The failure to fathom and narrate Ona's suicide reflects the failure to create a narrative of race-based political protest against the Leongs' race, class, and gender marginalizations. Three characters figure positions in the process of articulating—and disrupting—race-based politically oppositional discourse. The narrator of the novel and oldest daughter, Leila, figures the voice of Asian American critique and its commitment to race-based political protest. The process of her narration is a trope and an example of constructing race-based political critique. An apparent subject of that critique is Leon, who among other family members suffers dearly under racial discrimination. Though Leon is the apparent beneficiary of race-based political critique, he figures its disruption, committing himself to other desires. To put it another way, in the project of building race-based political critique, Leon is unnarratable. A more profound unnarratability is seen in Ona. Her unfathomable suicide creates an epistemological void that impels a rethinking of Asian American studies' political models and assumptions. She, like Leon, is a subaltern subject of the national polity, a figure from which and for whom race-based political critique is built. However, she emerges as the subaltern subject of Asian Americans studies too, depriving the field of the tools, and the solace, of tidy race-based political schemes.

Leila's narration tries to critique the racialized class inequities that shape Chinatown life, as well as the representational history that effaces them. Lowe writes that the imperatives of capitalist development turn Chinatown's private spaces into annexes of gendered, racialized labor exploitation. Notably, the Leongs' home space is "legibly imprinted" by Mah's work as a garment factory seamstress who routinely brings work home to make a living wage (168–69). The home becomes a factory outpost where she enlists her daughters' help. In turn, the factory becomes a home where the girls seek their mother in order to carry on everyday family affairs and are again enlisted to increase Mah's production.

The Leongs' family life is also structured by racializing, gendered pressures that contribute to Leon's physical and economic absence as male head-of-household. Racially excluded from the mainstream labor market, he is either out at sea as a temporary shipping laborer or wandering around Chinatown seeking odd jobs. In between, he lives in a male boardinghouse, partly to escape family strife, but also to be available to ship out or take on other casual labor. Leon is a modern-day Chinatown bachelor. The labor nativism and other legal and social discriminations that relegated nineteenth- and early twentieth-century Chinatown men to menial work might have abated, and the antimiscegenation laws and immigration exclusion of most Chinese women that made these men "bachelors" have been repealed.[1] However, exclusionary practices obtain in Chinatown's contemporary development as an underground sector of the global economy, a sector that is built upon and sustains a racialized, itinerant, casual labor market.[2] As Juliana Chang notes, Leon is only a nominal family man, a relationally and economically transient laborer like his bachelor forbears (110–33).

This portrait of the Leongs makes *Bone* a welcome departure from the Orientalist pabulum that pervades Chinatown's representational history. It contravenes the culturalizing ethnographic imperative, which obscures and naturalizes Asian American experiences of structural class inequity by caricaturing Asian American life as merely and ahistorically cultural. As discussed in chapter 2, these ethnographic caricatures abstract Chinatown into a synchronic ethnic enclave, a cultural oasis rich with Orientalist exotica, but unmoored from the structural pressures of race and class. In *Bone*, Leila bristles at such obfuscations: "I looked out at the streets and saw the spidery writing on the store signs, the dressed-up street lamps with their pagoda tops. . . . So this is what Chinatown looks like from inside those dark Greyhound buses . . . this is what tourists come to see. I felt a small lightening up inside . . . our inside story is something entirely different" (144–45).

The "inside story" that Leila prefers registers Chinatown's history and contemporary development as a racialized ghetto formed by anti-Chinese laws, public policy, social practices, and imperatives of local and global capitalist development. It tells Mah's story as a sweatshop woman and Leon's as a bachelor laborer, refusing erasure or naturalization by the "spidery writing" of the Chinatown book and its ethnographic counterparts in history and public policy. By articulating these "inside stories," Leila articulates politically oppositional critique. Leila's critique is keyed to Ona's suicide, which is not definitively caused by her family's structural ghettoization, but is deeply nested in it so that telling Ona's story is also a narration of the racialized class inequities of Chinatown life.

This narrative-political project relies on the racial-political concord of its subjects, their willingness to voice the same story as Leila's, or at least to be obedient subjects of her narration. But those who share the experience of racialized, gendered exploitation impede the telling of her story, evincing a fracturing of narrative and political desire. Specifically, they reproduce the culturalisms that obscure a structural portrait of Chinatown's racialized class inequities. This reflects a lack of racial-political uniformity that racial-political essentialism takes for granted. The recalcitrant subjects are Leila's own family members, rendering family a trope for racial-political concord. Family, related by blood and imagination, is the organizing entity through which private issues of racial-cultural fealty figure public issues of racial-political solidarity.

Chinese Families

Narrating Ona's suicide entails narrating the racialized, gendered class inequities in which her life was nested. As mentioned, Leila's attempt to tell this "inside story" is an attempt to construct a racial-political critique, especially against the culturalisms that efface Chinatown's material history. Leila is interrupted by culturalisms both within and outside the text. She begins to sketch Chinatown's racialized class landscape by noting that Ona jumped off the Nam Ping Yuen, a building in a mid-twentieth-century housing project constructed for Chinatown's working class. Leila explains: "*Nam* means south and *ping yuen*—if you want to get into it—is something like 'peaceful gardens'" (14). Leila's voice is ironic and bitter, denoting the disjunction between the building's name and the strained lives, and death, that the housing project indexes. Leila is keenly aware that her listeners will not hear this gap, that her depiction of Chinatown's socioeconomic landscape can be easily refashioned along the more palatable, readily available semiotics of culturalist exotica ("peaceful gardens"). Interrupting herself with the prickly, metadiegetical "if you want to get into it," Leila anticipates and defends against readers' expropriation of her translation as an offering for the tourist's glossary.

Within the text, Leila's attempt to contextualize Ona's suicide is derailed by similar culturalist fantasies. These fantasies are structured around caricatures of Confucianistic family practices, such as the solicitous worship of dead relatives and the exacting discipline of living ones. One of Ona's white coworkers suggests that suicide was Ona's only escape from draconian Chinese family discipline, asking Leila, "Are your parents really that strict?" (110). Within her family, Leon attributes the suicide to culturalist family ethics, believing that it is posthumous retribution for his failure to return the bones of the family patriarch, Grandpa Leong, to China. Leon also suggests that the suicide is the forewarned consequence of Ona's own violation of cultural patriarchy. Leon had demanded that Ona break up with Osvaldo Ong, whose father, Luciano, had swindled Leon in a laundry business. Leon prohibits the relationship because of Luciano's betrayal, but he draws his authority from culturalized patriarchal ethics. Getting "dangerously old-world about his control over Ona," that is, claiming his authority as a Chinese father, Leon demands Ona's obedience if she wants to remain his dutiful Chinese daughter (172).

Ona's suicide is thus turned into a Chinese suicide. It is taken as a cipher of Chinese family culture and is also culturalized as being caused by it. These culturalizations divert the suicide from its racialized class context and interrupt Leila's "inside story," her racial-political critique that seeks to make that context visible. They make Leila defend herself

preemptively ("if you want to get into it") and at other times simply halt
her narrative. For instance, Leila is often left speechless vis-à-vis Leon's
fierce insistence on his culturalized ethics, and in response to Ona's
coworker's preconfirmed inquiry about Chinese family discipline, she
retreats into weary silence, tired of correcting stubbornly held culturalizing distortions (149, 111).

That Leon culturalizes Ona's suicide shows that it is not only gawking
exoticists, but also Chinatown's own who impede the construction of
racial-political critique. Leon is discursively wayward, a figure of unnarratability. This is reflected in his physical waywardness, his constant
wandering off on feckless expeditions, which makes him difficult to find,
much less narrate. His expeditions include his quest to find Grandpa Leong's bones, now irretrievably lost, having been shuttled around after the
gravesite lease expired; and his chasing after Osvaldo to scapegoat him
for Ona's death. These spatial wanderings serve his culturalist beliefs.
If only he can find Grandpa Leong's bones and return them to China,
or if only he can blame Osvaldo for leading his filial daughter astray,
his and Ona's cultural violations can be redeemed and his culturalist
family ethics restored. Leon's spatial wanderings disrupt Leila's story on
the narrative level (she must stop telling her story to find him), as well as
on the epistemological level. They enact a culturalist epistemology that
obscures a structural portrait of Chinatown's racialized class inequities,
disrupting Leila's telling of that story, that is, her construction of racial-
political critique.

This is not to villainize Leon or overdetermine his intentionality. He
willfully culturalizes Ona's suicide, but is not scheming to disavow or
exacerbate his family's poverty and labor exploitation. At times, Leon is
strongly politicized. For instance, though he culturalizes Ona's suicide,
he also blames it on America's "big promises" and its "breaking of every one": "'America,' he ranted, 'this lie of a country!'" (103). Moreover,
his culturalisms are compensatory, trading in racial empowerment for
gender privilege, as I detail below. Nonetheless, Leon's reproduction of
culturalisms unsettles Leila's attempt to construct a critique of Chinatown's class inequities. Though it is mitigated by his occasional critique
of the state and the compensatory character of his desires, his reproduction of culturalisms unsettles the assumptions that racialized subjects
uniformly share the desire to articulate political critique.

Culturalisms are more intentionally used to hinder racial-political
critique by Luciano Ong, Leon's business partner and, to Leon, an imagined family member. Luciano and Leon set up the Ong & Leong laundry

together, but the venture collapses because Luciano cheats Leon. He does so by exploiting the culturalist family ethics that Leon clings to in his rationalizations of Ona's suicide. In his relationship with Luciano, Leon relies upon a hierarchical fraternalism, deferring to Luciano as *Dai Gor*, or "big brother" (165). This is an imagined kinship relationship based on shared race and culture. It presumes the loyalty and goodwill of familial relations that are not based on biologically shared blood, but on the bonds of sharing race and the attendant culture—on co-ethnic bonds. Leon defers to Luciano's authority and goodwill as a Chinese big brother, in exchange for Luciano's obligation to take care of Leon's interests as a co-ethnic underling. The two men enter into business the "old world" way, with no legal paperwork, but just a handshake and Leon's unconditional racial-cultural faith in his Chinese brother (171). Leila and Mah are wary of this arrangement and rightly so. Leon's faith in co-ethnic bonds gives Luciano the cover to filch the laundry's investment money and siphon its revenue.

Leon and Luciano are participating in an imagined kinship network in which cultural ethics structure economic behavior. This economic kinship network is an extension of Leon's culturalized vision of family through which he filters Ona's suicide. Leon construes economic behavior as being driven by Chinese culture, more precisely, by the loyalty and goodwill that are presumed to arise from the bonds of shared race and culture. Ironically, then, though Leon's reproduction of culturalizations vis-à-vis his daughter's suicide disrupts racial-political essentialism, here he puts forth a racial-*economic* essentialism. Luciano does not question Leon's culturalized vision of cultural, ethical, and economic family, but rather exploits it.

The organization and drawbacks of the economic kinship system that structures Leon and Luciano's partnership echo the premises and problems of the "ethnic enclave economy theory." As detailed in chapter 2, the theory claims that racialized immigrants, excluded from the mainstream labor market or relegated to its dead-end secondary sector, form an alternative enclave economy comprised of co-ethnic labor and business networks. Spaces like Chinatown become sites of "co-ethnic cooperation," trust, loyalty, and goodwill between employers and employees animated by bonds of shared race and culture, which jump-starts the upward mobility of bosses and workers alike (Zhou 4–13, 119–51).

The ethnic enclave economy theory adds significant nuance to perceptions of Chinatown. It represents Chinatown as a dynamic, cultural-economic space of ethnic agency, instead of a blighted ghetto where workers have little opportunity or will to self-determination. The theory also recovers Chinatown from the Chicago school model and its privileging of assimilation; Chinatown is not an inferior "species" formation that will (and should) dismantle as immigrants acculturate. The ethnic enclave economy theory also subverts the neoliberal, multiculturalist commodification of ethnicity, by empowering Chinatown's routinely commodified subjects to self-reify their culture for economic gain. It is a strategic culturalization: culture is literally an economic asset rather than, as in the Chicago school, a class pathology. For someone like Leon, who experiences continual racialized labor exploitation and exclusion, a co-ethnic economic partnership like the Ong & Leong Laundry is a hopeful alternative, a path to upward mobility chartered with a trustworthy Chinese brother.

But in the ethnic enclave economy, co-ethnic cooperation can be a cover for co-ethnic exploitation. Exploitation at the hands of co-ethnics can be refashioned into a temporary unpleasantness that workers can count on to be eventually and benevolently rectified by trustworthy bosses. Co-ethnic cooperation can also be used to neutralize political protest. Peter Kwong notes that cooperation among co-ethnic employers includes the sharing of blacklists of activist workers, who are branded as race-traitors (95). The rhetoric of ethnic loyalty is often folded into a kinship ideology like Leon's. For instance, during a 1984 restaurant strike in New York's Chinatown, supporters of the restaurant owner urged: "[T]his situation could be resolved without resorting to American courts. After all, we are all the offspring of our ancient emperor Wang-te. . . . [I]t is wrong to fight among us brothers" (qtd. in Kwong 139–40).

The intra-ethnic suppression of political protest shows that there is a lack of a uniform racial-political desire within Chinatown. This is partly attributable to an internal class divide, between better-off, profit-motivated business owners and exploited, low-wage workers. But Chinatown class divides do not provide an exclusive or exhaustive map of racial subjects' political positions. Workers who are exploited under co-ethnic cooperation can be committed to it, in spite of their rational interests, as demonstrated in *Bone* by Leon's self-defeating faith in Luciano as *Dai Gor*. Likewise, not all business owners are economically insidious, nor can the entirety of Chinese American ghettoization be pinned on them. Chinatown small business owners are often only relatively better-off than their workers, as well as ghettoized themselves, in that they turn to Chinatown ventures because of their racial exclusion from the mainstream labor market. Even if their businesses do enable a degree of upward mobility, they tend to have lower median incomes than whites with the same level of skills and education (Zhou 130–39). These various configurations of race, class, and political sensibility show that the fault lines of racial-political desire are not easily drawn. Racial-political essentialism does not hold.

Brotherhood: its bonds and obligations falsely promise and cheat Leon of his cultural-economic dream, but also manifest that race is a political mask. Everyday social relations tell us that the relationship between race and politics is not unmessy. However, if it is palatable enough to recognize how we live, we have been more stubborn in how we read. Drawing on Anne Cheng's, David Eng's and Shinhee Han's discussions of racial melancholia, Juliana Chang argues that Leon figures the nation's "melancholic remains," "illegible and illegitimate remainders of history" that refuse symbolic, affective, and bodily incorporation into the national narrative of modernity. As these dogged leftovers, subjects like Leon enable counternarratives that recognize, for instance, that capitalist modernity hinges upon racialized labor exploitation (113). However, these leftover subjects are also illegible as imperfect vehicles of the counternarratives. They mark the continuing need for counternarratives, but also ask us to consider the impediments to creating them. If Leon represents the stubborn detritus that the nation cannot fully kill off symbolically or materially, subjects like him at times kill themselves, or at least their socioeconomic prospects, with the perpetuation of culturalisms and the attendant self-defeating obstruction of racial-political critique. Ona's death is thus important not only because its narration is interrupted, but also because it is self-inflicted. Suicide figures the complicity of the Chinatown underclass in hastening its political-economic death.

Endogamy and Death

Withholding the consolation of narrative and the solace of racial-political critique, *Bone* demonstrates that race is an insufficient category of political protest. What, then, is the shape of the political future, especially when it is contravened by death, the political-economic suicide of racialized subjects who perpetuate the silencing of their exploitation? *Bone* paradoxically imagines a political future through this racial-political death, and its figuration through Ona's actual death. The loss of Ona's body, as well as the narrative body that does not hew to political expectations of race, generate in particular an antiheterosexist political future. This political future forestalls the reproduction of racial-political essentialisms, as well as literal acts and logics of heterosexual reproduction that underwrite political neutralization. My discussion of the latter does not seek to make racial-political essentialism more whole, but to make visible—and call into question—the relationship among race, heterosexuality, and politics. This is not to bankrupt race as a political framework or to offer airtight alternatives, but to truss some of the buckling points in the relationship between race and politics. Those buckling points are borne upon racialized women's bodies, namely on their heterosexual, biological, reproductive labor.

Death is generative in *Bone* because the text is deeply suspicious of reproduction. Reproduction causes death. The reproduction of culturalisms cultivates figurative death, a political death, as seen in the debilitation of Leila's efforts to construct racial-political critique. The destruction of racial-political critique begets socioeconomic death; culturalist obfuscations of structural ghettoization perpetuate labor exploitation and class inequity. Culturalisms beget this political-economic death through the sexual discipline of racialized women's bodies. Specifically, heterosexual gender obligations are necessary to create and sustain Leon's culturalist ethics of ethnic-economic family. Leon's economic kinship network is organized around an ethos of endogamy—he demands that economic relations are kept within the racial-cultural Chinese family. This metaphor of endogamy is not just a metaphor. Leon needs the obedience of Chinatown women to racial-biological endogamy to sustain his cultural-economic ethics and culturalized ethics more generally. Leon's ethics of endogamous, economic kinship and its attendant culturalist depoliticizations are prescriptions for heterosexuality.

This mandate for heterosexuality manifests in Leon's prohibition of Ona's relationship with Osvaldo. Leon demands that Ona break up with Osvaldo because Osvaldo's father had swindled Leon in the laundry business ("Crooked father, crooked son" [172]). But he also forbids the relationship because it threatens the purity of his endogamous ethical family. This ethical destabilization is screened through the threat of biological impurity. Osvaldo has non-Chinese lineage (his mother, Rosa, has Peruvian heritage), encoding the threat of miscegenation in his romance with Ona. Leon's hostility toward miscegenation is evident in the vocabulary of racial-biological purity that he uses to prohibit Ona and Osvaldo's relationship: "I forbid you to see that mongrel boy" (169).

This racist animosity marks a radical change of heart. Leon previously embraced Osvaldo, so much so that he called him "son" (169). Yet Leon's *volte-face* bespeaks a consistency, of the intransigence of his culturalist faith. Recall Leon's blind trust in Luciano as a co-ethnic brother. This is shibboleth enough to welcome Osvaldo into the fold, despite his not being "purely" Chinese. Implied is that Osvaldo has inherited his father's cultural-ethical Chinese-ness, demonstrated in Leon's interpellation of Osvaldo as his own heir, an appropriate "son" for his cultural-ethical family. But if Osvaldo was Chinese enough through the presumed racial-cultural ethics of his father, Luciano becomes inadequately Chinese through the body of his son. Maligning Osvaldo for his racial impurity is a way to discredit Luciano's cultural-ethical purity. If Osvaldo is a racial mongrel, then perhaps his father is a cultural-ethical mongrel—someone who cheated Leon because his cultural ethics are not fully and adequately Chinese. This supposition denies the possibility of co-ethnic exploitation. Rather than seeing Luciano as having exploited his co-ethnic trust, as breaking the fiction of cultural-ethical family, Leon holds fast to his culturalisms, attributing Luciano's deception to his implied cultural-ethical tainting. Luciano's previously unseen, un-Chinese ethics are literally embodied in his son's tainted racial body, the manifest, bodily sign of the cultural-ethical impurity that Luciano enacts. Luciano is unscrupulous because he is not *ethically* Chinese enough, seen in that his son is not *ethnically* Chinese enough.

Osvaldo's racial-biological body figures violations of cultural-ethical purity, but it is Ona's body that is surveilled to curb them. Leon's command that Ona break up with the "mongrel" expresses his desire for cultural-ethical endogamy through a demand for his daughter's racial-biological endogamy. If bodily, racial impurity is the sign and cause of cultural-ethical deficiency, Ona's relationship with Osvaldo, insofar as it encodes miscegenation, threatens to propagate the biological underpinnings of cultural-ethical impurity. Ona's body must be managed. It is the vessel through which racial-biological purity and the attendant cultural ethics are to be preserved or polluted. Given that culturalisms neutralize political protest, women's bodies are turned against themselves, commanded to beget their own political-economic death.

The instrumentality of racialized women's biological bodies in sustaining depoliticizing culturalisms makes visible that culturalisms are underwritten by an imperative to heterosexuality. It is against this context that Ona's suicide signifies and enacts more than foreclosure, of healing and political critique. Given the cost of perpetuating a certain kind of racial life—the silencing of political critique by the heterosexual production of endogamous ethics and bodies—*Bone* turns toward the trajectory of death. The relationship among politics, biological reproduction, sexuality, and death is addressed by Lee Edelman, who also sees heterosexual biological reproduction as a means of political silencing. For Edelman, contemporary politics, no matter how apparently progressive, reinstantiates a conservative, specifically heterosexist, social order. This is because politics is ethically structured and discursively expressed as a "fight for the children": the fantasy of "the Child" is the "perpetual horizon of every acknowledged politics, the fantasmatic beneficiary of every political intervention." Politics is an imperative to heterosexuality, to preserving the value of producing children and of the underwriting heterosexual, social-biological relations. Politics is thereby hamstrung by an ideology of "reproductive futurism," an imagination of the political future as committing and recommitting to ethical and biological relations of heterosexual reproduction (1–3).

The heterosexual imperatives of reproductive futurism take on additional dimensions in the racialized world of the Leongs. Here, the political future is calibrated by a "racial Child." The racial Child is the "fantasmatic horizon" of Leon's endogamy; it is the fantastical figure of racial, cultural, and ethical purity. As such, it is the producer and product of the racial-sexual discipline imposed on Ona, the sign and material body of the racially pure heterosexual genealogy that is to promise cultural-ethical purity. The racial Child, like Edelman's abstract Child, reinstantiates retrogressive social orders, in this case, the racial hierarchies and the attendant class stratification naturalized by culturalist ethics. Recall Kwong's description of how a restaurant strike in New York's Chinatown was suppressed through the discourse of kinship, through the appeal that employees and bosses are all "offspring of the ancient emperor Wang-te" (139–40). This rhetoric seeks to quiet protest by interpellating workers as Chinese children, more precisely China's children, who, assembled under a common racial-national biology, are obligated to cultural-ethical solidarity over political protest. An important difference, then, between the racial and abstract Child is that the former does not feign progressive politics but, as the vessel of depoliticizing culturalisms, manifestly undoes them. The racial Child is the abstract Child unmasked. It neutralizes politics without claiming the alibi of doing the opposite.

Death contravenes the fantasy of the racial Child and its depoliticizing, ethical, and biological apparatus of heterosexual reproduction. In the simplest of terms, by killing herself, Ona withdraws from the economy of racial-biological endogamy. This is not necessarily her motivation, but it is an important effect. Ona already threatened to break her family's lineage through her relationship with Osvaldo, the "mongrel," but her suicide actualizes the break by destroying the body that is commanded to bear endogamous children and ethics.

But death is no guarantee of withdrawal from a depoliticizing, heterosexual, culturalist economy. Gayatri Spivak's discussion of another suicide, of Bhuvaneswari Bhaduri, an unmarried, female Indian independence activist, is illustrative here. Bhuvaneswari was assigned to assassinate an enemy, but wanting neither to execute the murder nor disobey her group, killed herself instead. Spivak notes that colonialist scripts would read the suicide in the genre of *sati*, the self-immolation of widows on their husband's funeral pyre; the self-inflicted death of any woman without a husband manifests the barbaric routines of Indian cultural patriarchy. Yet ironically, it was Bhuvaneswari's activist community that rehearsed these scripts, by reading the suicide as a response to unrequited love or spinster melancholy. These narratives, like *sati* discourse, inscribe the woman's body in the sexual-semiotic economy of culturalized, heterosexual male possession (307–8).

Spivak's famous point is that the subaltern cannot speak. The subaltern subject is not inherently or guaranteed to be political, but must be discursively constructed as such, evident in that they can be denied such a construction. Bhuvaneswari's body, even in death, is made to bear depoliticizing, culturalist, gendered ethics by being read as the sign of not fulfilling them—the racialized, gendered body can confound rather than enable political speech. This political neutralization is effected by subjects who are assumed to be political, by Bhuvaneswari's fellow activists whose shared subaltern status does not manifest a uniformity of political desire when gender and sexuality are taken into account. Even in death, depoliticizing culturalisms stubbornly refuse to die.

If the fact of death is not enough to counteract cuturalisms, the manner of Ona's suicide prevents their reproduction. Beyond withdrawing her body from Leon's endogamous economy, Ona kills herself in a way that precludes the posthumous culturalization of her body. Jumping off the Nam Ping Yuen mangles her body, which then requires cremation, disheartening the mourners who seek something tangible onto which to invest their grief. Cremation also forestalls the post-mortem narrativization of her body, furnishing no body to serve as an artifactual object lesson of the tragic consequence of violating heterosexual culturalist ethics. If the physical condition of death contravenes the racial-sexual management of Ona's body, the manner of her suicide contravenes her body's narrative and epistemological management.

Ona is a recalcitrant child who refuses to give biological and epistemological life to depoliticizing culturalisms. Withdrawing bodily and epistemologically from her father's endogamous economy, she refuses to bear the racial Child and its culturalist political neutralizations. That the terms of racial depoliticization are enfigured in the heterosexual imperative to produce the racial Child makes visible the embeddedness of sexuality and race. Sexuality is at the center of racial problematics, and racial relations can preserve the privilege of heterosexuality. Race, in turn, can map a more particular terrain of sexuality. These intersections can help us imagine interventions into heterosexist, racial-political neutralizations. They do so by suggesting a turn to the relationship between race and the queer. Edelman looks to the queer, as well as to death, to counteract the regressions of politics-as-reproductive-futurism. However, Edelman concludes that the intervention of the queer and death into politics is to render politics effete, to show that there is "No Future," as pronounced by the title of his study. In contrast, my use of the queer and death seeks to enable a political future. Ona's death is a queer death that generates, rather than evacuates, political possibilities. This difference stems from the differences in social relations—and social exigencies—that are immanent when the role of race is accounted for in the queer.

The Political Future and Queer Exogamy

In Asian American studies, modest attention has been given to the queer as a mode of politics. David Eng argues that turning to the queer will "engage[], renew[] and render[] efficacious" Asian American politics and Asian Americans as political agents (225). Such renewal is necessary because of at least one stumbling block—the inability to count on race to impel political protest. This is not an essentialization of the queer as political, nor is this to premise the queer exclusively on sexual identity. Rather, Eng posits the queer as a critical methodology that is capable of looking at "multiple axes of difference in highly dynamic ways," and that is "an organizing topos that affirms rather than effaces a host of alternate differences," yet enables the organization of new and flexible "coalitional possibilities" (216, 225). Other axes of difference can honor this heterogeneity (though some better than others, as my discussion of the inadequacies of race shows), and the queer can certainly be homogenizing. The point is that the queer is a productive choice of critical lens that has an effective capacity to shore up the sags of race-based politics.

Imagining politics through the queer might be a critical choice, but it is not an arbitrary one. The queer constitutively structures Asian American subjectivity and sociality. Eng and Nayan Shah point out that Asian Americans have entered the U.S. polity and space as queer formations. Of note are the Chinatown "bachelor societies" that were institutionally constructed, but politically oppositional. They subverted social management by modeling antinormative practices of homosociality and homoeroticsm (Eng 17–19; Shah 77–97). Mid-twentieth-century liberalizations of immigration and citizenship laws enable Asian American social formations to develop along normative models, but the queer remains a constitutive mode of Asian American political oppositionality. The queer emerges as such in response to the heterosexism and homophobia that underwrite one of the most vocal modes of Asian American oppositional discourse. I am referring back to the *Aiiieeeee!* editors' political "sensibility," which Eng and many others point out recuperates racial subjectivity, especially that of emasculated Asian American men, through an aggressively masculinist, homophobic discourse. Inasmuch as Asian Americans seek a capacious terrain of politics, this heterosexism and homophobia must be contested, and is immanently contested through the queer. Inasmuch as the *Aiiieeeee!* editors' heterosexist and homophobic political model, as roundly criticized as it is, nevertheless underwrites our dominant political rubric—the racial-political essentialisms that I delineated at the outset of this essay—the queer is necessary to craft a more nuanced political practice. The queer is not essentially political, but given the genealogy of Asian American oppositional discourse, it is essential to Asian American politics.

Edelman's critique of "reproductive futurism" does not address race, but its insights enable the imagination of Ona's death as a queer death that has a relationship to politics. But because I seek to account for race, I reach the different conclusion that the queer and death generate rather than destroy politics. For Edelman, the queer embodies death as the act and figure that reject the constitutive heterosexism of politics. Queer sexuality is an act of death in that it entails sex that does not presume or aspire to biological reproduction. The queer is a figuration of death in that it embodies the death drive, the move toward instability and dissolution in the Lacanian realm of ontology and meaning. The queer shatters the fantasy of stability in the Imaginary, the realm of meaning, identity, and social form, which, being engendered by teleologies of production, is subtended by the logics of heterosexuality. As a set of figural relations derived from sexual relations without reproductive aims, the queer is thereby a figuration of nonproductivity that does not wend toward the Imaginary and social form, but destroys it instead. The queer "figures the place of the social order's death drive," embodying and exerting an energy of negativity and dissolution against the heterosexually underwritten instantiation of Imaginary form. This energy is radical and relentless. Not merely an antidote to the heterosexist social order, the queer is the antithesis of social order itself, "the negativity opposed to every form of social viability" (6–8, 9, 3).

Politics, as a channel through which heterosexist form and social order are produced, as evidenced by its production of and constitution by the Child, is the particular heterosexist social form that the queer destroys. Since politics produces social form and is a version of social form, the queer as the negation of social form is inherently antipolitical. The intervention of the queer, for Edelman, is therefore its destruction of politics—not just retrogressive politics, but all politics, insofar as all politics are a version of heterosexually produced social form (therefore all politics are retrogressive). However, Edelman's critics note that the queer need not be opposed to politics in toto because all politics are not inadequate—or unnecessary—in toto. Moreover, Tim Dean points out that linking the queer with the antisocial is not to place queerness outside of the empirical world of the social, but to exploit strategically the elements of homosexuality that trouble the disciplines of the social (826–27). This is particularly important for racialized subjects, like those represented in *Bone*, because their battle is not to opt out of the social but, as subjects who are persistently stripped of social, political, and economic legibility, to write themselves in (for better or worse and not without revising the social along the way). Factoring race into "reproductive futurism" helps to imagine for racialized subjects a political future, the foreclosures of which are crises, not resolutions.

Bone gestures toward the queer as a mode of political futurity through its suspicion of not just endogamous reproduction, but of heterosexual reproduction more generally. Ona's suicide repudiates her father's endogamous mandates, but her death also defeats a possibility for *exogamous* sociality. If endogamy mutes politics, it might follow that exogamy does the opposite, as a reproductive and social act that crosses rather than crystallizes racial-biological and cultural-ethical boundaries. This is demonstrated by discourses and practices of cross-racial coalition-building, an important and effective strategy in race-based politics. As a way to minimize fractures and hierarchies of class, gender, and sexuality within a racial group, cross-racial coalition-building is a favored mode of political organizing and critical inquiry. This sociopolitical mixing can be metaphorized as a kind of exogamy, the miscegenation of sociopolitical relations to amplify the shared voices of individual racial groups while indexing the continuing centrality of race, for racial groups individually and in their aggregation as a nonwhite collectivity. As with endogamy, exogamy as a trope for sociopolitical relations is rooted in the racial-biological relations from which the trope derives. Cross-racial political alliances are often born out of the intimacy of interracial relationships or through the multiracially identified interests of interracial individuals. The political implications of biological exogamy are intimated in Ona and Osvaldo's romance. Their cross-racial, social-sexual relationship tropes and enacts the sociopolitical crossing of racial boundaries, and their potential reproduction of miscegenated offspring is symbolic of building a cross-racial genealogy.

This potential, however, is short-circuited by Ona's death. Ona's death rejects the discipline of endogamy, but it also cuts off the possibilities of producing an exogamous political future, insofar as the latter requires the reproductive labor of her body. Ona's death derails this exogamous potential because though exogamy might be a more effective race-based political model, it remains linked to the chauvinistic ethics of heterosexuality. If cultural-ethical endogamy demands racialized women's obedience to racial-biological endogamy, exogamy as a trope for sociopolitical mixing can be seen as freeing women to participate in racial-sexual behavior outside the bounds of masculinist racial prescriptions. However, cross-racial political alliances born out of racial-biological exogamy maintain the obligation of women's bodies to heterosexual reproductive demands, even if for politically progressive purposes. A political future imagined through Ona and Osvaldo's miscegenated offspring entails the continued requisition of women's bodies—erecting a political future upon a fantasy of a cross-racial Child. Whether because endogamy is silencing or because exogamy is an imperfect alternative, *Bone* turns us toward a politics dissociated from the reproductive functions of the heterosexual body.

If the queer is stereotyped as being "sterile, unproductive, antifamily and death-driven" (Dean 827), it would further destroy the already destroyed Leong family. But recovering normative nuclear familiality is not an option either. After all, the ethics of family fuels the Leongs' grief. Instead, through Ona's death, the drive toward death and dissolution of the queer productively aggravates the Leongs' family degeneration. Ona's death destroys her family by queering it. It repudiates the heterosexual imperatives embedded in endogamous familiality and exogamous alternatives. Ona's death as a queering death is not merely a theoretical celebration of negativity and destruction. It emotionally and materially helps the Leongs recuperate their ruined lives, specifically by impelling them toward the production of queer family relations. Ona's death takes us from the queer destruction of family to its queer production.

Generative, queer family relations are most notably found between Rosa (Luciano's wife and Osvaldo's mother) and Mah. Unlike the many broken relationships in *Bone*, theirs is abiding. Spending long hours working together at a sweatshop, the women become "like sisters" (164). The language of sisterhood is important for it invokes and claims a cross-racial political bond. Rosa, we recall, has Peruvian lineage, her adulterated body originating the racial-biological and cultural-ethical contamination mapped onto her husband and son. By considering themselves "like sisters," Mah and Rosa imagine a kinship network, like Leon does with Luciano, but one with political possibilities. Mah and Rosa create a familiality of gendered cross-racial bonds born out of the conditions of work. Sisterhood as such is a prevalent discourse and mode of political organizing that frames the activism of racialized female laborers. Sisterhood discourse can have the disciplinary effects of the brotherhood that structures Leon and Luciano's relationship, but the imagined kinship community that Mah and Rosa model is animated to challenge, not compound, racialized, gendered labor exploitation. For instance, in Miriam Louie's interviews with female laborer-activists, Julia Song of the Korean Immigrant Workers Advocates (KIWA) notes that to build trust with exploited female restaurant workers she claims the role of *onni*, or protective, older sister figure. She does so not to depoliticize them (or to exploit, as Luciano does as *Dai Gor*), but to motivate them for political action. Notably, Song is *onni* not only to Korean workers. Advocacy groups like KIWA initially formed around racial-cultural identity, but have flexibly adapted to organize around shared, cross-racial exploitation within a workplace, for instance, challenging Korean bosses on behalf of Asian and Latino workers (Louie 181, 157). Mah and Rosa's relationship represents the empirical seed of these sisterhoods. They are cross-racial familialities crafted at work to do political work.

As cross-racial coalitional formations, these sisterhoods might be a form of heterosexist political exogamy. On the contrary, they contravene the heterosexual requisites of exogamy because they are queer sisterhoods. This is intimated in the erotic charge of Mah and Rosa's re-lationship: "They joked that they sewed more than they slept, and sewing side by side, they were more intimate with each other than with their husbands" (164). Mah and Rosa's erotic intimacy is an erotic domestic relation. As mentioned, for Mah the home becomes a factory and the factory becomes a home, turning the workplace into a domestic space that, as we see, is overlaid with a same-sex erotic charge. Mah and Rosa's relationship thereby models a form of "queer domesticity," to use Nayan Shah's phrase. Shah uses this term to describe domestic arrangements in San Francisco's early twentieth-century Chinatown. Because of im-migration and citizenship laws, these arrangements were characterized by densely inhabited household units of unrelated, unmarried Chinese men (the homosocial and homoerotic "bachelor society"), with the few women unidentifiable as wives and mothers, though more identifiable as prostitutes. These arrangements transgressed heterosexual nuclear family norms. Chinatown residents were thereby pathologized as "sexu-ally maladjusted" and "delinquent and deficient of normative aspira-tions" to monogamous, heterosexual marriage. "Queer domesticity" thus describes homosociality and homoeroticism as well as delinquent heterosexuality. Queer domesticity as such is generative, Shah argues. Specifically, it enables the cultivation of networks of domestic care and intimacy outside the bounds of conjugal heterosexual reproduction. It enables the cultivation of queer familialities (82–85, 78).

As a cross-racial political familiality crafted outside the political-sexual economy of racial-cultural heterosexuality, Mah and Rosa's rela-tionship models what I call "queer exogamy." The women form a queer sisterhood that does political work. Queer exogamy diverges from Edel-man's trajectory of the queer as politically effete. Rather, because these relations are queer they do political work, given the depoliticizations of heterosexual familiality. Louie's laborer-activist interviewees articulate the connections between politics and queer familiality. For instance, María Antonia Flores turns away from heterosexual domesticity by turning to the sisterhood of La Mujer Obrera. Heterosexual domesticity teaches her to be a self-sacrificing Mexican wife, a role that naturalizes her exploitation in her factory job ("When you are just sitting there lis-tening to your husband, you think it's perfectly natural that you have no rights as a woman, as a person") (qtd. in Louie 91). Flores rejects heterosexual domesticity because it is depoliticizing ("just sitting there listening"), and turns to a familiality that is queer in that it is homosocial and politicized. Queer sisterhoods emerge as the dialectical result of a contradiction of masculinist, culturalist family ideology that perpetuates racialized, gendered exploitation. These women remain committed to the ideology of family, but of a family that is more capacious and politically effective than is prescribed by heterosexual normativity.

All the *Bone* women, Mah, Rosa, and Ona, gesture to the cutting off of heterosexual biological production of family (not incidentally, Nina, the middle sister, has had an abortion). But they model the propagation of a rearticulated family organized by politicized queer sisterhoods. Queer sisterhoods enable a mode of production, the production of family and politics that Leila cannot create through the category of race. This is not to idealize queer familiality. Juliana Chang points out that Leon and Luciano's relationship is figured as a romance and courtship, seen in Leon's eroticized admiration of Luciano's body, and his eager, lady-in-waiting type anticipation of their meetings (122–23). Yet in this case, the same-sex eroticism serves Leon's demand for biological and ethical endogamy, amplifying the depoliticizing norms of heterosexist family. Mah herself is not an airtight figure of queer exogamy. She ultimately leaves her job at the sweatshop to run a children's clothing shop (the "Baby Store"), suggesting an endorsement of heterosexist reproduction. However, Mah keeps the shop in less than perfect repair, even foregoing to change the old storefront sign, which still reads "Herb Shop" (20). Leila puzzles over this ineffective business strategy, and her boyfriend concludes that Mah "wants to hide" (20). The Baby Store is Mah's cover. It provides her the cover of participating in the logics of heterosexual normativity but, insofar as her behavior is economically irrational (not properly advertising her heterosexist wares), she resists being fully pulled into reproducing the depoliticizing norms of heterosexual family.

The queer sisterhoods described above refract racial as well as sexual norms. Their erotics extend through the terrain of race to engender cross-racial familialities, which draw from the queer to provide alternatives to the depoliticizations of racialized heterosexuality. They are queer exogamies.

Destroyed Narratives

Ona's suicide impels a queer, exogamous mode of imagining and living race, politics, and family. It traumatically destroys a normative nuclear, particularly culturalist, model of Chinatown family, which is nonetheless destroying itself via the self-neutralization of politics. "Chinatown" emerges as metalepsis, the signifier of an idea and a place that is only fictively Chinese insofar as it disappoints racial-cultural fantasies as well as racial-political ones. But Chinatown also enables the imagination of queer exogamous familiality, which is not a fail-safe mode of politicization, but one way that racialized, gendered subjects can make themselves legible, particularly when they are invested in erasing each other. Queer politics offers an alternate mode of narrative, of enabling racialized subjects to write themselves into the social. The queer enables a generative destruction, the production of alternatives to race-based political critique through the destruction of the heterosexist culturalisms that immanently destabilize that critique. This drive toward legibility is paradoxically enabled by the textual and physical unavailability of Ona's body. The absence of her physical body confounds the construction of textual bodies, either as culturalist scripts that perpetuate racialized, gendered exploitation and the propagation of biological bodies that feed these scripts, or as the race-based political critique that seeks to voice oppositionality, but cannot fully do so.

That Ona's death thus turns us away from heterosexist culturalist Chinese family and its attendant depoliticizations is indexed by *Bone*'s backward, halting chronology. This reversal of narrative temporality is accompanied by a generational reversal—instead of families and futures generated through Ona, as a representative of the second generation, the generation of hope and progress in immigrant narratology, *Bone* turns us back to Mah and Rosa, to the first immigrant generation, whose values and bearings are typically coded as outmoded, dying, and defunct. However, it is through acts and hermeneutics of death and degeneration that *Bone* imagines a political future. This enables the generation of a productive formation out of the traumatic damage of Ona's suicide, a suicide that is Chinese insofar as it is taken as a code for culturalist visions of Chinese family, but that is ultimately not Chinese enough, in that it cannot be narrated through the racial-political essentialisms we assume to gainsay these culturalisms. Ona's death impels another kind of Chinese suicide, the turning away from the racial-political essentialisms that we have relied on, to good end, but that have limited efficacy in imagining a political future. We learn this through *Bone*, a novel about failure, not of Ona or of the possibility of healing for her family, but of the narratives we have relied upon to tell our stories.

In 2005, two entrepreneurial behemoths, Google and Microsoft, were entangled in a battle over intellectual property. At issue was Google's hiring away of a Microsoft executive, Kai-Fu Lee, to head Google's rapidly expanding China operations. The intellectual property in question was Lee's technological and business expertise, which, having been developed as an employee of Microsoft, was claimed by Microsoft as company property. As claims to Lee's expertise were fought over, other possessions of his emerged as central to the dispute. Also at stake was Lee's racial body, his value as an authentic Chinese subject who inhabits and commands the racial, cultural, and linguistic codes that could help Google penetrate the China technology market. Lee was being battled over as a valuable commodity of race and ethnicity, a commodity that he himself was expected to self-exploit and trade, and through which he would rise in the ranks of the technology world as well as a powerful, elite, transnational class. At Google, Lee is the entrepreneurial giant's "ethnic entrepreneur," what Viet Nguyen describes as a subject who trades upon his race and culture to gain social and material privilege (3–19). Race and culture being his commodities, Lee is an ethnic entrepreneur in that he is an entrepreneur of ethnicity.

The figure of the Asian American ethnic entrepreneur unsettles the conventional relationship among race, culture, and class. Whereas for most racial groups it is axiomatic to associate race with class disadvantage, for Asian Americans ethnic entrepreneurship suggests that race *improves* class, that it confers class privilege. For Asian American studies, ethnic entrepreneurship impels attention beyond canonical figures configured by orthodox relationships between race and class. It demands that we pay attention to not just nineteenth-century "yellow peril" coolie laborers, but also to figures like Kai-Fu Lee, who destabilize the idea that race is a categorical class liability.

Two particular kinds of ethnic entrepreneurship invert the relationship between race and class. The first is characterized by Kai-Fu Lee, for whom race is a valuable socioeconomic asset. Here, the "ethnic" in "ethnic entrepreneurship" is more than a descriptor of the entrepreneur's racial-cultural body. It denotes that ethnicity is a commodity, and that the entrepreneur's particular enterprise is trading that commodity, through which he obtains class privilege. The second form of ethnic entrepreneurship examined here is Asian American small business ownership—particularly Korean American small business ownership. What can we learn from the curious fact that so many Korean Americans run mom-and-pop grocery stores, convenience stores, liquor stores, and the like, especially in urban black ghettos, a phenomenon that became a matter of national crisis during the 1992 Los Angeles riots?[1] For Korean American shopkeepers, there is also a syntactical reconfiguration of the "ethnic" in "ethnic entrepreneurship." "Ethnic" in this case denotes causality, suggesting that Korean Americans are entrepreneurs *because* they are ethnic. Korean Americans are culturalized as shopkeepers, their small business ownership constructed as a racial-cultural proclivity. To the extent that Korean American shopkeepers have become symbols of Asian American upward mobility (even though the failure rate of small businesses is quite high),[2] especially as a foil to their impoverished African American customers, these ethnic entrepreneurs are testimony that racial-cultural difference does not necessarily hinder class mobility. Culturalized as shopkeepers, they are iconicized as figures of upward mobility not in the absence of race, for instance, through the color-blind rhetoric that typically structures exceptionalist American Dream discourse, but in the salient presence of race. Korean American ethnic entrepreneurs provide another instance of how racial-cultural difference ostensibly improves class.

That race can improve class warrants skepticism. For one, if race brings class privilege, it does so for some racial subjects, but not all. Kai-Fu Lee might enjoy class privilege on account of being Chinese, but this is less so for some of his co-ethnics in China. Who will be the technology drones punching out code or the wage laborers building the physical and service infrastructure to support Google's presence in the Chinese technology frontier? How might the advantages of a Kai-Fu Lee come at the expense of his co-ethnics? What are the ethical obligations of ethnic subjects to each other in the process of securing class privilege or pursuing upward mobility? The entrepreneur of ethnicity as a commodity is burdened by these questions of ethnic loyalty and betrayal. Selling his ethnicity as a commodity can result in and depend upon the "selling-out" of his co-ethnics (Nguyen 3–19), for instance, upon perpetuating the idea and practice that a class of racialized subjects is available as and amenable to being cheap and exploitable labor. If race enables class privilege, it does so unevenly, enabling the privilege of some while amplifying its disciplining effect for others.

Race also works unevenly, but in a different way, in enabling class advancement for the second type of ethnic entrepreneur under discussion. Small business ownership has been touted as Korean Americans' particular track to upward mobility. It is constructed as such through culturalizations, through the idea that there is something about Korean race and culture that causes Koreans to be mom-and-pop shopkeepers. These culturalizations are dubious, as is the desirability of small business ownership as a route to upward mobility. This form of ethnic entrepreneurship is a form of class containment and discipline. It is a limited and limiting niche that results from American racial exclusions rather than Asiatic racial virtues. Specifically, small business ownership enables Korean Americans to advance economically, but it keeps them marginalized socially and politically. It evinces a reconfiguration of our contemporary racial equilibrium in which racialized subjects are conceded economic advancement as a literal buy off for quiescence in social and political domains. I describe this uneven condition as a "fracturing of class spheres." It is a condition of economic mobility denuded of social and political mobility. Fractured in this way, class mobility through small business ownership is a disciplining form of upward mobility that impels a reassessment of how we define and what we aspire to as class mobility. If there is an argument to be made that fractured class mobility is better than nothing, its untenability was made clear during the 1992 Los Angeles riots, when Korean Americans were abandoned by social and political institutions as their stores burned to the ground, and when they became embroiled in what was dubbed "black-Korean conflict." These problems, and others, of Korean American shopkeepers make their upward mobility through ethnic entrepreneurship an instance not of racialized class success, but of racialized class failure.

Chang-rae Lee's *Native Speaker* draws us into these worlds of ethnic entrepreneurship in which race has an apparently positive impact on class, but not without qualifications. As a spy novel *cum* immigrant rags-to-riches story, *Native Speaker* interweaves the two types of ethnic entrepreneurs' respective negotiations of ethnic loyalty and fractured class mobility. Scholarship on *Native Speaker* focuses on the role of the protagonist, Henry Park, a second-generation Korean American and professional spy, as a trope for the ethics of immigrant integration into the American polity. John Kwang is also a well-discussed figure; the novel's councilman of Queens, New York, he attempts the heroic work of enfranchising racialized immigrants in the political sphere. Of note are Min Song's contextualization of these questions through the traumatic crucible of the 1992 Los Angeles riots, as well as Crystal Parikh's and James Lee's discussions of the ethics of ethnic betrayal that underwrite Henry's spy work and force an examination of Asian American class privilege. Also of interest are Tina Chen's focus on Lee's reworking of the spy novel genre, and You-me Park and Gayle Wald's attention to the novel's invisible female figures upon whom the male characters rely for sociopolitical legitimation.

Here, I foreground class and the ethics of class mobility, which I screen through questions of genre, in this case the ethnographic genre of the "Chinatown book," which can operate as a spy genre. I also call attention to *Native Speaker*'s invisible figures, namely one who is invisible in plain sight—Henry's unnamed, widowed father, a wealthy proprietor of a handful of ghetto grocery stores. Henry's father represents the culturalized, upwardly mobile Korean American ethnic entrepreneur. He is invisible in that when he is remarked upon he is a launching point from which to illuminate Henry's quandaries, with little or perfunctory attention to the peculiarities and specifics of his work as a small business owner. In addition, while other readings of the novel focus on Henry's betrayal of John Kwang, whom Henry is assigned to spy on, I focus on Henry's betrayal of his father, of whom Kwang is meant to be a better shadow. Like Song, though *Native Speaker* is set in 1980s New York City and its suburbs, I extend the temporal and spatial discussion to 1992 Los Angeles. The 1992 Los Angeles riots bring the complexities of Korean American small business ownership into sharp focus, as well as provide an apocalyptic extratextual ending to *Native Speaker*'s investigation of the predicaments of class mobility for ethnic entrepreneurs.

Native Speaker stages a confrontation between the two types of ethnic entrepreneurs that I described. The first type of ethnic entrepreneur, for whom ethnicity is an entrepreneurial commodity, is figured through Henry Park and his job as an "ethnic spy." Employed by Glimmer & Co., a mercenary espionage firm that specializes in providing ethnic spies to rout out the schemes of co-ethnic targets, Henry is charged to exploit his and his targets' shared sense of racial-cultural identity in order to infiltrate their lives and trust. Henry trades his ethnicity as a commodity, an enterprise through which he secures his success as a white-collar professional, but at the cost of selling out and betraying his co-ethnics. Henry's spy work positions him to betray his father, who figures the second type of ethnic entrepreneur, the Korean American shopkeeper for whom ethnicity is an entrepreneurial causality. A wealthy immigrant merchant, Henry's father embodies a cluster of what the text represents as Korean characteristics, of which his grocery work is a natural emanation—he is represented as being an upwardly mobile small business owner because he is Korean. However, this upward mobility is fractured. Henry's father has little purchase in American life besides his wealth: "bound to 600 square feet of retail ghetto space" (182–83), he is socially marginalized and, as becomes of grave concern in the text, invisible as a subject in the political realm. As such and through allusions to the 1992 Los Angeles riots, Henry's father is put forth as an admonitory figure that warns racialized subjects against the false comforts of accepting mere economic advancement as an adequate condition of class mobility.

These two kinds of ethnic entrepreneurs are brought into confrontation in that the one, Henry as a spy/entrepreneur of ethnicity as a commodity, determines the conditions of legibility, and the empirical effects of that legibility, of the other, the culturalized Korean American shopkeeper. This determination is effected through the ethnic nature of Henry's spy work, which in assuming that ethnic subjects share a ready, even primordial, racial-cultural bond reinforces the idea that ethnic subjects can be distilled to a racial-cultural essence. Henry's essentialization of his targets culturalizes them, making their racial-cultural difference the attribute of their actions, histories, and possibilities. Henry thereby perpetuates the culturalizing logic that naturalizes his father's job as a ghetto shopkeeper. We meet Henry agonizing over the ramifications of his spy work. They make him a traitor not only to specific persons within the parameters of his professional assignments, but also to his larger co-ethnic community, in that he perpetuates the epistemology and disciplining effects of culturalization. Will Henry continue his spy work? Will he continue to betray his fellow Asian Americans within his job and as an agent of epistemology? Specifically, will he betray his father by perpetuating the idea that Korean Americans are culturally inclined to be small business owners? The discipline of this specific culturalization is that it obscures the structural constraints that lead Korean Americans to small business, which render it a limited and limiting niche, not an expansive economic opportunity. Culturalizations also obscure the structural effects of small business ownership, namely the fracturing of class spheres that had such devastating consequences in 1992 Los Angeles. Will Henry perpetuate these obfuscations, the limited social legibility, this tunnel vision of Korean Americans?

This chapter expands my focus to more conceptual and relative forms of Asian American ghettoization that obtain beyond the conventional economic and spatial segregation. I do not focus on the physical-economic space of an impoverished Korean American ghetto, but on the ghetto of small business ownership, which I characterize as a racially defined and racially confining economic activity. I also focus on an epistemological "culture ghetto," which naturalizes Korean American participation in small business ownership. These different kinds of ghettoization extend across geographical class spaces, including an upscale white suburb where Henry's family lives, and across economic standing, to include upwardly mobile Asian Americans. This is not to deracinate the concept of ghettoization or wrest it away from subjects who suffer under its spatial and economic effects. Rather, it is to complicate our understanding of class, to examine how class discipline operates beyond physical and material indices, especially when improvements in those indices can be used as proof that race and class are "over," that American classlessness is alive and well because some racialized subjects achieve a degree of economic and spatial mobility. The case of upwardly mobile Korean American shopkeepers shows that though some Asian Americans are economically privileged, it is important to look at the condition of that privilege, namely to see the failure of economic advancement to bring racialized subjects full social and political inclusion. This fractured class condition certainly makes Korean American merchants better-off than those with little economic, much less social and political, hope, but it nevertheless evinces an important aspect of how racialized subjects are disciplined by class—not through their exclusion from upward mobility, but through their attainment of it.

A few other notes on ghettoization: the Korean American ethnic entrepreneurs that I discuss do not live in Korean American ghettos, but they spend their hours in other ones, namely the African American ghettos where they set up shop. They do so to the extent that the rapper

Ice Cube has lamented that these spaces are being turned into "black Korea[s]." Korean American merchants' ghettoization in upward mobility is a privilege compared to their black customers' conventional ghettoization, but the spatial and economic intersection of these groups enables us to see how different forms of ghettoization work across race and space. In addition, though I highlight the damage suffered by Korean Americans during the 1992 Los Angeles riots, I do not mean to minimize the severe costs borne by African Americans and Latinos. Rather, the damage inflicted upon these several groups must be addressed simultaneously, as my discussion of black-Korean conflict makes evident. Korean American small business owners are one node through which we can apprehend multiple configurations of ghettoization, while addressing the paradox of ghettoization in upward mobility.

I begin by delineating how Henry's spy work/ethnic entrepreneurship limits the conditions of legibility of Korean American shopkeepers to culturalized ethnic entrepreneurs. The questions of social legibility encoded in Henry's job make his spy work a process of authorship. How can Asian Americans author or make legible their places in the American polity, in this case, beyond the position of the culturalized ethnic entrepreneur? *Native Speaker* addresses this question through literal authorship, by figuring Henry's spy work as a kind of Asian American writing and Henry as an Asian American writer. I start with an account of Henry as a writer, as well as an account of Henry's writer, Chang-rae Lee, and their roles in the enterprise of Asian American authorship and the ramifications of such in making Asian American class situations legible.

Writing as Spying

Native Speaker, Chang-rae Lee's debut novel, revolves around the anguish of Henry Park over his marriage, his son's childhood death, his relationship with his greengrocer father, and his job as a spy. Troubled by the invidious consequences of his work, the personal and professional ruin, and sometimes murder, of his targets, Henry struggles over whether he should continue being a spy. Because his spy work depends on exploiting his and his co-ethnic targets' shared racial-cultural identity, his agony is that much more acute; Henry feels like a traitor to his race. The ethical pressure of this ethnic spy work becomes unmanageable when Henry is assigned to John Kwang, a darling of New York City politics who is currently a councilman from Queens and the favored frontrunner in the upcoming mayoral race. Kwang is the antithesis of Henry's father; Kwang is polished, public, political, and, most important, he aspires to do more than run a ghetto small business. Henry agonizes over whether to betray a man whom he takes as a better figure of Korean American masculinity, as well as of immigrant upward mobility. Nonetheless, Henry delivers the coup de grâce by uncovering a list of undocumented immigrants participating in a loan club administered by Kwang. Kwang turns out to be a decoy (finding and deporting the undocumented immigrants are the goals of Glimmer & Co.'s clients, the Immigration and Naturalization Service), but his political career is destroyed as additional scandals unfold. Henry's negotiations of his race betrayal are troped through his relationship to language, the question of whether he or other immigrants can be "native speakers" whose linguistic enfranchisement would index their social, political, and economic enfranchisement. Henry's quandaries are also screened through his attempts to reconcile with his prickly father, who dies by the end of the text; with his white wife, Lelia, a speech therapist who has left him; and with the memories of their dead son, Mitt. Henry resigns from his spy job, makes a melancholy peace with his wife, the memories of his father and son, and his role in destroying Kwang. The novel closes with Henry working as Lelia's assistant in teaching English to immigrant children.

Lee's novel is also a meta-novel, a narrativization of the processes of Asian American authorship. Henry's spy work is a literary endeavor. His specific task is to cozy up to his co-ethnic targets so that he can write a "register," a detailed character portrait, which is then submitted to their foes, the clients with whom Glimmer & Co. contracts. These profiles are to be dispassionate, but they are also to be ethnic—they are to impart the targets' ethnic character, a "grit of an ethnicity" (141). Henry as a spy is thereby a writer, specifically an ethnographic writer, in that his goal is to "come away with some [ethnic] spice or flavor under [his] nails" (141). We recall that Henry as a spy is also an ethnic entrepreneur, an ethnic subject who trades his ethnicity as a commodity. By weaving these roles together—spy, ethnic entrepreneur, and writer—*Native Speaker* codifies and critiques the processes of Asian American literary production under the ethnographic imperative. As an Asian American writer, Henry is to be a native informant, conjuring up cultural portraits for the scrutiny and edification of his readers. That he is also an ethnic entrepreneur suggests that ethnographic writing is a kind of ethnic entrepreneurship, a business of trading upon the author's ethnicity as a commodity for the multiculturalist literary market. By making ethnographic writing a form of spying, *Native Speaker* makes visible an ethical quandary underwriting the ethnographic genre, the quandary of selling out or betraying one's ethnic community by reducing it to Orientalist caricatures.

The ethics of Asian American ethnographic literature concern not only Henry as the writer in the novel, but also the writer of the novel, Chang-rae Lee. Lee's position in the enterprise of Asian American authorship makes him a kind of spy as well. *Native Speaker* made quite a splash when it was published in 1995. It boasts a long list of accolades, including the Hemingway/Pen Award for first work of fiction, the Barnes and Noble Discover Great New Writers Award, and the Before Columbus Foundation's American Book Award. In 1996, it was chosen as the American Library Association's Notable Book in the fiction category and was one of two finalists in a 2002 attempt to create a citywide reading program in New York City. The author also enjoys much renown: in 1999, he was anointed by the *New Yorker* magazine as one of the twenty best writers under the age of forty; his subsequent books have been anticipated with much fanfare (his third is now in talks with Hollywood producers); and he is currently a member of the distinguished creative writing faculty at Princeton University. Lee has apparently "arrived." However, if Lee has been summarily inducted into the pantheon, no small feat for a previously unknown talent and an Asian American one at that, what exactly is being sanctified? If Chang-rae Lee has arrived, where is he going? For that matter, where did he come from?

The apparent appeal of Lee and his novel is evident in the kinds of awards he has won. On the one hand, Lee is a great new writer who has written a good book that appeals to a wide readership. On the other hand, it is not difficult to spot a strong delimitation in the praise of *Native Speaker*. If we take a snippet of the Before Columbus Foundation's mission statement as an indication—to "promot[e] and disseminat[e] contemporary American multicultural literature"—it becomes apparent that an important component of *Native Speaker*'s praise is praise of an ethnic author's ethnic achievement. The Before Columbus Foundation's interest in multicultural literature does not seek to marginalize ethnic writers as only ethnic writers. On the contrary, its mission is to press upon the American literary canon to include ethnic literature as constitutively, not supplementarily, American (Before Columbus). Notwithstanding, the reviews of *Native Speaker* reflexively categorize the novel as an ethnic writer's ethnic story. Min Song notes that the *New York Times* adulates the novel as "a lyrical, edgy, and perceptive tale of the second-generation foreigner, the child of immigrants stranded in a no-man's land between the old culture and the new." Likewise, the *New Yorker* is intrigued by the text's working over of "the tortured ethnicity of the immigrant" (Belluck; Klinkenborg 77).[3] The pantheon that *Native Speaker* has been inducted into is the pantheon of the ethnic immigrant story, a subcategory of literature that is by no means a lesser form of aesthetic achievement, as the Before Columbus Foundation points out, but one that is structured by social and aesthetic expectations that nonetheless tend to marginalize such literature as supplementary offerings to the American canon by secondary Americans.

A main way that Asian American literature is made to conform to the ethnic immigrant genre is through the ethnographic imperative. As an immigrant story, a work like *Native Speaker* is expected to be an ethnographic story, to offer an authentic "insider's view" into an Asian culture that authors and characters are assumed to embody. Jessica Hagedorn quips that Sven Birkerts in his *New York Times* review of her 1993 anthology, *Charlie Chan Is Dead*, acts more like an immigration official than a literary critic when he, "obsessing over the writers' bloodlines," criticizes the anthology for not clearly demarcating the racial-cultural identities of the included writers (qtd. in Koshy 331). Birkerts complains: "The author biographies that accompany the stories are too often useless. We puzzle over whether a writer is foreign- or American-born, and frequently we find ourselves playing the 'guess the ethnicity from the name' game" (17). Birkerts is aware that the goal of Hagedorn's anthology is to do away with stereotypes, of Asian Americans and of the literature that they write, but his claim that it is "inexcusable" to leave readers confused over authors' racial-cultural identities suggests a return to old literary expectations (17). If this is not an explicit call for ethnographic literature, it is an implicit one, marked by the desire for ethno-biography, a demand for a clear explication of the authors' racial-cultural identities as a way to frame what kind of "insider's view" readers can expect.

The ethnographic criteria by which Asian American literature is judged are evident not only in the praise given to *Native Speaker* (that it marvelously illuminates an immigrant's "tortured ethnicity"), but also in the errant quibble. The criticism of *Native Speaker* focuses on how the novel is not ethnographic enough, especially on how the novel's illuminations of immigrant life are weakened by the spy story, as if, as James Lee points out, anything beyond the immigrant story in Asian American literature is a detraction (246–47). Song calls attention to *New York Magazine*'s assessment: "*Native Speaker* . . . is an artful mediation on ethnic identity, fractured loyalties, and cultural confusion that is bundled inside a not-entirely-plausible spy thriller" (Goldberg 46). The ambiguous sense of the reviewer's "artful" is instructive here. If the word is meant as a compliment, praising the novel for its skillfully crafted renditions of "ethnic identity, fractured loyalties, and cultural confusion," the usual ethnographic stuff of ethnic identity, which while acknowledged as overlaid with complexities of loyalty and confusion, still stands as primary over the clumsy and, according to the review, secondary spy story. If the reviewer finds the immigrant story "artful" in the sense that it does not strike him as genuine, what he seeks perhaps is more ethnic identity and less cultural "fracturing" and "confusion," an amplification of a fixed racial-cultural truth. In either case, the review speaks a desire for authentic ethnography as a criterion of Asian American literary aesthetics. Such readings turn literary critics not only into immigration officials, but also, in the estimation of the *Aiiieeeee!* editors, into "sociologists and holy Joes, picking at the bones of our poetry and tearing the lids off our prose, looking for a mastodon frozen stiff in a block of ice" (Chan et al. xxiii).

If imaginative limits are placed on *Native Speaker* and Asian American literature more generally, Lee's novel is a story about those limits. *Native Speaker* narrativizes the pressures of the ethnographic imperative through Henry's role as a spy, ethnographer, and writer. The ethnographic pressures on Asian American literary production are codified in the instructions that Henry is to follow when writing his registers: "I am to be a *clean writer*, of the most reasonable eyes, and present the subject in question like some sentient machine of transcription. In the commentary, I won't employ anything that even smacks of theme or moral. I will know nothing of the crafts of argument or narrative or drama. Nothing of beauty or art. And I am to stay on my uncomplicated task of rendering a man's life and ambition and leave to the unseen experts the arcana of human interpretation" (203, emphasis in original). Glimmer & Co.'s demand that Henry be a "sentient machine of transcription" means that he is to do little more than create registers or character portraits that capture his subjects' ethnicity, to do little more than come away with "some [ethnic] spice or flavor under his nails" (141). The ethnographic imperative likewise demands that Asian Americans writers be "sentient machine[s]." They are to create dispassionate cultural portraits unencumbered by the "crafts of argument or narrative of drama," for instance, by the "vexing questions" that Etsuko Sugimoto's work was praised for omitting, as discussed in chapter 2. Henry is likened to an Asian American writer-as-native-informant, who is charged merely to "register" for his reading audience an authentic ethnographic record.

These ethnographic portraits, for Henry and for Asian American writers in general, are of course not dispassionate. That Henry as a native informant is also a spy bespeaks the ethical charge and treasonous potential of ethnographic writing. By figuring spying as a kind of writing, *Native Speaker* brings into focus that writing is also a form of spying, that embedded in the project of ethnic writing are questions of loyalty and betrayal. These questions are immanent in the project of ethnic knowledge production more generally, as Crystal Parikh delineates in her discussion of the minority intellectual. Likening the minority intellectual to *Native Speaker*'s ethnic spy, Parikh argues that Henry floats in a "ghostly" in-between space of ethical obligations to his co-ethnics and of selling them out to unsympathetic audiences. Defining the minority intellectual/spy as an ethnic studies scholar who produces antihegemonic knowledge, Parikh argues that this figure, on the one hand, produces antiracist knowledge in support of disenfranchised minority communities, from which he came or for which he claims to advocate. On the other hand, the minority intellectual is disarticulated from his disenfranchised community by virtue of his privilege, for instance, as a member of the privileged realm of the university, which, moreover, can co-opt and neutralize antiracist discourses by turning them into defanged expressions of multiculturalism (261–62). Parikh's description of this in-between position as "ghostly" and spylike is apt. The minority intellectual is a skulking, dislocated presence that seeks to "spook" or antagonize normalizing ideologies, but keenly feels that his work may be spooking himself and his co-ethnics. He has become the deliverer of racial knowledge that can be manipulated to shore up the usual racial hierarchies. This betrayal is amplified when the treasonous transmission of racial knowledge confers privilege on the intellectual/spy, like cachet in the university for being an expert on racial knowledge (279). Because this privilege is gained by virtue of the intellectual's position as the gatekeeper of ethnic knowledge, and because he is a gatekeeper by virtue of his assumed racial inhabitation and access to ethnic communities, the ethnic intellectual is, as Nguyen argues, self-exploiting his ethnicity as a commodity through which to gain class privilege (3–19). The ethnic intellectual/spy is thus an ethnic entrepreneur—an entrepreneur of ethnicity as a commodity—who sells himself as a metonym and gatekeeper of his racial community, which he in turn sells out for his own class gain, through the offering of potentially damaging racial knowledge.

As a minority intellectual, then, Henry is also an ethnic entrepreneur. He sells his ethnicity as a commodity to be traded for his class gain, for his success as a white-collar professional, in contrast to his father's demeaning greengrocer job. That his ethnic entrepreneurship is also spy work and a form of writing bespeaks the treasonous potential of ethnic knowledge production. Henry's construction of Asian American subjectivity and experience via his registers brings into focus that the production of knowledge about Asian Americans positions the ethnic producer of knowledge to be a co-ethnic traitor. Because his writing work is reductively ethnographic, a project of extracting a "grit of ethnicity," Henry's betrayal is the perpetuation of an epistemological simplicity, the ongoing straitening of Asian American ontological possibilities to nothing more than an ethnic "spice or flavor." The criticism, then, that the spy story of *Native Speaker* detracts from its immigrant story is wrong. *Native Speaker* does not fail because it is a spy story; it succeeds because it is one. Its ethnographic immigrant story is a spy story, a story of an ethnic subject spooking his own to extract reductive, ethnographic portraits for his readers' consumption.

There are empirical consequences to Henry and other Asian American writers' spylike ethnographic writing. Ethical choices in textual production condition empirical class positions and possibilities. A main effect of reductive ethnographic literature is the culturalist obfuscation and subsequent neglect or condoning of the structural constraints on Asian American class situations. In Henry's case, his spy work/ethnographic literary project/ethnic entrepreneurship naturalize Korean American merchants' ethnic entrepreneurship as a racial-cultural proclivity, obfuscating the structural constraints that have led Korean Americans to small business and that make this niche a form of class discipline. This is not to say that literature forms class relations exclusively or deterministically, but that it is an important means, as a textual project in itself as well as an element of the more general project of ethnic knowledge production, through which Asian Americans can author their class possibilities.

Nigerian Umbrellas (Ethnographic Surveillance Part I)

Henry's registers/ethnographic writing culturalizes his subjects, portraying his targets' psychology and motivations as determined by their cultural inhabitation. This is evident in the basic premise of the registers' usefulness, that by getting at the core of the targets' ethnic ontology, their psychology and motivations can be unlocked and some vulnerability exposed. Dennis Hoagland, Henry's boss, puts it simply: "To be a true spy of identity . . . you must be a spy of the culture" (206). The assumption that an ethnic individual is wholly calibrated by his ethnic culture is articulated by one of the targets of ethnography himself, Emile Luzan, a pro-Marcos Filipino psychiatrist whom Henry is assigned to early in the text. Posing as an analysand, Henry is encouraged by Luzan, who is eager to bond with Henry as a fellow Asian American, to filter his psyche and being through a "cultural dimension," to "cast it all, if you will, in a broad yellow light" (133).

Luzan's adherence to culturalizing logics makes him an easy target, the "medallion of sweet-ass veal" to Henry's "wolf" (43). Henry, however, is an anguished wolf, not only because there are profoundly inimical consequences to his culturalizing writings (Henry's registers lead to Luzan's murder, and an earlier assignment to a Chinese dissident results in the dissident's "disappearance"), but also because they destroy the capaciousness of the ethnic self. Henry's culturalizing registers destroy the idea that an ethnic subject can be anything more than the sum of his ethnic parts, that his life possibilities cannot exceed an essentialized cultural ontology. This includes the suggestion that Asian American class possibilities are culturally prescribed. Specifically, the culturalizing logic of Henry's registers suggests that Henry's father is a small business owner because he is Korean. This distresses Henry because it naturalizes for his father, and reflects back onto Henry and other Korean Americans, what Henry considers is a limited, constraining, and even shameful job. Henry's shame over his father's small business work stems from the indignity of his father having to work as a greengrocer even though he has a master's degree in engineering from Korea, and also from the appearance that Henry's father exhibits little other ambition. Though Henry's father has built up his business from one ghetto grocery store to several stores around the city, "those five stores defined the outer limit of his ambition, the necessary end of what he could conceive of himself" (183). Even more unsettling for Henry is that his father's limitations might not be personal shortcomings, but are representative of the shortcomings of Korean Americans more generally. Gruff, emotionally withdrawn, reticent, surly, and weighted down by "han," a Korean folk concept that refers to something like quiet, dignified perseverance in the face of relentless, unwarranted suffering, Henry's father is an aggregation of what the text represents as Korean masculinist stereotypes. These characteristics disqualify him from having a more expansive career—and, as we will see, a more American career—but make him a natural fit for the crude work of running ghetto grocery stores, of returning wordlessly, day after day to the "stink and sweat of ruined vegetables" (136).

Henry's father's work in running a small business is thereby conflated with, or at least represented as a fitting match for, his cultural behavior. The conflation of cultural and economic behavior is emblematized in an offhand comment made by Lelia, Henry's white wife. Puzzling over why there are so many Nigerians selling umbrellas on the streets of New York City, she concludes: "I guess it makes sense. . . . Desert peoples being sensitive to rain" (213). Like Henry, Lelia is figured as a cultural ethnographer, a figuration that clarifies that the ethical problems of Asian American ethnography are not disembodied, intra-ethnic problems, but symptoms of a white gaze that compels the ethnographic drive in the first place. Lelia is the "standard-bearer" in *Native Speaker*'s racial-cultural economy, specifically of language, as she is a speech therapist (12). More generally, she represents the power of whiteness to adjudicate and surveil. Introduced in the text as a "woman of maps" (3), she makes Henry, the ethnic ethnographer, an object of ethnography himself. This description refers to the many maps that Lelia collects and studies, even draws on her own, in preparation for an international jaunt she will take in order to gain perspective on her troubled marriage. However, it also reflects her bearing toward her Korean American husband, toward him as a map whose ontological topography she wants to schematize. Lelia's main contention in her marriage to Henry is that she cannot schematize him. She wants to "know" him, gain access to the secrets of his spy work as well as to his racial-cultural difference. The familiar marital complaint of not "knowing" one's spouse is a trope for the ethnographic project of routing out and fixing a racial-cultural ontology. That Lelia needs to "know" in this way confirms Henry's mother's suspicions that this "lengthy Anglican goddess"—the "standard-bearer"—would "measure [Henry] ceaselessly . . . continually appraise [their] vast differences, count up the ways" (15). As this type of ethnographer, Lelia's assessment of Nigerian umbrella-selling is apt ("Desert peoples being sensitive to rain"). Though this attribution is somewhat contextually informed, inasmuch as it takes the Nigerians' desert climate into account, it effaces the structures of diaspora that make Nigerian immigrants street peddlers of sundry goods in the first place. Lelia's comment turns contextual factors into an implicitly cultural attribute of a "people."

Sharing this culturalizing logic, Henry's spy work conflates Korean American small business owners' cultural and economic behavior. The culturalization of Korean American small business ownership is evident in flippant stereotypes as well as scholarly study. Some explanations are Koreans' distrust of outsiders due to centuries of homeland invasion, which lead to preference for autonomous economic activity and working with co-ethnics; a Korean tradition of "buying and selling" carried over to diasporic sites; and the use of the *ggeh*, a loan club or rotating credit association, that gives Korean Americans ready access to the start-up capital necessary to invest in small businesses (Zia 94–95; Yoon 25; K. Park 59).[4] The *ggeh* has particular significance as it is invariably mentioned in analyses of Korean American small business ownership. Its role is ambiguous as documentation varies widely, due to blurry categorization (such as mixed usage of *ggeh* pools for personal and professional use) or individuals' reluctance to report participating in it because they think it is illegal.[5] Nonetheless, this cultural practice is consistently identified as central to small business participation. If the *ggeh* is not the crux of raising capital, it is the crux of postulations that attribute economic behavior to cultural behavior.

These arguably cultural behaviors play arguable roles in leading Korean Americans to small business ownership, but they cannot be disarticulated from their national and transnational structural contexts. In-Jin Yoon offers an understanding of Korean American small business participation in which culture plays a role, but interacts with diasporic structural factors. For instance, instead of a Korean cultural tradition of "buying and selling," Yoon shows that a more important factor is that the majority of Koreans who availed themselves of the 1965 liberalization of U.S. immigration laws was comprised of middle-class immigrants with financial and social capital (education and professional skills) who faced exclusion from the mainstream U.S. professional labor market. Small business ownership provided an intermediate opportunity between, on the one hand, exclusion from stable, well-paying professional jobs because of language difficulty, racial discrimination, and the lack of recognition of foreign degrees and training; and, on the other hand, working in low-paying wage jobs with little room for advancement. Small business ownership was available as an intermediate opportunity because white ethnic immigrants who previously ran urban small businesses were retiring in the 1970s and 1980s, when Korean immigration to the United States was at its peak, and because there was and continues to be a lack of services to poor urban neighborhoods that mainstream companies consider to be high-risk investment areas. Korean Americans could avail themselves of the market demand for small businesses because as middle-class immigrants they had the financial resources and professional skills to perform the complex work of running a shop (Yoon 53–57).

Korean immigrants thereby entered and became dominant in the small business niche because the opportunities were structurally available; because they had the financial resources and skills to avail themselves of these opportunities, as well as the goal to enter small business; and because of their racial exclusion from the mainstream professional labor market (Yoon 43–47). Once engaged in small business, Korean Americans do indeed draw upon their racial-cultural identity, for instance, by cultivating co-ethnic solidarity to facilitate business relationships. However, as Yoon and Pyong Gap Min argue, this use of culture is the result of being structurally located in the small business niche, not the cause (Yoon 45; Min 218–19). Korean American small business participation is a structural adaptation, not a cultural predilection. Korean Americans are no more inclined to be a mom-and-pop shopkeeping "people" in the same way that Nigerians are no more inclined to sell umbrellas because they are culturally attuned to rain.

If Henry continues his spy work, he perpetuates a culturalizing logic that enables the attribution of a racial group's economic activity to cultural inhabitation. Exploiting his own and others' Asian ethnicity to do so, Henry as an entrepreneur of ethnicity as a commodity is poised to corroborate the idea that Korean-ness is an entrepreneurial causality. This is an ethnic betrayal in that perpetuating this limited legibility of Korean American shopkeepers confines them to the small business niche, not only by suggesting that they, like Henry's father, do not aspire to more because they are culturally incapable of doing so, but also by obscuring and legitimating the structural factors that lead and limit Korean Americans to small business.

The culturalization of Korean American small business ownership casts a false sheen. It suggests that Asiatic virtues fortuitously dovetail with American exceptionalism. Insofar as entrepreneurship embodies the American bootstrap mythos and its claim that economic success is readily gained by sowing a bit of hard work in the free market, the culturalization of small business synchronizes exceptional foreignness with exceptional American-ness to suggest that ethnic entrepreneurship is an ideal, natural, and fortuitous path to Asian American upward mobility. However, if culturalizations obscure the structural causes that lead Korean Americans to small business and that make the niche a limiting one, the boosterism of small business obscures a structural effect of Korean American ethnic entrepreneurship. It obscures the "fracturing of class spheres," a condition of economic mobility stripped of social and political mobility, that characterizes the upward mobility obtained through ethnic entrepreneurship. The fracturing of class spheres makes manifest that upward mobility through small business ownership is an inadequate class condition. If this fractured condition seems imperfect but livable because small business owners have at least advanced economically, the 1992 Los Angeles riots show that this condition has devastating consequences. These consequences demand a reassessment of the kind of upward mobility to which racialized immigrants have been aspiring and have been led to aspire.

"The Inalienable Rights of the Immigrant": The Fracturing of Class Spheres and the 1992 Los Angeles Riots

It is crucial to understand ethnic entrepreneurship as a racialized, limited, and limiting economic activity, as an adaptation to a discriminatory labor market and not, as American exceptionalist discourse would have it, as a testament to America's free-market meritocracy. In a 2002 presentation given to Philadelphia's Asian American community, the then secretary of labor, Elaine Chao, unveiled with much fanfare a program called GATE, "Growing America Through Entrepreneurship." GATE is intended to help open the doors of small business ownership to Asian Americans, for instance, by providing Asian language translations of administrative forms, training for aspiring shop owners, and expedited loans from the Small Business Administration. Chao touted small business ownership as testament to American ideals of freedom (at least the freedom to participate in small-scale capitalism) and identified Asian Americans as culturally suited for entrepreneurship. Asian Americans are model minorities whose exceptional Asian cultural values of hard work and perseverance dovetail with exceptional American practices of free-market democracy.

Omitted from such boosterism are the racial exclusions that make small-scale entrepreneurship neither a freely given economic opportunity nor a racial-cultural proclivity, but rather a product of racial discrimination in the labor market. In tension with Henry's culturalization of Korean American small business ownership is his recognition that his father's job is the result of racial discrimination:

> [My father knew] he could only get so far with his face so different and broad.... [He had to] discard his excellent Korean education and training ... set straight his mind and spirit and make a life for

his family . . . retool his life to the ambitions his meager knowledge of the language and culture [of America] would allow, invent again the man he wanted to be. He came to know that the sky was never the limit, that the true height for him was more like a handful of vegetable stores that would eventually run themselves, making him enough money that he could live in a majestic white house in Westchester and call himself a rich man. (333)

Small business ownership is recognized as a regulation, a "retooling" of Henry's father's dreams to fit the U.S. labor market, which does not recognize his ambitions, education, and training. Issues of language bar Henry's father from better opportunities, as do issues of culture (if we believe that his gruff Korean-ness makes him essentially mismatched for professional work). But these are not detached from racial discrimination. Simply put, Henry's father knew "he could only get so far with his face so different and broad." Racial discrimination creates a not so transparent glass ceiling that makes small business ownership the upper limit of Henry's father's economic opportunity, the "true height" being not the "sky," but downward mobility, given his skills and education, to a "handful of vegetable stores."

Nevertheless, under the ceiling of small business ownership Henry's father can "call himself a rich man." Indeed, he is a rich man, wealthy enough to live in an upscale white suburb and give his family all the material benefits of upper-middle-class life. However, his economic advancement does not erase the discriminatory effects of his race. The latter not only propels downward mobility relative to Henry's father's skills and education, but also straitens the shape and condition of his relative upward mobility. Henry's father's upward mobility is a form of class discipline. This is not only because it is capped at ethnic entrepreneurship (the "true height"), but also because it is capped at economic advancement. Despite his wealth, Henry's father remains socially and politically marginalized because of his race. For instance, though the Park family has the money to live in a "majestic white house in Westchester," the family members must "mince delicately about in pained feet through our immaculate neighborhood, we silent partners of the bordering WASPS and Jews, never rubbing them except with a smile, as if everything with us were always all right, in our great sham of propriety, as if nothing could touch us or wreak anger or sadness upon us" (52).

Race keeps the Parks socially disenfranchised despite their economic enfranchisement. Despite their upper-middle-class financial status, they are social outsiders, or at least tolerated racial others who should not disrupt the upper-middle-class social fabric, signified here by their wealthy white neighborhood.[6] The Parks might be able to perform assimilation to white middle-class norms, "a great sham of propriety," but they are not welcomed into the sociality that sanctifies those norms and that, at any rate, does not appreciate too intimate of a racial "rubbing."

Race also keeps Korean Americans politically disenfranchised, invisible as subjects in the political realm, either as valued constituents of elected representatives or as grassroots political agents who imagine and claim a place in civic society. In Henry's father's case, his political disenfranchisement is partly the result of self-will. He explicitly eschews civic engagement, seen in that "the sole right he wanted was to be left alone . . . so that he could just run his stores," and in his denigration of others', especially African Americans', political activism as "useless" (196). However, this political self-silencing is a defensive stance of resignation. It is born from Henry's father's a priori erasure as a political constituent who matters, as an Asian American constituent who might get swept up from time to time in the "troubles of white and black people," but who does not see himself and his interests reflected in or by his representatives (196). Councilman Kwang, who tries to be that representative, acknowledges Henry's father's disenchantment with the political process: "The rights people could say to him, 'We're helping you, too . . .' but how did he ever see that in practice?" (196). Self-willed or imposed, the political disenfranchisement of Asian Americans is of central concern in *Native Speaker*. This is why the novel counters Henry's father's political invisibility and silence with a figure like Kwang, someone who aspires to and succeeds in becoming an Asian American political leader.

Parsed in this way, Henry's father's upward mobility is structured by a "fracturing of class spheres," the failure of economic advancement to be coterminous with social and political advancement. How is this fracturing a form of class discipline? How is the social and political constitutive of class? Why should social and political marginalization be understood as part and parcel of class inequity? Scholarly study and everyday life remind us that class is measured by more than economic indices. Raymond Williams, in his genealogy of "class," describes how our modern understanding of the term derives from the convergence of two strains of usage, a sociopolitical usage and an economic usage. The first, developed under the upheavals of the American and French revolutions, was used to make a sociopolitical distinction. For example, "middle class" came into parlance to subvert the binary between aristocrats and the rest of society, over which the former had power and indiscriminately lumped together as the "common people." Economic connotations adhere to "middle class," but Williams argues that its usage had a primarily sociopolitical animus, the creation of a different scheme of rank and position that gave the "masses" greater sociopolitical power and value. Other terms denote economic position. During the Industrial Revolution, "working class" was meant to indicate that such a class was economically "useful" and materially "productive," in contrast to an idle aristocracy or the "professional classes" and "trading classes" whose economic activity is not the result of productive labor, that is, of "work." There is significant overlap in these sociopolitical and economic usages of "class." Economic position is tied to sociopolitical position and value, and the latter is tied to the economic rewards to which different social classes have access. This overlap is indexed, as Williams points out, in our modern sense of the concept of class, to which we often attach "socioeconomic" in order to capture that class is comprised of some combination of the sociopolitical and the economic (*Keywords* 62–65).

That the sociopolitical is constitutive of class can also be framed through Pierre Bourdieu's discussion of symbolic or social capital, sanctified social attributes that mark high social standing or membership in a privileged social class (75). Bourdieu focuses on social capital in the sphere of taste and aesthetics, but there are other forms of value and power in realms of social standing. Of concern here are the social capital of racial social standing, and of value and power in the realm of electoral or grassroots politics. Insofar as these forms of value are social capital, and insofar as social capital is constitutive of class, inclusion and power in the political realm as well as in a racialized social hierarchy are constitutive of class.

This sketch of some important thinkers' theorizations of class shows that class is a multisphered concept and relation. If, as Williams notes, class is comprised of some combination of the sociopolitical and economic, then it is not exclusively equivalent to or fully captured by either. Accordingly, class advancement cannot simply be understood as economic advancement, but must include sociopolitical advancement. In the case of immigrants socially and politically marginalized by race, class advancement entails sociopolitical inclusion and enfranchisement.

This all seems agreeable enough: given that the term "socioeconomic class" is a set piece of contemporary class vocabulary, the multisphered character of class does not go unrecognized. However, what is disavowed is that these spheres can be fractured. They are assumed to operate in concert, but they do not do so dependably, especially when race is a factor. American class ideologies are fundamentally premised on a multisphered understanding of class, but are also structured to deny that those spheres can be fractured, as a way to deny that empirical experiences might not live up to national class ideals. For instance, the American bootstrap ethos is premised on the understanding that class is not merely an economic condition, but an economic condition enabled by social and political conditions, namely the exceptional national conditions of social and political egalitarianism. The American ethos of economic egalitarianism, the idea that economic mobility is available to all who try, that America is a classless society or at least has an economic hierarchy that can easily be scaled, is based on the claim of social and political egalitarianism, that in an exceptional democracy none is fettered by social and political discriminations that would hinder economic pursuits. The conditions of sociopolitical egalitarianism are constitutive of America's economic egalitarianism. The social and political are constitutive of class, in that economic classlessness is predicated on social and political classlessness.

This multisphered understanding of class is fundamental to American national identity, but so is the disavowal that the spheres can be fractured. This disavowal is achieved through conflation and synecdoche. A product of the blended discourse of exceptional social, political, and economic egalitarianism is an ideological conflation, a conflation of the nation's social and political identity with its economic system—a conflation of democracy and capitalism. This conflation is evident in the connotations that adhere to the term "free market," the commitment to which is so often bandied about as a sacred national virtue. In that usage, "free" does not merely describe that the market is to work without state interference, but also evokes a more expansive idea of liberty, of the social and political freedom of those who participate in and support the market. Thomas Frank describes this conflation of capitalism and democracy as "market populism," the belief that the economic freedom of markets is equivalent to the sociopolitical freedom of individual citizens; or that the market, put forth as the site of democracy, free as it is, expresses the freedom of the citizen (xiv–xvii).

The conflation of capitalism and democracy thereby engenders a synecdoche in which the freedom of capitalist enterprise is used as a stand-in for sociopolitical freedoms. Some of the most nationalist discourses rely on this conflation and synecdoche. For instance, in response to the September 11, 2001 attacks on the World Trade Center,

President George W. Bush described the attackers as "enemies of freedom." He declaimed that they had enacted hostility to democracy by attacking a "symbol of American prosperity" ("Statement by the President"; "Address to a Joint Session"). The World Trade Center might be a "symbol of prosperity," but it most certainly is an icon of free enterprise and a material site of hypercapitalism. By positioning an attack on a capitalist site as an attack on democracy, Bush's rhetoric parlays a site of capitalism into a symbol and site of democracy, suggesting that capitalism and democracy are equivalent. This rhetoric also makes capitalist freedoms synecdochic of sociopolitical freedoms. The destruction of a symbol and site of the economic freedom that is one part of America's democratic structure (insofar as the right to hypercapitalism is an economic freedom) is put forth as an attack on democratic freedom as a whole. A week after the September 11 attacks, the New York Stock Exchange published an announcement in the *New York Times* informing readers that the Exchange would be reopened. The announcement states that "a bell will be rung" on the trading floor, as is the custom to signal the opening of business, and ends with the proclamation: "[L]et freedom ring." The bell of American democracy is rendered as being rung by the bell of capitalist enterprise.

The conflation of capitalism and democracy, and the synecdochic use of economic freedom might be harmless, even a cause for celebration, if they bore out—America would be an exceptional nation, indeed, if it offered its subjects the package deal of sociopolitical democracy and economic freedom. But this conflation and synecdoche do not hold, especially when race is a factor. It need not be rehearsed that the freedom of the market does little to produce or sustain the social and political freedoms of individual Americans, such as racialized laborers who are routinely exploited in the name of capitalist freedom. Even when racialized subjects do benefit from the market, for instance, by making money through entrepreneurship, this economic freedom does not fulfill the conditions of its synecdoche. If Henry's father is an example, his being rich but, because of his race, socially and politically marginalized, the situation of the Korean American shopkeeper shows that economic freedom hardly obtains or expresses social and political freedoms.

Economic aspects of class cannot be extracted and overdetermined to stand in for its social and political aspects. To put it another way, economic advancement and mobility are not representative or encompassing of sociopolitical inclusion and enfranchisement. Rather, for racialized immigrants like Korean American shopkeepers, economic advancement is a *disembodied* synecdoche of sociopolitical inclusion. The association is empty.

The fractured upward mobility of Korean American shopkeepers suggests the need for a more cautious assessment of racialized immigrants' upward mobility. If class is multisphered, as core American class ideologies themselves claim, upward mobility for racialized immigrants must not be an exclusively or falsely metonymic economic phenomenon. This is not to tilt class analyses toward nonmaterial capital over economic capital, but it is to forestall a premature declaration that racialized class containments have been surmounted, that American mythologies of classlessness have been vindicated because some racialized immigrants can advance economically. It is also to imagine and demand more capacious lives for racialized immigrants who, like Henry's father, might resign themselves to the seductive fiction that (limited) economic mobility alone is a sufficient condition of upward class mobility.

Fractured upward mobility is not only insufficient, but it is also dangerous. *Native Speaker* makes the latter visible by linking Korean American shopkeepers' upward mobility to the 1992 Los Angeles riots: "[W]e [the Park family, ought to act like] . . . everything with us were all right . . . [t] hat we believed in anything American, in impressing Americans, in making money, polishing apples in the dead of night, perfectly pressed pants, perfect credit, being perfect, shooting black people, watching our stores and offices burn down to the ground" (52–53).

Korean American shopkeepers' fractured upward mobility is referenced here in the description of the Parks as "perfect" minorities, which invokes the image of the model minority, a minority that works hard ("polishing apples in the dead of night") and does not stir up trouble. In fact, the model minority thesis codifies the fracturing of class spheres. One of the first media articulations of the model minority thesis states: "At a time when Americans are awash in a worry over the plight of racial minorities, one such minority, the nation's 300,000 Chinese Americans, is winning wealth and respect by dint of its own hard work. . . . Still being taught in Chinatown is the old idea that people should depend on their own efforts—not a welfare check—in order to reach America's 'Promised Land'" (Peterson 73). Published in a 1966 edition of *U.S. News & World Report*, this proclamation is well recognized as a thinly veiled backlash against the civil rights movement, a contrasting of obeisant, bootstrapping Chinese Americans with unruly blacks, who demand national attention to their "plight." We also see that the model minority thesis instantiates a fracturing of class spheres. It positions Asian

Americans as being economically mobile ("winning wealth"), but in a way that keeps them quiet socially and politically. This is reflected in their eschewing of the "welfare check": in contrast to agitating African American civil rights activists, upwardly mobile, model minority Asian Americans eschew speaking out in the political sphere to demand recognition as social subjects worthy of state care.

"Being perfect," being a model minority who submits to fractured upward mobility, is apposed to "watching our stores and offices burn down to the ground," a reference to the 1992 Los Angeles riots. This apposition can be read as a causal relation. Korean American shopkeepers could only "watch" as their livelihoods burned because they were socially and politically powerless. They were not considered socially valuable subjects deserving of institutional resources, like police and fire department services, which were systematically withheld from South Los Angeles where Korean American shops were located. In fact, Police Commissioner Daryl Gates instructed Fire Chief Donald Manning to focus resources on white, wealthy suburbs like Santa Monica, Beverly Hills, and West Hollywood, remarking that South Los Angeles and the neighboring Koreatown were not a "top priority" (Cho 202). As a result, Korean Americans disproportionately suffered the financial damages from the riots. Of the $1 billion in damages, $400 million were sustained by Korean Americans. They suffered nearly half the losses, even though they comprised only 2 percent of the South Los Angeles population (Louie 141).

This "malign neglect," in Omi and Winant's phrase (99), this discounting of Korean Americans' social worth, was compounded by their lack of community or electoral political power. If Korean American shopkeepers found themselves discounted as social subjects worthy of institutional resources, they had few voices in the political sphere to say otherwise. There was no one, Elaine Kim points out, in the "corridors of Los Angeles, Sacramento, and Washington DC" voicing the needs and distributing resources on behalf of Korean Americans ("They Armed" 10). Perhaps this political invisibility was the result of self-will, as we saw in Henry's father's intentional rejection of politics. Indeed, Korean Americans were characterized by the media as apathetic or too busy with work to get involved in politics. But this political invisibility was also imposed. The scant political voices that did exist were categorically ignored. No community leaders were asked to contribute to the political dialogue until civil rights lawyer Angela Oh insisted that she be interviewed on the television news program *Nightline*. When Korean Americans appealed to political institutions, for instance, for post-riot aid, they were pointedly denied. The former commerce secretary Ronald Brown said of a federal grant to rebuild South Los Angeles: "Not a penny will go to the Koreans" (qtd. in Zia 190).

If Korean American shopkeepers are upwardly mobile subjects who have (limited) economic rights,[7] they hardly had, but sorely needed, other rights; social rights as valuable social subjects with claims to institutional protection and resources, and political rights as subjects who could claim a voice in the political sphere to demand those resources. In Anna Deavere Smith's *Twilight*, these needs are inchoately articulated by Mrs. Young-Soon Han, whose liquor store was destroyed in the riots: "Until last year I believe America is the best. . . . I really realized that Korean immigrants were left out from this society and we were nothing. What is our right? Is it because we are Korean? Is it because we have no politicians? Is it because we don't speak good English? Why? Why do we have to be left out? . . . We don't get any! Because we have a car and we have a house. And we are high taxpayers. Where do I finda justice?" (246).

Mrs. Han identifies the social and political invisibility of Korean Americans ("[We] were left out from this society," "[W]e don't have any politicians") and connects it to race ("Is it because we are Korean?"). Most important, she recognizes that economic advancement obscures Korean Americans' social and political invisibility: "Why do we have to be left out? . . . We don't get any [rights]! Because we have a car and we have a house. And we are high taxpayers." Mrs. Han critiques the false synecdoche of economic freedom put forth by the conflation of capitalism and democracy, and by American myths of classlessness. The right to make money hardly effectuated rights in the social and political spheres during the Los Angeles riots. Shop owners like Mrs. Han experienced the violence that emerged from the gap between the freedom to make money, and the liberty of social and political inclusion that supposedly enables economic freedom. "These were the inalienable rights of the immigrant," as Lee ironically notes in *Native Speaker* (47), the right to make money through a limited and racialized niche, a right that is an empty placeholder for the social and political rights that it is assumed to encompass.

Ethnographic Surveillance Part II: Black-Korean Conflict

If Commerce Secretary Brown's excision of Korean Americans from sociopolitical redress appears harsh, it is because Korean Americans were perceived as instigators rather than as victims of the riots. This perception was generated by the mainstream media's culturalization of the riots. The media anchored the riots to black-Korean conflict, to tension between Korean American ghetto shopkeepers and their poor black customers. The media culturalized this conflict, representing it as a result of a clash between Korean and black culture, as well as the pathologies of both. These culturalizations are a form of ethnography and, as such, a form surveillance. As in Henry's spy work, the media's culturalization of Korean American merchants was a means of discipline. In this case, the discipline was to assign blame, to suggest that the riots were a tragedy of Korean Americans' own cultural making.

Given the complexity of race and class relations that the 1992 Los Angeles riots made visible, one would think that they would force a deep national self-reckoning. The riots showed that race and class conflicts in America are not merely a matter of black versus white, and that interracial allegiances cannot be easily assumed. African Americans were enraged at the acquittal of the police officers who beat Rodney King, at another instance of the white disregard for black life, but they expressed their rage by looting Korean American–owned stores. At the same time, some blacks fiercely protected Korean American stores. Latinos, who make up a significant part of the workforce in Korean American shops, also participated in the looting, destroying the sites of their livelihoods. Scholarship on the riots by and large recognizes the complexity of the event. Min Song writes that the riots opened up a space to understand the "social wounding" that is both cause and effect of the interwoven "dwindling of the white middle class, the daily misery of poor urban blacks, and the influx of immigrants from all over the world" (12). Like others, Song understands the riots as a gnarled manifestation of long-standing and sedimented structures of racial inequality, under which African Americans bear the brunt of white-led institutional racism and in which Korean immigrants have entered as complicating, difficult-to-categorize figures. Claire Jean Kim calls this embedded institutional racism "racial power," "the racial status quo's systemic tendency toward self-reproduction, [which] finds concrete expression in a variety of political, economic, social and cultural processes that tend cumulatively to perpetuate White dominance over non-Whites" (2). Racial power, that is, white racial power, has produced a "triangulated" racial order in which the inequities experienced by blacks under the power of whiteness are mediated by Asian Americans. Moreover, presumed to be foreigners, Asian Americans are perceived as undeserving of the civic rights of both whites and blacks. However, they have gained a higher economic status than blacks, creating a complex racial tension (16).

The Los Angeles riots resulted from the boiling over of the knotty, tense relations of these several races across a spectrum of class positions, relations that resist the usual schematization of racial conflict (as conflict between blacks and whites), and of class conflict, in which race is axiomatically accompanied by economic disenfranchisement. The riots also manifested a fissure in white racial power, the untenability of a triangulated racial order in which African Americans have been routinely ghettoized, and Korean Americans are ghettoized to the niche of small business and to fractured upward mobility. Disadvantaged under whites, but advantaged over blacks, Korean Americans are intermediaries and, as many have noted, scapegoats of black-white tensions.[8] The riots were caused by the intersection of African and Korean Americans' different ghettoizations, both of which are produced by the triangulating racial power of whiteness that puts these two groups in tense relation.

The mainstream media found a more compelling story in the bottom two-thirds of this triangulation. Zooming in on and sensationalizing black-Korean conflict as the root cause of the riots, the media pushed the question of white racial power out of sight. The black-Korean conflict frame positions Korean American shopkeepers as instigators of the riots, as mercenary predators who, deriving economic advantages from the exploitation of poor blacks, invited black resentment and retribution. As the media commonly iterated, black-Korean conflict results, for instance, from Korean Americans charging higher prices for inferior goods to customers who do not have other places to shop; or because Korean Americans cultivate vice culture in black neighborhoods by proliferating the number of liquor stores there. Overlaid onto this depiction is animosity toward Korean Americans because they are racial foreigners, outsiders to the nation who have "invaded" black communities to make money. That Korean Americans do not typically live in the ghettos where they set up shop gives credence to the "invading foreigner" narrative. Korean Americans are accused of being uninterested in developing community relationships with their customers, to whom they are rude and racist. This perception of Korean Americans as expropriative mercenaries finds a historical precedent in the attitude toward Jewish shopkeepers earlier in the twentieth century. James Baldwin writes of Jewish shopkeepers in 1960s Harlem: "It is bitter to watch the Jewish storekeeper locking up his store for the night, and going home. Going, with *your* money in his pocket, to a clean neighborhood, miles from you, which you will not be allowed to enter" (34, emphasis in original).

If the black-Korean conflict frame constructs the riots as a violent expression of black anger at Korean American exploitation, it constructs the Korean American response as equally violent. Shopkeepers responded by "shooting black people," as Lee writes in *Native Speaker* (53). "[S]hooting black people" refers to an effect of the riots. Deprived of social and political protections, Korean Americans armed themselves and perched atop their shop roofs to fend against looters, an image that was widely broadcast to sensationalize Korean Americans as dangerous vigilantes. "[S]hooting black people" is also a cause of the riots, the phrase alluding to the a priori troubled relationship between merchants and their customers. The phrase alludes in particular to the 1991 shooting of Latasha Harlins, a black teenager who was killed by a Los Angeles convenience store owner, Soon Ja Du, over an allegedly stolen carton of orange juice. Du was found guilty, but given the strikingly light sentence of a five-hundred-dollar fine, probation, and community service. In the black-Korean conflict frame, Harlins's shooting is the riots' backstory. Though the riots were incited by the acquittal of the Los Angeles Police Department officers who beat Rodney King, Harlins's murder was a central narrative reference point, the video of which, captured by a surveillance camera in Du's store, was repeatedly broadcast alongside the video of King's beating. The brutality that incited the riots (King's beating and the police officers' acquittals) was displaced onto another brutality (Harlins's murder and Du's light sentence). The latter became an emblem of black-Korean conflict, receding the Rodney King beating from view and foregrounding Korean Americans as the riots' instigators and villains. Violent tension between Korean American merchants and black customers is real and demands attention. However, the black-Korean conflict frame foreshortens the riots to an interracial class war that does not account for the role of white racial power and its triangulation of racial relations that creates conflict between Korean and African Americans in the first place.

At the center of the black-Korean conflict frame is a culturalizing epistemology that misattributes the conflict to Korean culture. This is evident in the "invading foreigner" narrative, in which Korean American merchants are constructed as "invading" because of their culture. Namely, in the same way that Korean Americans have been construed as being culturally inclined to small business ownership, they are construed as being culturally inclined to mercenary expropriation. The latter is manifest in common negative stereotypes of Korean American merchants. For instance, they are cheap Asians who would do anything for a buck, or clannish, insular Asians who are rude and antagonistic to their customers because they refuse to or are incapable of assimilating so-called American norms of gregariousness. Sympathizers of Korean Americans also culturalize the conflict between merchants and customers. They explain that rudeness or disrespectful treatment of customers of any race is a misunderstanding of Korean-Confucianistic mores of politeness; merchants throw change on the counter instead of placing it in hands because for Asians such physical contact is an inappropriate gesture of intimacy; and banter with patrons is an affront to Asiatic mores of privacy (Zia 94–95).

The mainstream media gave credence to these culturalizations through what quickly became the standard images of Korean Americans during the riots. Alongside the surveillance camera video of Du shooting Harlins, two main images dominated the media coverage. As Elaine Kim describes in *Sai-I-Gu*, Dai-Sil Kim Gibson's 1993 documentary about the riots, Korean Americans were represented as either "[male] merchants on the roof [of their stores] with guns, apparently ready to shoot anybody . . . with the implication that they cared only about their property, that they didn't care about human life or the communities . . . where their stores were located"; or "screaming, begging, crying, yelling, inarticulate—not speaking but just hysterical—mostly female shop owners who were begging people not to destroy their stores" (qtd. in Jung Sun Park 211). On the one hand, Korean Americans were framed as cold-blooded money mongers. Having been willing to kill before the riots over the price of orange juice, they were now heavily armed atop their shop roofs, once again favoring property over human life. On the other hand, they were strange hysterics, their babbling cries in a mixture of Korean and broken English rendering them incoherent agents of language as well as incoherent subjects of the nation, that is, as decidedly other and foreign. Together, these media images suggest that Korean Americans' cold-blooded money mongering is tangled up with their foreignness, that they are not only mercenary predators, but also that they are so because they are Korean.

Whether to defend or to denigrate, the culturalization of black-Korean relationships reduces the riots to an occasion for armchair ethnography. The riots became an opportunity to ponder Korean Americans' cultural difference rather than to confront the effects of white racial power. The culturalization of the riots through the black-Korean conflict frame is an empirical instance of the disciplining power of ethnography that is mapped through Henry's spy work in *Native Speaker*. Ethnographic culturalizations not only naturalize Korean Americans as small business owners, but also naturalize their culpability in the difficulties that arise from working in this niche. The *Los Angeles Times* reports: "[T]he ancient financial network that sustained [Korean American small business owners] was helpless against Thursday night's onslaught of street crime" (Shiver and Garcia). The "ancient financial network" refers to the *ggeh*, the informal money club that, as discussed above, is frequently identified as a cultural practice that leads Korean Americans to ethnic entrepreneurship. But why would the "ancient financial network" help combat the riot looting? What does it have to do with the riots at all? This disjunctive invocation of the *ggeh* betrays the belief that culture structured the riots. A cultural practice, the *ggeh*, is being pondered for its inability to quell the violence, as if culture were the riots' solution. The belief that culture structured the riots also enables the blaming of Korean culture for being the riots' cause.

Obscured are the structural reasons that Korean Americans are ghetto shopkeepers and poor blacks their customers. Pyong Gap Min and Andrew Kolodny draw from Edna Bonacich's work to characterize Korean Americans as "middleman minorities."[9] Middleman minorities emerge in societies where there is a formal or informal status gap between elites and the underclass. This gap is often filled by groups that are racially distinct in the region, such as by Jews in Europe, Chinese in Southeast Asia, and Indians in Africa. The middleman minority fills this gap economically, providing goods and services through marginal occupational niches that are shunned by elites, either as intrinsically distasteful work or as work that is distasteful because it requires direct contact with the underclass. The middleman minority thus occupies an intermediate socioeconomic class status. They are socially and economically privileged over the underclass, but are subject to hostility from above and below, from the elites because of their racial difference and often foreign national status; and from the underclass for the same reasons, as well as because of the underclass's resentment toward the middleman minority's relative class privilege (Bonacich 583–84).

The grievances of the underclass are not surprisingly directed at the middleman group. The underclass's misery seems to be produced by the middleman, given the middleman group's economic, spatial, and social proximity. However, it should not be lost that the middleman minority position is precisely a middleman position, an intermediary role that indexes a triangulation in which the power of the elites should not recede from sight. Of concern here is that the racial power of whiteness produces a black underclass and a Korean American middleman class, with the latter doing the "dirty work" of serving the underclass, for instance, of opening convenience stores and corner groceries in black ghettos, which white businesses shirk. Baldwin presciently describes the middleman minority phenomenon in his previously mentioned comments about African Americans and Jews. Baldwin's examination of African American bitterness against Jewish shopkeepers comes from a 1967 *New York Times Magazine* piece entitled "Negroes are Anti-Semitic Because They Are Anti-White." Baldwin describes the social, spatial, and economic imbalance that African Americans live and observe, seemingly at the hands of Jewish shopkeepers. But as the title of his essay suggests, he contextualizes black-Jewish tensions within a broader frame in which whites figure into the equation. Baldwin argues that it is not Jewish shopkeepers per se who exploit American blacks, but the larger structures of racial inequity that white society produces and preserves. These structural inequities are what create a black underclass that is spatially, socially, and economically segregated from privileged whites, but in close contact with Jews who, not being as disadvantaged as blacks, but also not as advantaged as whites, took on the intermediary social and economic position of running ghetto small businesses (33).

Baldwin critiques the racial triangulation and white racial power that Claire Jean Kim names as such and shows to be persistent and urgent problems nearly a half century later. Whereas it was once the Jews in black American ghettos who were "caught in the middle,"[10] it is now Korean Americans who are the "new Jews" or, as Lee puts it in *Native Speaker*, the "Oriental Jews" (53). Obscuring the larger picture of triangulation and racial power mistakenly locates African American grievances in the spatially and economically proximate, readily visible middleman minority shopkeeper. The middleman minority theory does not exhaustively or exclusively define Korean American shopkeepers' position in the American race and class landscape.[11] However, its overall strokes do much to shift the frame of the Los Angeles riots away from black-Korean conflict and its underwriting culturalizations toward a critique of racial power and racial triangulation.

Notwithstanding the complexities of white racial power and racial triangulation, Korean American shopkeepers' gains do often translate into African Americans' losses. Individual shopkeepers might indeed treat blacks poorly and exploit them, perhaps because of racism or as a way for

shopkeepers to preserve their relative privilege in their triangulated configuration, perhaps even to align themselves with or aspire to the whiteness from which they are excluded. In other words, Korean American
shopkeepers are not immune to being complicit in perpetuating white
racial power and thereby creating conflict with African Americans.
However, if this is so, it is still white power and not Korean culture that
is at the root. Baldwin writes that if the Jew, or in this case the Korean,
needs to be "singled out" for amplifying the misery of poor blacks, it is
"not because he acts differently from other white men, but because he
doesn't" (37, 39).

Culturalizations are powerfully disciplining. They render Korean
American shopkeepers as both virtuous and vicious,[12] as ideal entrepreneurial subjects who testify to American mythologies of classlessness;
but also as foreign parasites who interfere with this classlessness by
amplifying the difficulties of the black underclass. African Americans
are also culturalized in this equation. The black-Korean conflict frame
reduces them to inveterate, and in the case of the riots, looting indigents,
shoring up the familiar neoconservative attribution of black disenfranchisement to an African American culture of poverty and criminality;
or to black cultural impoverishment, the lack of a productive, sustained
culture that can bootstrap African Americans out of the underclass.[13]
These media portraits share the culturalizing logic of Henry's spy work
in *Native Speaker*. And, like Henry's ethnographic registers, the media's
culturalized portraits are a form of surveillance. They are not neutral
or objective, hardly "clean," but censure Korean Americans as the riots'
villains. The attribution of the riots to black-Korean conflict is anchored
to an explicit form of surveillance—the security camera in Soon Ja Du's
store that captured Du shooting Latasha Harlins. Here we have the record of what might be taken as a truly dispassionate, documenting eye,
a camera. However, its "register" is used as an emblem of black-Korean
conflict and its underwriting culturalizations. This ostensibly unmediat-
ed record becomes a surveilling ethnographic record. It captures a mercenary Korean American shopkeeper and a thieving African American
in their ostensibly natural states.

"The Ancient Financial Network" and Other Unhappy Endings

If ethnography and its culturalizations have such damaging effects,
what are the alternatives? How might culturalizing obfuscations be coun-
tervailed so that the structural dynamics of small business ownership,

namely Korean American shopkeepers' racial triangulation under white racial power and their fractured upward mobility, both of which had such devastating consequences during the Los Angeles riots, be made more visible? How can Korean Americans gain a richer legibility and place in American social, political, and economic life? How might they write themselves into the polity beyond the position of inveterate, model minority, ethnic entrepreneurs? How can Korean Americans claim authorship of their own subjectivity? How can they claim an ethical power of self-authorship, one that is not complicit with structures of power and epistemologies of surveillance?

Native Speaker presents no easy alternatives or happy endings. At the close of the novel, Henry quits his spy job. He is no longer able to bear his mode of authorship, his complicity in disciplining fellow Asian Americans. This might suggest that Henry ultimately takes an ethical stance against his spy work, against its culturalizations and ethnographic surveillance that have such damaging epistemological and material effects. However, quitting his spy job does not so much let Henry abjure or reform the logics of culturalization as it allows him to wash his hands of them. Though Henry removes himself from the economy of ethnographic surveillance, he takes no heroic action against it, leaving Glimmer & Co. to carry on its culturalizing surveillance apace. Perhaps Henry is intrinsically powerless to intervene in his employer's schemes. If we believe Henry's boss, Dennis Hoagland, personal accountability is feckless and personal agency a pipe dream: "[S]omeone is always bigger than you. If they want, they'll shut you up. They'll bring you down" (46). Vis-à-vis Glimmer & Co.'s culturalizing operating strategy, Hoagland's pronouncement suggests that culturalizations are simply too big, too entrenched, too much of common wisdom for Henry or anyone else to contest. Hoagland takes an existential view. He declares that his company and employees have no ethical responsibility or agency because they neither create nor instantiate anything. They merely execute inexorable truths: "There's no real evil in the world. It's just the world" (46). Culturalizations are just the way of the world. Henry has little agency or moral burden to reform them.

If we do not believe Hoagland, then Henry's final actions do have ethical implications, if not because Henry leaves Glimmer & Co., then because of the alternative path he chooses. After quitting his spy job, Henry becomes his white wife's assistant in her freelance speech therapy work, helping her teach immigrant children how to speak English. Lelia, we recall, is the "standard-bearer," the measure and measurer of full inclusion into American life (12). This full inclusion is troped through language: Lelia, with her effortless, masterful English, is a fully enfranchised American subject, in contrast to someone like Henry's father, who speaks poor English and accordingly remains on the margins of society. This full inclusion is social, political, and economic, as I have been discussing, and, of course, cultural. In the same way that Henry's father's marginalization is linked to his Korean cultural difference, Lelia's inclusion is wedded to her possession of the dispositions of dominant white culture. What constitutes white culture is not quite defined in *Native Speaker*, but it is at the root a condition of unremarkability. Lelia describes herself as an "average white girl" with "no mystery," no intrigue of cultural difference (10). Simply put, to inhabit white culture is to be part of the mainstream, to be behaviorally, and in the symbology of the novel, linguistically unmarked.

If English language fluency is an emblem of inclusion into mainstream white culture, then the ethnic immigrant's attempt to attain English fluency is a symbol and means of assimilation. Henry's choices at the end of the novel demonstrate that he has embraced this assimilatory path. Henry's main qualification as a spy/ethnic entrepreneur is his racial-cultural difference, which he trades as a commodity. Quitting his job suggests that Henry eschews his differential status; he no longer wants to be a spy, to be the racial-cultural outsider that qualified him for the job. His new goal, which the title of the novel suggests has been his fundamental aspiration all along, is to be a "native speaker." Henry wants to be unremarkable like Lelia, not a spy who can spot ethnic difference because that difference can be spotted in him, but a generic subject who has assimilated into mainstream white culture. Henry appears to have achieved this goal because, if English fluency is a mark of assimilation, he speaks English well enough to become Lelia's speech therapy assistant.[14] By taking on this teaching work, Henry directs other immigrants to the same path. Through a pedagogy of English, he drafts them into a pedagogy of assimilation.

Given that cultural difference is a liability for Korean Americans, capping their upward mobility at small business ownership and making them the Los Angeles riots' villains, Henry's assimilatory linguistic project might forecast a more hopeful future for his immigrant students. Wouldn't it give them a chance to transcend their foreign culture and thereby avoid being locked into (culturalized) socioeconomic paths and embroiled in culturalized interracial class conflicts? The problem with this forecast is that it relies on the premise that assimilation propels immigrant advancement. This premise echoes that of the Chicago school model of ghettoization that was discussed in chapter 2. In that model, socioeconomic dynamics are culturalized. Whether it is to say that ethnic culture is deterministically limiting (the cause of ghettoization) and mainstream white culture is deterministically liberating (the means to upward mobility), structural socioeconomic dynamics are obscured. Likewise, Henry's direction at the end of *Native Speaker* suggests that the trammels of immigrant life, its problems —and now its solution—is located in the realm of culture. Insofar as his assimilatory linguistic path figures as the means to full, or at least better, inclusion into the polity, Henry continues to locate the authorship of Asian American subjectivity in the privatized realm of culture.

It might be argued that Henry's path is not wholly assimilatory, that the last line of the novel suggests a more complex future. In teaching immigrant children English, Henry and Lelia teach something to themselves. They are to learn how to respect their students' native languages and attendant cultural differences: "[Lelia] calls out each [name] as best she can, taking care of every last pitch and accent, and I hear her speaking a dozen lovely and native languages, calling all the difficult names of who we are" (349). That Lelia, the "standard-bearer," takes care to respect her students' differences softens the novel's assimilatory push. However, this more complex, and notably multicultural, direction is undercut by the couple's previous failure to carry though such a multicultural pedagogy. I refer here to the death of Henry and Lelia's son, Mitt. His mixed-race body described as "beautifully jumbled and subversive and historic," Mitt embodies a multicultural ideal (103). Mitt is killed by a group of white neighborhood kids who dog-pile him. The symbolism is obvious: Mitt is suffocated by the weight of whiteness, the "pale little boys [that] crush" him, drowning out the "attempt of his breath . . . calling us from the bottom of the world" (106–7). It is no matter, then, that individuals teach themselves and others to speak "difficult names." The force of whiteness is too powerful, too heavy, and will insist on compressing the world into its own image.

This leaves us with John Kwang as a model for an ethics of ethnic behavior. Rather than being mired in culturalizations, under which ethnic subjects are either limited by their cultural difference or liberated by their assimilatory sameness, can Kwang address and account for the structural constraints of race and class that are levied by white racial power? He tries to do so as a councilman of the immigrant-heavy Queens. He seeks for his constituents opportunities that extend beyond

mere economic advancement, namely that secure social and political enfranchisement; and that unsettle the culturalist pigeonholing of racialized immigrants' socioeconomic possibilities. That these opportunities
are within reach is evident in that Kwang can be a politician at all. He
is of the same immigrant generation as Henry's father, but Kwang has
transcended the ceiling of small business ownership to become a powerful political leader. Moreover, he is not merely a minority politician
catering to the narrow interests of his ethnic borough. Kwang has broad-
based appeal, demonstrated in that he is the favored candidate in the
upcoming mayoral race. Kwang attempts to suture Korean Americans'
fractured class spheres and break culturalized glass ceilings. He is both a
model and agent of these goals. Kwang commands an expanded legibility for himself and seeks to do the same for his constituents. He seeks to
write them more fully into the polity, to give them "a broader foreground
from which [they] might naturally emerge" (148).

Kwang offers an alternative to Henry's paths of ethnographic treason or assimilation. He figures a different kind of authorship, a way for
ethnic subjects to write themselves into the polity that moves beyond
Henry's culturalizing binary. As this kind of Asian American author,
Kwang is resistant to Henry's mode of authorship. He is an illegible, even
inconceivable, subject to Henry. Henry has trouble ethnographizing him
for his registers because Kwang, unlike Henry's father, does not seem
to be deterministically constrained, socially, economically, and politically, by Korean culture: "[Henry] had never even conceived of someone
like him. . . . [Kwang was] not just a respectable grocer or dry cleaner
or doctor, but a larger public figure who was willing to speak and act
outside the tight sphere of his family. He displayed an ambition I didn't
recognize, or more, one I hadn't yet envisioned as something a Korean
man would find worthy of energy and devotion." Kwang is a "Korean of
the future" (139).[15]

The problem with Kwang as a "Korean of the future" is that the novel
ultimately does not allow him to escape the filter of culturalizations.
Kwang might appear to have trumped the culturalizations of Korean
culture, but this image is predicated on his taking up of the culturalizations of American culture. It turns out that Kwang's improved future,
like that of Henry and of Henry's speech therapy students, is predicated on assimilation. This is evident in the close association that *Native
Speaker* makes between political participation and Americanization.
Kwang is able to be a politician only because he has stunningly Americanized. In contrast to Henry's father, who is represented as embodying

gruff, insular Korean masculinity, which renders him ill-equipped to navigate a world beyond his "600 square feet of retail ghetto space" (155), Kwang has Americanized himself out of this Korean unsociability. He adopts behaviors and characteristics that the novel codes as American. He is exceedingly personable, able to hob-nob, and able to charm his way through the complex electoral system. Kwang is also Americanized in body. Instead of "the brief choppy step of our [Korean Americans'] number," Kwang strides in "luxurious . . . lengths," radiating an "American executive" and "power broker" aura (137–38). Language figures Kwang's assimilation as well. In contrast to Henry's father's stuttering barks and silence, Kwang commands the locution of a native speaker, moving "perfectly . . . through the sounds of his words" and taking on the linguistic gestures that Henry "recognizes as Anglo" (179–80).

The formula at work is that Korean culture marginalizes while assimilation to American culture offers inclusion and power. Recalling Henry's assimilatory path, we see that Kwang has likewise swapped one subjectivity-determining cultural field for another. He leaves culturalizing logics intact. Because his political participation is linked to his Americanization, Kwang reinforces the idea that Korean culture is containing and American culture is liberating. This undermines his achievements. Kwang might be a model of and advocate for a more expansive legibility for Korean Americans, but only as one who assimilates and implicitly for those who do the same.

It could be argued that Kwang's assimilation is subversive, a strategic performance of mainstream cultural norms used to gain sociopolitical power and inclusion. Indeed, there is an element of performance in Kwang's Americanization. When Henry observes Kwang's "luxurious lengths," he also describes them as "borrowed." Likewise, the "Anglo" gestures of Kwang's elegant English seem learned and "stylized" (138, 180). In fact, Henry suspects that Kwang's assimilation is a mask. For instance, Henry notes that Kwang's "American executive" style is achieved through costume. Kwang's "power broker" suit fits only because it "must have been retailored from their lanky western proportions to flatter his short Korean legs." Henry thinks that there is something inauthentic about Kwang's impeccable English too. Henry conjectures that there is "a mysterious dubbing going on" that guards against the revelation of an "errant tone, the flag, the minor mistake that would tell of his [Kwang's] original race" (137, 179).

However, the gap between Kwang's assimilation and his suspected hidden Korean-ness points less to subversive performativity than to a tragic, incomplete donning of costume. Kwang's assimilation does turn out to be a mask. He does possess a hidden Korean-ness that he has not fully evacuated. Kwang's incomplete assimilation is represented as his fatal flaw, to which he eventually falls victim. Kwang's assimilation-as-mask manifests whenever his political power is challenged. When one of his rallies is smoke-bombed, Kwang's impeccable English betrays its "errant tone." During the chaos, he hastily and ungrammatically mouths to Henry: "I'm okay. No worry." Kwang's English then disintegrates altogether when, shuttled away from the scene, he mouths "thank you" to Henry *in Korean* (155). Kwang also betrays his false assimilation in one of the novel's pivotal scandals, the bombing of his office, which kills an aide and a custodial worker, and which is linked to Kwang's association with a Korean gang. Devastated, Kwang cloisters himself at home in the Korean American enclave of Queens, comforting himself by singing maudlin Korean folk songs. When he finally emerges, he takes Henry to a Korean bar in Manhattan's Koreatown, where, in keeping with Korean masculinist indulgences, waitresses are paid to fawn sexually on male customers. After leaving the bar with one of the Korean waitresses, Kwang gets into a car accident, the investigation of which reveals that the waitress is an undocumented minor.

This chain of events reveals that underneath his assimilatory sheen Kwang remains irrepressibly Korean. We even learn that he stores kimchee in the basement of his home. This emblematizes Kwang's cultural bearing: his Korean-ness is quintessential, but concealed. But it is not fully concealed as in his unguarded moments, Kwang reflexively turns to Korean culture, whether by singing Korean folk songs or patronizing Korean sex-service bars.[16] These events destroy his political career, not just because they are generic scandals, but because they reveal that Kwang is culturally unfit to be an *American* politician. The scandal of carousing with an undocumented sex worker is enough to ruin any politician, but for Kwang it especially indicates that he is involved in a Korean underworld, that he remains at the core tied to a world of racial-cultural difference. If we remember the cultural determinism that Kwang and Henry's assimilation instantiates—Korean culture marginalizes while assimilation to white mainstream culture enables more expansive opportunities—we see that Kwang's downfall bears out the logic of this culturalizing formula. When Kwang exhibited American cultural behavior, he was rapidly gaining power and presence in the political realm, but when he reverts to his Korean-ness, his possibilities crumble.

The linchpin of Kwang's downfall, then, is none of the individual scandals per se, but his inability to transcend Korean culture. This attribution further crystallizes when, most damningly, Kwang is found to be involved with a central symbol of Korean Americans' culturalization—the "ancient financial network," or the *ggeh*. Henry's spy work uncovers that Kwang, notwithstanding his impressive Americanization, has been administrating a long-standing and elaborate *ggeh*. Kwang's *ggeh* is multiracial, its funds raised by and distributed to any of his immigrant constituents who needs a boost. Henry filches Kwang's list of *ggeh* participants and submits it to Glimmer & Co. as his parting swan song. Many of the participants are undocumented immigrants and are then deported; the *ggeh* list is given to the Immigration and Naturalization Service, which turns out to be Glimmer & Co.'s client. The *ggeh* is not illegal. However, it irredeemably ruins Kwang's career because it adds an additional stain of cultural difference to his image, sullying the Americanization that is needed, according to the logic of the novel, to be a successful agent in the sociopolitical sphere.

That such a polished, meticulously self-manufactured figure like Kwang would engage in a homespun and culturally alien operation like the *ggeh*, or would be so imprudent as to frequent a Korean sex bar and have dealings with a Korean gang, seems hard to believe. But this is consonant with the cultural determinism with which *Native Speaker* begins and ends. Kwang is ultimately an obedient subject of Henry's ethnography. He cannot help but to partake in Korean cultural practices, foolish as they turn out to be. Henry remarks of Kwang's *ggeh*: "the idea of the *ggeh* occurred as second nature to him" (334). This second nature turns out to be Kwang's first nature. It leaves him vulnerable to the inevitable exposure of what "anthropologists and pundits alike . . . might have called his *natural state*" (176, emphasis in original). Kwang's regression to Korean culture also undoes his linguistic gains, which had marked his advancement beyond the culturalized limits of small business ownership. As the scandals unfold and to the horror of his spin doctors, Kwang refuses to give a public speech to repair his reputation. Previously articulate and charmingly public, that is, quite a "native speaker," quite an American who inhabits and claims the culture of power, Kwang suddenly reveals himself to be no different than Henry's father, withdrawn, insular, silent—and Korean. Kwang turns out to be just another ethnic immigrant who might have done better than to fly above his cultural limits. Indeed, he is ultimately incapable of doing better than what is prescribed by his natural cultural state.

Native Speaker ends with Dennis Hoagland being right all along.

Culturalizations are always "bigger than you. . . . They'll bring you down" (46). Korean Americans cannot, it turns out, author their subjectivity beyond culturalizations. Despite Kwang's expertly tailored suit, his Korean legs will be bared. Kwang did not or could not fully take up the lessons of Henry's pedagogy of assimilation. If only Kwang had really acculturated, he would have obviated the scandals that ultimately destroyed his career and continued his work of advocating for and modeling Korean Americans' sociopolitical legibility. If only Korean American shopkeepers in South Los Angeles were willing to pick up American cultural behaviors like making eye contact or chit-chat with customers, or if only they had Americanized themselves out of small business in the first place, they would not have been entangled in the 1992 riots. At any rate, these attempts will yield little, as we see with John Kwang. *Native Speaker* ends with a warning—resign yourself to your racial-cultural difference and its limits, even as—especially if—you dare assimilation. Learn, as Kwang tragically does, that as with the odor of the pungent kimchee stored in his basement, Korean Americans cannot escape or fully evacuate their stink.

6 / Indian Edison: The Ethnoburbian Paradox and Corrective Ethnography

In the title story of Jhumpa Lahiri's *Unaccustomed Earth*, Ruma, a second-generation South Asian American woman, lives in upper-middle-class suburban comfort. For her, "frugality [is] foreign" (3-4). This is a striking statement in that it reverses a common wisdom—foreignness usually makes frugality familiar. The immigrant, the foreigner, is an icon of saving, having alighted upon a new land with few financial resources, yet with the fierce resourcefulness of hard work and thrift that vindicates the American Dream mythology and makes Asian Americans its object lesson. In Lahiri's story, and in contrast to the narratives of Asian American ghettoization in the preceding chapters, Asian Americans have "arrived." They have arrived economically and spatially, ensconced in financial stability, if not luxury, in the spatial emblem of class comfort, the American suburb. The problem of Asian American ghettoization can be resolved.

Ghettoization is typically an urban problem so it is not surprising that suburbanization and the economic well-being it codes offer an immanent solution. Yet suburbanization has its limits, as I detailed in chapter 5. Moreover, suburbanization as a solution to ghettoization iterates the culturalization of class. Suburbanization codes cultural assimilation, at least in the common form presented in the example of Lahiri's story. Ruma is married to a white man, which symbolizes her distance from her Bengali heritage, and the suburb she lives in is reflexively depicted as white. These dynamics rehearse the link between assimilation and upward mobility. Upward mobility is diverted onto the private terrain of culture, as is, in turn, ghettoization. This culturalization also fates ethnic difference to obsolescence. Is the antidote to ghettoization always the deracination of culture? Is the suburb only white?

The "ethnoburb" is the dialectical alternative to urban ghettoization on the one hand, and to suburbanized, assimilatory upward mobility on the other. It is an alternative in terms of class as well as culture, putting Asian Americans in relationship to class in a way that does not bloat culture, so that ghettoization is privatized, or that attenuates cultural difference, so that assimilation remains fused to upward mobility. "Ethnoburb" is a term coined by geographer Wei Li to describe suburban formations with pronounced ethnic populations, ethnic character, and ethnic affluence. Ethnoburbs are sites like Monterey Park, California, dubbed the "Chinese Beverly Hills," where Chinese-language signs and architectural styles have transformed the suburban landscape. The ethnoburb gives immigrants the best conditions of culture and class. It is a site of upward mobility, yet it enables the preservation and cultivation of cultural community. The ethnoburb is an alternative aspirational destination of ghettoized immigrants and a corrective to the chauvinism of assimilatory suburbanization. Frugality is foreign, and foreignness does not axiomatically stand in for the need for frugality.

The ethnoburb is not only an end of a journey, but also the beginning of one. Some ethnoburb residents are immigrants who follow the conventional rags-to-riches trajectory. Securing suburban middle-class comfort is the culmination of their hard work; the ethnoburb is their reward. However, the space is also populated by those who bypass this familiar path, by Asian migrants who are already wealthy and begin their American lives in suburban comfort. The growth of the latter group was conspicuous in the 1980s, the decade when ethnoburbs became highly visible. Intensifying globalization brought great wealth to Pacific Rim nations, resulting in the formation of sizable middle and privileged classes in Asia. The migrants among them had the means to settle directly in the suburbs, to "leapfrog the core" (Li 41). The ethnoburb is populated by model minorities as well as moneyed minorities.

The ethnoburb appears to be a better and different racialized class formation. It breaks the link between upward mobility and assimilation, while also calling attention to the political-economic power of Asians in the United States. Wealthy Asians in America are not simply obeisant, politically disenfranchised model minorities, as I discussed in chapter 5, but are proxies of mighty nations that shape, if not command, global political economy. Yet these images and experiences of ethnoburb formation risk feeding an old problem—the obfuscation of Asian American experiences of class inequity. They are not obfuscated by culture per se, via the culturalization of class, but are obfuscated because the celebration of the ethnoburb is a foreshortening. Celebrating the ethnoburb as a mark of Asian Americans' class "arrival," their notable surmounting or bypassing of ghettoization, not only forgets those who never make it to the ethnoburb, but also forgets those who experience class inequity *within* the ethnoburb.

This is the paradox of the ethnoburb. Though an essential feature of the space is the presence of conspicuous middle and upper classes, the ethnoburb also needs an underclass. Though the ethnoburb is a site and emblem of notable Asian American wealth, it is also the site of persisting, if not intensified, Asian American ghettoization. A central insight of Li's model is that the ethnoburb is not a homogenously class-privileged space, but a highly class-polarized space (148, 46). The pronounced class stratification in the ethnoburb is forgotten not only in celebratory, but also deprecatory, images. For instance, a white Monterey Park resident, resentful of the influx of Chinese Americans into the suburb, relates that he has heard that it is common practice for Chinese immigrants to troll through the area with satchels of cash in hand, accosting residents with offers to purchase their homes (in Fong 38). This tale reflects the belief that Asian immigrants who come to the ethnoburb are universally and unvaryingly well-off. This belief ignores that the ethnoburb does not categorically index the end of class inequity for Asian Americans but is, counterintuitively, where class inequity can begin.

Suburban Sahibs: Three Immigrant Families and Their Passage from India to America, by S. Mitra Kalita, confronts us with the ethnoburbian paradox. The text is a narrative record of the lives of three families in the Indian ethnoburb of Edison, New Jersey. The text is keenly attentive to class. Its chapters are organized by class and its structural contexts. They toggle among the stories of the three families, the Kotharis, the Sarmas, and the Patels, each of whom signifies a stage en route to the American Dream. The families' class situations are contextualized within local and global structures and relations, such as the influence that transnational trade and H-1B visas have had on Indian migration. *Suburban Sahibs* is what I describe as "corrective ethnography." It is a record of sociality, like the cultural ethnography I have been critiquing, but one that fills in the gaps and unmasks the obfuscations of the "Chinatown book" to present a detailed class portrait. *Suburban Sahibs* is a class ethnography.

That the three families represent stages en route to the American

Dream, that there are differences in economic conditions in the ethno-burb, renders *Suburban Sahibs* a fuller portrait of the ethnoburb than is captured by nicknames like "Chinese Beverly Hills." For some of the "suburban sahibs," the ethnoburb is, paradoxically, the site of impover-ishment and downward mobility. This makes the ethnoburb a site of in-tra-ethnic class divides, giving the space another paradoxical character-ization. The ethnoburb is a site where class difference and contention are originated, not a placid resting point that marks the end of class striving.

As "corrective ethnography," *Suburban Sahibs* does not idealize cul-ture. In "Indian Edison," culture is an economic asset that produces inequitable economic outcomes, and a social construction that is a false salve to economic inequity. Notwithstanding, it is an enticement to co-ethnic community, a central draw of ethnoburb formation. These functions of culture echo those in the ethnic enclave economy model. Indeed, the ethnoburb is a form of ethnic enclave economy. But as such, the ethnoburb is remixed, its similarities to the ethnic enclave economy model bearing important differences. For one, the class divides in the ethnoburb are more pronounced and span a wider spectrum. Second, culture as an instrument of class stratification needs to be recognized, rather than obscured, to understand how this social formation develops. The ethnoburb is not a ready solution to Asian American ghettoization, but schematizes the problems of it.

I foreground what Li describes as the ethnoburb's "class heterogene-ity" or, more to the point, class stratification, in order to recommend a cautious assessment of apparent forms of Asian American upward mo-bility. I began to do so in chapter 5 and continue here in order to forestall the conclusion that race and class no longer discipline Asian American lives. *Suburban Sahibs* shows that new forms of Asian American upward mobility engender pitfalls as well as possibilities, and that class advan-tages create forms of class confinement. This is not to claim that Kalita's text is exhaustively or infallibly corrective, but its attention to the down-sides of the ethnoburb offers one model of authorship in which Asian American experiences of class inequity are written into the polity.

Indian Ethnoburb, Suburban Chinatown, Asian Beverly Hills

The New Jersey section of "usindiainfo.com" provides a list of helpful links for Indians who have recently moved to the northern and central New Jersey area. The list includes "Facts and History of New Jersey," "NJ Symphony Orchestra," "Liberty State Park," and "Six Flags Adventure

Site." The Web site helps Indians settle into their new place of residence, providing information to facilitate their integration into New Jersey's social fabric. This information suggests an assimilatory ethic. It edifies Indians about and encourages them to participate in established, non-ethnically marked American social institutions. However, the Web site also offers an extensive collection of links of a different kind. Under "Indian Necessities," there are hundreds of links to New Jersey's Indian-owned businesses, such as restaurants, grocery stores, travel agencies, and law offices. "Indian Places of Worship" lists fourteen local Hindu and Jain temples. Indians have come to New Jersey, but New Jersey has certainly become Indian.

The suburb of Edison, in Middlesex County in central New Jersey, is conspicuous as a place of Indian settlement. In *Suburban Sahibs*, Kalita offers a history of the town and its transformation by Indian Americans. Until the later twentieth century, Edison was a working- and middle-class community of military employees and ethnic whites. The latter dominated the area after World War II when large corporations like Ford, Revlon, Johnson & Johnson, and the New York Times Company set up offices and factories in Middlesex, along the suburban industrial park model. In the 1970s and 1980s, Indians began to migrate to this area in increasing numbers. They did so because, for one, macro sociopolitical changes, namely the 1965 liberalization of immigration laws, enabled South Asians, among many other Asian ethnic groups, to migrate to the United States in large numbers. Local conditions made Edison and the nearby townships particularly appealing. Edison is at the crossroads of several highways to New York and Philadelphia, both of which are within convenient commuting distance; and while Edison offers access to these urban centers, it has the common advantages of the suburbs, such as better-funded schools, safer neighborhoods, and lower residential density. From 1990 to 2000, the Indian population in New Jersey more than doubled from 79,440 to 169,180. In Edison, it tripled in that decade from 6,000 persons to almost 17,000, as the white population of Edison shrank (9, 38, 12, 10). The presence and influence of Indians in Edison and neighboring towns are reflected in the Amtrak stops in this area. They are peppered with advertisements featuring Bollywood stars hawking phone cards and bank services in English, Hindi, and "Hinglish."[1]

Many of the Indians in the New Jersey suburbs labored through the conventional path of rags to riches, starting out in the ghettos of nearby cities and moving into the suburbs as their occupational and financial progress allowed. Their upward mobility was facilitated by their possession of significant human capital resources, such as the ability to speak English, due to British colonization, and high levels of education. By some tabulations, 97 percent of Indian immigrants have a high school education and 75 percent are college graduates, compared to 80 percent of the general U.S. population who have finished high school and 30 percent who have college degrees (Kalita 11).

High education levels suggest that Indian immigrants could also have settled in the suburbs directly. These immigrants were likely already part of a professional middle class before migration and therefore likely to have possessed the attendant financial capital, enabling them to bypass the "rags" stage of immigrant upward mobility. Direct suburban settlement was amplified by the influx of South Asian immigrants during the 1990s technology boom, especially under the H-1B visa program that was established to shore up the shortage of U.S.-born technology labor. In 1997, 65,000 H-1B visas were allotted to highly skilled foreign technology professionals, a quota that was nearly doubled to 115,000 in 1999. Of the first 65,000 visa holders, half were Chinese and Indian (Kalita 77–78). Many firms that recruited under these visas were headquartered in sprawling suburban campuses, making settlement in nearby suburbs a logical choice. For instance, the Sarmas of *Suburban Sahibs* settle directly in Edison after Shravani Sarma is recruited by Global Consultants in Parsippany, New Jersey. Global Consultants is a "body shop," a high-tech employment agency, which places Shravani with AT&T and then Lucent, firms that are also located in the New Jersey suburbs (Kalita 78, 85). Corporations hungry for technology labor recruited aggressively in Asia, wining and dining potential employees and facilitating the logistics of their travel to and settlement in the United States. These efforts, plus the relatively high salaries, channeled technology workers like the Sarmas to places like Edison via a "gold-paved entry," in Kalita's words, that led South Asians straight to the suburbs (65). The emergence of the ethnoburb thereby unsettles, as Li notes, the succession models that conventionally structure conceptions of ethnic upward mobility. Rather than being the destination arduously worked for from the way station of the ghetto, the suburbs are "ports of entry" for ethnic immigrants, especially for those who already enjoy professional middle-class status in India (47).

Other immigrants took the more familiar path of climbing up the socioeconomic ladder. When Indians began moving in, Edison was a modest and atrophying town. Its commercial strips consisted of mom-and-pop businesses owned by white ethnics, businesses that were dwindling because they were not taken up by successive generations. Certain locales became "decrepit strips," including the Oak Tree Road area, which is now the vibrant center of Edison's Indian commerce. Indian immigrants took advantage of the then low property values as well as took the risk of setting up shop in shabby areas (Kalita 12, 41). They also took residential risks, buying houses in undesirable neighborhoods. *Suburban Sahibs* relates that the Kotharis buy a house in Avenel, a town near Edison that was affordable because it was the site of a sex-offender prison. As more and more Indians took these risks, businesses started to thrive and commercial and residential property values soared, turning modest Middlesex towns into upscale suburbs. If Indian Americans are concentrated in wealthy suburbs, it is not only because they brought wealth to America but also, as Kalita notes, because they created wealth here (39, 41).

How was this wealth created? Why did businesses and residential communities thrive, becoming not only increasingly wealthy, but also increasingly Indian? To put it another way, how did Edison, New Jersey, become an Indian ethnoburb? As mentioned, the ethnoburb is Wei Li's model of a suburban space that has conspicuous clusters of ethnic business and residence, as well as pronounced ethnic affluence. The majority of ethnoburb residents do not necessarily belong to the dominant ethnic group, but that group is dominant because it has a pervasive influence on the space's landscape, architecture, commerce, residential patterns and culture (Li 1). Li's research focuses on Chinese American ethnoburbs in California's San Gabriel Valley. They include Monterey Park, described by Timothy Fong as "the first suburban Chinatown" in his monograph of the same name. Li points out, however, that spaces like Monterey Park are not merely Chinatowns transplanted into the suburbs, but disparate social formations formed under the convergence of national and global economic imperatives, immigration and other race-related public policies, and local socioeconomic and political conditions (x, 1).

For Edison, the factors that led to its development as an Indian ethnoburb include: the demand for foreign labor during the 1990s technology boom, the 1965 immigration reforms as well as the H-1B visa program established in the late 1990s, the accessibility of Edison to major metropolitan areas, and the availability of initially affordable businesses opportunities and residential real estate. But what makes the ethnoburb an ethnoburb is not that these factors merely brought Indians to the suburbs, but that they brought middle-class and wealthy Indians to them, and also created well-off Indians within this space. Li's point that the ethnoburb is not, in her example, a "suburban Chinatown" is the point that the eth-noburb is not a ghetto merely transplanted to a suburban space. This is an easy to miss, but crucial distinction. Li is defining "Chinatown" in "suburban Chinatown" as a ghetto. She is defining it as a space of class inequity, instead of using it as a metonym for "cultural community." The ethnoburb is not a "suburban Chinatown," that is, a suburban ghetto, because in addition to pronounced ethnic character and ethnic popula-tion, the ethnoburb is characterized by pronounced ethnic wealth. The San Gabriel Valley ethnoburbs of Li's study are characterized by the high socioeconomic status of their residents, the majority of whom are white-collar workers. Here, a third of Chinese immigrants hold professional jobs, in contrast to all immigrants in Los Angeles County, of whom only 16 percent are professionals (119, 125). Simply put, ethnoburbian immi-grants are "highly educated, relatively affluent, and well-housed" (148).

If the ethnoburbs of the San Gabriel Valley are not "suburban Chi-natowns," perhaps they are "Chinese Beverly Hills," another popular alias of Monterey Park. On the one hand, this nickname is a compli-ment, a reflection of the economic power of Asian migrants, whose racial congregation need no longer be associated with ghettoization. Timothy Fong notes that Frederick Hsieh, a prominent area realtor, popularized the nickname in the late 1970s when he used it to market Monterey Park to potential migrants in Taiwan. The target audience was wealthy Tai-wanese, who commanded the economic power to afford a "Chinese Bev-erly Hills" address (29). On the other hand, this nickname is laden with accusation and resentment. When coupled with the tale recounted above about Chinese immigrants cruising neighborhoods with sacks of money, it suggests predation and invasion. In the 1980s, when Monterey Park was emerging as a "Chinese Beverly Hills," the suburb was also roiled in a slow-growth movement. The movement did not always overtly express, but heavily implied that Chinese Americans were unwelcome, under the pretense that they were causing overdevelopment. Sonia Gerlach, Mon-terey Park's planning commissioner, as well as the interim president of the pro–slow growth RAMP (Residents Association of Monterey Park), equated overdevelopment with the encroachment of "Chinese money" (Fong 92). Likewise, community activist Frank Arcuri warned of "Chi-nese people" who have so much money that "they can buy our city, buy our economy" (qtd. in Fong 113).

The class resentment and anxiety expressed in these comments cre-ate an equivalence between race and economics. Being Chinese is a metonym of (threatening) wealth, the alarming sign of having money.

This equivalence is expressed by Asian Americans themselves. During the slow-growth controversy, longer-established Monterey Park Chinese Americans, who had moved there via the conventional rags-to-riches path, distanced themselves from the newer, already wealthy Chinese immigrants who were settling directly in the suburb. They agreed with the slow-growth proponents that these wealthy Chinese immigrants were blighting the suburb with aggressive economic behavior (Fong 67). Their conspicuous wealth was also distasteful because it was not the result of the time-honored crucible of racial-economic struggle. One longtime Chinese American Monterey Park resident complains: "When I first came to LA, I lived in Chinatown, went into the [military] service, came out, worked in a lot of jobs, and step by step I moved to Monterey Park. It took how many years? Thirty, forty years? It seems like these immigrants . . . want to live in Monterey Park as soon as they get off the boat. Not the boat, now they come by airplane" (qtd. in Fong 66). These sentiments indicate that there is a diversity of Asian American economic experiences. However, their point is that such diversity is becoming extinct, giving way to a jet-setting, economically rapacious throng.

In Edison, New Jersey, where politicians find it expedient to end their speeches with "Jai Hind" ("Long live India") (Kalita 20), similar class resentments reflect the assumption that Indians are a pack of wealthy, invading foreigners. The rapid growth of the Indian population in the 1980s coincided with an increasing number of hate crimes and the emergence of groups like the "Dotbusters," street vigilantes who were connected to several high-profile racially motivated murders of Indians (Kalita 43–44). These racist hate crimes were also conditioned by class. Race serves as the readily accessible and visible axis through which to express hate toward Indians, but at the core is class resentment. A white Jersey City resident unequivocally articulates the class basis of anti-Indian racism: "I been [sic] in this country all my life and they [Indians] come in and plop down two hundred thousand dollars for a house" (qtd. in Kalita 42).

Such resentment creates an image of ethnoburbian Asian Americans as pervasively—and perversely—wealthy. There is certainly a great deal of ethnic wealth in Edison and other ethnoburbs. Indeed, the presence of ethnic wealth is a primary characteristic of an ethnoburb as delineated by Li. However, foregrounding this wealth, to the extent that the ethnoburb is perceived as constituted only by the well-off, denies Asian American experiences of class inequity. It does so by not only minimizing attention to those who do not have the wherewithal to settle in or create an ethnoburb, but also by minimizing attention to those who are impoverished within the ethnoburb. This sounds like a paradox—impoverishment in the ethnoburb? But, as we will see, it is class stratification, not uniform class privilege, that gives rise to the ethnoburb. Inasmuch as "Beverly Hills" is a metonym for uniform wealth, if the Asian American ethnoburb is not a "suburban Chinatown," it is not an "Asian Beverly Hills" either.

The Class-Divided Ethnoburb

The ethnoburb is visible as a class-divided space by understanding it as a space that is "somewhat like" and "so much like." By this I mean that the ethnoburb takes on its unique characteristics vis-à-vis its relationship to other models of ethnic class formations. It approximates characteristics of these other models, sometimes to unsettling degrees. As such, the ethnoburb becomes visible as a paradoxical formation, as a highly class-divided space that is as much a space of "arrival," of upward mobility or of maintaining existing wealth, as it is of regression, of economic marginalization. The ethnoburb is materially and discursively formed against the main models of ethnic class formations, of "ghetto" and "ethnic enclave," as well as of the middle-class white suburbs that the first two are implicitly constructed against.

The ethnoburb is not a "suburban Chinatown," a ghetto located in the suburbs, because it does not fit into the model of the "ghetto." The ethnoburb is a space of wealth and the middle and privileged classes, unlike the ghetto, which is a space of impoverishment and the underclass. The ethnoburb is also a voluntary formation, not one of forced segregation (Li 45).[2] Thus the main difference is a class difference overlaid with agency. The ethnoburb is a place of voluntary settlement that reflects class privilege. This is the privilege of class achievement; for rags-to-riches residents, the ethnoburb is a place that coronates their class ascendance. It is also the privilege of class entitlement; for wealthy migrants, the ethnoburb is a space that they create to reflect and tend to their class advantages.

The ethnoburb is unlike the ethnic enclave for the same reasons. "Ethnic enclave," as I have been discussing it, is an alias for "ghetto." It is a different name for the same empirical space (for instance, Zhou describes New York's contemporary Chinatown as an ethnic enclave, while I characterize it as a ghetto, but we are discussing the same physical space). The ethnoburb is unlike the ethnic enclave because like the ghetto (because the ethnic enclave is the same space as the ghetto), the

ethnic enclave is a space of impoverishment, the underclass, and structural spatial-economic segregation. However, the ethnoburb is similar to
the ghetto/ethnic enclave in that it is a visibly racialized class formation
of cultural difference.

As a racialized ethnic class formation, the ethnoburb is not equivalent to the middle-class white suburb, notwithstanding the spatial and
economic similarities. The racialization of and cultural difference in the
ethnoburb are important factors that draw wealthy immigrants to this
space. Ethnoburbs provide the benefits without the costs of the white
suburbs. They enable the sustenance of middle-class and privileged living standards without demanding assimilation. Li describes the ethnoburb as something in between the ghetto/ethnic enclave and white suburb (1). It is not dominated by poverty, yet it does not impel assimilation.

This sketch of the ethnoburb sounds like a vindication of the ethnic enclave economy theory. As mentioned, I equate the ghetto with
the ethnic enclave because the latter is an alias of the former, because
they are the same empirical space. But there is an important discursive
difference: even as "ghetto" refers to the same physical space as "ethnic
enclave," each label has its own vocabulary and visions of class. Parsing
out the vision and vocabulary of "ethnic enclave" aids in parsing out
the specificities of the ethnoburb. The main likeness between the ethnic enclave and the ethnoburb is that they are both ethnic economies
built upon the consumer demands of and business practices among co-
ethnics. As such, the ethnoburb, like the ethnic enclave economy, offers
an alternate condition of middle-class or privileged life. Profiting from
co-ethnic economic relations, ethnoburb residents, business owners,
and employees need not assimilate economically, spatially or culturally
into the white middle-class mainstream.

The ethnoburb, like the ethnic enclave economy model, thereby subverts the Chicago school model of ghettoization and of upward mobility
that has heavily shaped the popular imagination. Cultural difference is
no longer a class pathology that mires ethnic subjects in ghettoization,
but a companion to upward mobility. Zhou describes this alternative
route to middle-class stability as "assimilation without acculturation,"
assimilation into the economic middle class without acculturation to
mainstream white cultural norms (5). Li modifies this claim, describing cultural dynamics in the ethnoburb as a "two-way street" (49). Inasmuch as no American social formation can be completely isolated from
the dominant white culture, inasmuch as assimilation always applies
an implicit pressure, the ethnoburb enables a fluid cultural duality in

which subjects might participate in assimilation, but in which they also have access to a middle-class space that allows them to participate in ethnic difference. The ethnoburb enables its subjects to live culture along a "two-way separation-integration continuum along which groups can move in either direction [toward assimilation or cultural difference], instead of assuming a one-way process that transforms immigrants, at least figuratively, into white Americans" (Li 48–49).

The nonassimilatory direction of Li's "two-way street" suggests that the ethnoburb vindicates the ethnic enclave economy theory. The ethnoburb model retains the claimed subversion of the ethnic enclave economy model ("assimilation without acculturation") without suffering some of the qualifications. The ethnoburb solidly links nonacculturation with wealth and agency; it is a space of an ethnically self-defined, self-segregating middle and privileged class. In contrast, the ethnic enclave economy model does not fully bear out its subversion because the advantages claimed for its beneficiaries, namely, ghetto small business owners, are dubious. For one, ghetto small business owners are only relatively better-off. They are advantaged in comparison to menial laborers and the unemployed, but their economic situation is still characterized by want, as evidenced in the limits of small business entrepreneurship that I discussed in chapter 5. Moreover, ghetto small business ownership reflects involuntary segregation. It is a least worst alternative, as noted by Zhou's interviewees in New York's contemporary Chinatown. They state that: "It never occurred to me that I could work outside Chinatown," "To own a small business in [Chinatown] is all that I want and all I could possibly achieve," and "There are many different kinds of jobs available outside of Chinatown, jobs that pay much more. The question is, Can you get one?" (qtd. in Zhou 124, 139, 140). The ethnoburb is a more perfected form of an ethnic enclave economy. It is an improvement because it is only "somewhat like" the conventional ethnic enclave economy. Because of key differences (voluntary segregation, production of a solid middle class and of privilege), the ethnoburb replicates the core idea behind the ethnic enclave economy ("assimilation without acculturation") without suffering the latter's drawbacks.

If the near likeness of the ethnoburb and the ethnic enclave economy model vindicates the latter, other likenesses remind us of the shortcomings of the ethnic enclave theory. They also call attention to the shortcomings of the ethnoburb as an ideal and sign of the trending of Asian Americans toward surmounting or bypassing class inequity. Like the ethnic enclave economy, the ethnoburb is beset by class divides. This is the paradox of the ethnoburb—the space is an index of Asian Americans' class achievements and privilege, yet it is highly class-stratified. In fact, among the models of ghetto, ethnic enclave, and ethnoburb, Li describes the ethnoburb as the most highly class-stratified space (45).

Class divides arise in the ethnoburb for the same reasons that the ethnoburb develops as a space of wealth and privilege. Li writes that the ethnoburb "attracts ... ethnic millionaires [as well as] encourage[s] poorer people to immigrate for work" (43–44). The production of this dichotomy can be traced to the structural reasons for intensified Asian immigration in the 1970s and 1980s. Those reasons include changes in national and international policy and politics, such as the 1965 immigration reforms; political instability in Taiwan and Hong Kong; thawing relations between the United States and China; and the interwoven globalization of Chinese and U.S. economies (Li 87, 109–11). These factors favored the migration of the middle class and privileged. The 1965 immigration reforms selected for professional middle-class immigrants since one of their main preference categories was for highly skilled professional workers. The 1979 termination of formal diplomatic relations between the United States and Taiwan, and the scheduled return of Hong Kong to China in 1992, incited the wealthy business class to transfer their bodies and capital to the United States for safer keeping. Transnational economic development made it useful for Chinese businesses to establish "global outposts" in the United States (Li 35, 87–88, 109–12, 35). These middle class and wealthy migrants favored settlement in and created ethnoburbs. The ethnoburbs had the advantages described above, as well as the benefit of a familiar ethnic setting.

The same factors led to the increased immigration of less well-off Asian migrants. While immigration policy changes like those of 1965 selected for the professional middle-class, other immigration policies like the 1980 Refugee Act brought large numbers of migrants from impoverished, war-torn backgrounds. Often not voluntary migrants, they were socially and economically handicapped in the United States by the shock of displacement (Li 37). Moreover, as globalization has engendered the transnational travel of wealthy bodies and their capital, it has also created a class of "compulsory transnationals" or, in Viet Nguyen's phrase "compulsorily mobile aliens" (21). These subjects are disenfranchised by capitalist development in their home countries and in efforts to find better opportunities elsewhere find themselves exploited abroad. These immigrants also make an appearance in the ethnoburb because of the opportunity structures there—if global capitalism attracts a class of wealthy transnationals to the United States, it also creates a need for a class to serve them. The class dichotomy of the ethnoburb is drawn by a split of professionals and wealthy financiers on the one hand, and menial service workers on the other (Li 31).

This split is created by another fundamental condition necessary to ethnoburb formation: the ethnoburb is necessarily a place of both ethnic residence and ethnic business, of the "interdependence between the ethnic economy and the ethnic population" (Li 100). If the ethnoburb were only a space of ethnic residence, it would not necessarily be an ethnoburb. It would not likely congeal into a visible center of Asian American life. Li notes that if ethnic businesses and services were not available in the suburbs, suburban Asian Americans would seek them in other Asian commercial centers, previously and generally established in urban locales (100). Thus a suburb might emerge as housing a visible ethnic population, but it would not fully be a hub of ethnically characterized life, insofar as such lifestyles include ethnic commerce. In turn, if the suburb were not a hub of ethnic business, it would lose a powerful means of attracting ethnic subjects there and not necessarily grow into an ethnically marked space. Indeed, ethnic businesses are at the forefront of transforming suburban landscapes into ethnically characterized spaces. For instance, business signs in Asian languages are the visible emblems of the permeation of ethnicity in the suburbs and elsewhere.

Ethnic businesses create the need for and draw in co-ethnic menial workers. One of the hallmarks of the San Gabriel Valley ethnoburbs is the 99 Ranch Market chain of supermarkets, owned by Taiwan-based Tawa Supermarkets Companies, that specializes in Chinese foodstuffs (Li 106). Ethnic restaurants also abound, providing Asian migrants with culturally specific food. These businesses facilitate settlement in the United States as well as provide places for wealthy immigrants to spend money. Li points out that Tawa markets its stores as clean and modern facilities that hardly resemble the grungy mom-and-pop shops of the Chinatown ghetto in order to draw in a middle- and upper-class consumer base (108). However, there is an obvious need for a different class of immigrants to staff these businesses—the working class, working poor, and underclass, comprised of menial laborers and service employees. These classes are available because the labor needs of the ethnoburb economy dovetail with the structural patterns of class-stratified migration (100). As mentioned, immigration policy and global capitalism select not only for professional immigrants and wealthy transnationals, but also for "compulsory transnationals." This produces what Li describes as a "highly functional arrangement" in which the privileged class character of the ethnoburb is sustained by the availability of menial and service labor (148). If the presence and development of ethnic businesses are requisite for ethnoburb development, then, insofar as these businesses produce and rely on class stratification, class stratification is requisite to ethnoburb development.

The "functional arrangement" of class stratification necessary for ethnoburb formation resolves a fundamental contention among ethnic enclave economy theorists. As discussed in chapter 2, a main contention is whether the ethnic enclave economy should be defined as a place of residence or business. The first option skews for a depressed socioeconomic portrait, of widespread ghettoization, while the second produces an overly sanguine profile, because it foregrounds relatively better-off business owners. The ethnoburb model resolves this problem by defining itself as an ethnic enclave economy that is constituted by both business and residence. As such, the ethnoburb model neither denies ghettoization, nor masks class divides. Class divides are salient and must be recognized as a necessary condition for the ethnoburb to emerge at all.

Here we see another likeness between the ethnoburb and the ethnic enclave economy model. We recall that a flaw of the latter is that it minimizes class divides. Class benefits are skewed toward small business owners, who exploit their employees under the banner of culture ("co-ethnic cooperation"). The central intervention of the ethnic enclave economy model ("assimilation without acculturation") is built upon this central shortcoming. Only one class segment of the ethnic enclave economy assimilates economically without acculturating. Moreover, the economic assimilation of this class (business owners) depends on the hindered economic assimilation of the laboring class (the perpetuation of its economic disenfranchisement via co-ethnic exploitation). Co-ethnic exploitation is present, but not a centrally configuring dynamic in the ethnoburb, as is co-ethnic cooperation (I detail this further in the next section). The point here is that the ethnoburb, like the ethnic enclave economy—indeed, as a form of the ethnic enclave economy—is built on class divides. If the ethnoburb model vindicates the ethnic enclave economy model by being "somewhat like" it, by not suffering qualifications, it calls attention to the central shortcomings of the ethnic enclave economy by being "so much like" it, by being a form of ethnic enclave economy that calls out its reliance on class divides.

How do the likenesses between the ethnoburb and ethnic enclave economy unsettle the ethnoburb as an ideal and sign of the end of class inequity for Asian Americans? As a class-divided space, the ethnoburb signals for some of its residents and workers the beginning or continuation of class inequity, not the end of it. The class inequity constitutive of ethnoburb development makes it too much like another model of ethnic class formation. The ethnoburb is a "suburban Chinatown" after all. It is a ghetto in the suburbs, insofar as segments of its population are constitutively ghettoized.

If the suburbs prove to be a ghetto, why do economically disenfranchised Asian Americans migrate to them at all? How can they afford to live in the ethnoburb given the high cost of suburban living? What is the role of culture within ethnoburb formation? These questions are addressed, and the paradox of the ethnoburb's class-divided structure more closely rendered, in *Suburban Sahibs'* portrait of the Indian ethnoburb of Edison, New Jersey.

Tent Building: Ethnoburbian Ghettos

The class divides in Edison are expressed through the textual divisions that structure Kalita's "corrective ethnography." The experiences of *Suburban Sahibs'* three ethnoburbian families are interwoven in an alternating, tripartite structure. The text begins by introducing us to the Kotharis, a prominent family in social and business circles, who are known for their production of Navratri, an annual Hindu festival that the Kothari patriarch, Pradip, has turned into a spectacular ethnoburb-wide affair. Beginning with Pradip's October 2000 Navratri and ending with Election Day in 2001, the chapters alternate the Kotharis' story with those of the Sarmas, a young couple who have been recruited by technology firms under H-1B visas, and the Patels, a working poor family whose members shuttle form one low-wage job to another. The chapters roughly follow the order of Kothari, Patel, Sarma, and then back to the Kotharis again to repeat the sequence. With the Patels' story sandwiched in between the stories of the well-off Kotharis and Sarmas, the class divides of the ethnoburb, the ethnoburbian paradox, are thrown into relief. This class ethnography is cross-hatched with treatments of the relationship of class to culture.

The three families schematize ethnoburb demographics. The Kotharis represent the hardworking Indian family whose perseverance is rewarded with the comforts of suburban life. The Sarmas, in contrast, "leap-frog the core." Educated at prestigious Indian universities and recruited by well-paying technology corporations, they are not the proverbial "dollar-in-their-pocket" immigrants who begin their American lives in the urban, ethnic ghetto, but head directly to the middle-class suburb of Edison. However, Harish, the head of the Patel family, is this proverbial immigrant (though he actually has twenty dollars in his pocket [49]). He has faith in the American Dream, but the dream eludes him as he shuttles from one low-paying, menial job to another. He also "leapfrogs the core," living his poverty not in an urban ghetto, the more conventional port of entry in immigrant narratology, but in the well-to-do ethnoburb of Edison.

The experiences of the Kotharis and the Sarmas are emblematic of how middle-class and privileged Asian Americans come to and create the ethnoburb, via either a rags-to-riches trajectory or direct suburban settlement enabled by the possession of premigration financial and social capital. The Patels' case tells the less told story of economic marginalization in the ethnoburb, a story of the ethnoburb not as a space of privilege but of ghettoization. Kalita's attention to class divides in the ethnoburb makes her text a "corrective ethnography," not only because it is a class ethnography, an alternative to the culturalist pabulum produced under the ethnographic imperative, but also because it gainsays glib notions that ethnoburbs are "Asian Beverly Hills," signs and physical proof that ghettoization is a diminishing problem for Asian Americans.

For the Patels, Edison is a suburban ghetto (89). Harish immigrates to the United States in 1985, following the path of his brothers before him, one of whom is a civil engineer in Detroit and the other in a Ph.D. program at Duke University. Like his siblings, Harish has the human capital resources that should enable him to find professional opportunities. He is college-educated and in India was a midlevel manager at a bank (49). But Harish cannot find work commensurate with his education and professional skills. Kalita attributes this to bad timing (the late 1980s recession), the incompatibility of his Indian banking skills with U.S. banking procedures, and, despite his ability to speak English, his unintelligible accent (53). Harish suffers downward mobility, taking on menial jobs, such as unpacking boxes at a cosmetics warehouse and working as a gas station attendant. At one point, he takes on a second job as a security guard to make a living wage (54, 50). Harish's financial problems are compounded by his location—the expensive New Jersey suburbs. With savings from his minimum-wage and near-minimum-wage jobs, plus a loan from an employer, he pays six hundred dollars per month for a one-bedroom apartment where he lives with his wife and their two daughters. However, he cannot afford a car. His movements around the suburb are circumscribed (55).

Given his financial want, why does Harish choose to live in the expensive and inconvenient ethnoburb? One reason is that the ethnoburb offers cultural familiarity and community. He goes to New Jersey to connect with established relatives and Indian friends who help support him. Likewise, he chooses Edison and a particular housing complex there, the Hilltop Estates, because of its high immigrant population of mainly Indians (55–56). But Harish also goes to the New Jersey suburbs because those suburbs need him. He is needed as a service worker, the person who pumps gas for those who do own cars.

This connection—Harish's role as a service worker to wealthy Indians in the Edison ethnoburb—is not explicit in *Suburban Sahibs*, but it is encoded in the social relations that the text describes. The three families of *Suburban Sahibs* are connected through Pradip's production of Navratri. This cultural-religious festival brings together Indian Hindus of all classes: "Here, in suburban New Jersey, the 7-Eleven cashier and Amoco gas station attendant become dancing kings with whom bankers and computer programmers struggle to keep pace" (Kalita 15). Notwithstanding, Navratri is a highly classed project—it does not always erase class divides, but is built upon them. Kalita notes that "tents go up" and feet are pedicured (15, 19). Who are the agents beneath these passive linguistic constructions? Who are the laborers who set up the vast, unwieldy festival tents and who are the nail salon workers who beautify the bodies of festival dancers? Pradip reviews the lighting and heating contracts for the festival, indicating that there are electricians and HVAC employees, that is, a working-class population upon which Navratri relies (17). Pradip also checks in with the security guards in front of the tents (19). Might these security guards be like Harish, taking on a second job to supplement their income? Food vendors with delicious fare abound. Might the food be prepared with ingredients purchased from the local Shoprite, where Harish's daughter, Kajal, works as a cashier to supplement the family income (132)? Kalita notes that Navratri, traditionally a nine-day festival, is stretched across several weekends so that children do not have to miss school and parents do not have to miss work. But for some, like for the menial and working-class laborers who build and maintain the festival, the festival is site of more work, of weekends cherished not for the leisure they schedule, but for the opportunity for more labor hours to supplement low and modest incomes.

The Sarmas do not attend Navratri because they belong to a different Hindu sect, but their well-to-do lifestyle is nonetheless built upon the labor of service sector workers. The profile of the Sarmas differs from those of the other families in that it pays more attention to gender, highlighting the experiences of Shravani Sarma, nicknamed "Lipi." Lipi and her husband, Sankumani ("Sanku"), immigrate under H-1B visas, bringing with them their son, Chiku. Both husband and wife have full-time jobs (Lipi is a particularly sought-after technology worker), creating the need for child care and for the service workers in the day-care industry to provide it. For Lipi, child care is a necessary choice, not a necessity. Even when she is presented with the prospect of staying at home, for instance, during one period when it looks like she might get laid off, it is paramount that she find another job.[3] This is not because Lipi does not cherish her son, but because she is a determined career woman who does not want to be a housewife (123). Lipi's maintenance of herself as a middle-class professional, as the kind of subject who makes the ethnoburb an ethnoburb (a middle-class and wealthy space), and as a subject who does not subscribe to patriarchal gender norms, thereby requires the gendering of others' labor, of the child-care providers necessary for her to be a career woman. This is not to assume that all child-care workers are women (we are not told the genders of the Sarmas' child-care providers). The point is that insofar as child-care work is coded as feminized work, the ethnoburb's service sector is gendered.

Menial and service workers are present in the ethnoburb, though they are obscured from view by spectacular displays of wealth (Navratri is expensive to stage, and Pradip's production of it boasts his wealth), even as they are indispensable to producing those displays. Their residential presence is also preferred to be unseen. Kalita notes that many of Edison's poorer immigrants congregate in "Hilltop Estates," a suburban tenement complex, with its shabby interiors, lack of air-conditioning, junk piles, laundry hung in balconies, and youth gangs (86–89). The rents are relatively expensive, but more affordable than buying a single-family home. Many save costs by cramping numerous family members and friends into one unit. Hilltop Estates is an example of a "pocket of poverty" that Li observes is part of the ethnoburb structure. It is in a lower-income area created by low-paid workers who come to the ethnoburb for jobs (148). Kalita is more direct, describing the ethnoburb's "pockets of poverty" as "virtual suburban ghettoes" (89). Yet this description is not even that direct. The qualifier "virtual" is unnecessary; Hilltop Estates is an *actual* ghetto. It is a space of structurally imposed, racialized, class inequity. However, other qualifications are necessary. In my previous discussions of the term "ghetto," "structurally imposed" refers to macro-systems of law, policy, and social opinion that are imposed upon racialized subjects by the racial power of whiteness. In the ethnoburb, the structural imposition is within a voluntary and ethnic formation. The poverty and underemployment of impoverished ethnoburb residents can be the result of conventional structural discrimination. For instance, part of the reason Harish cannot find a white-collar job and must live in Hilltop Estates is because of a distaste for his accent in the mainstream labor market. However, the ethnoburbian ghetto as a space that results from structural discrimination is located in the voluntary (for the wealthier residents) ethnic formation of the ethnoburb. That voluntary ethnic formation exerts its own structural pressure. Within Edison, the impoverished have no choice but to live, indeed, be segregated and removed from sight and consciousness, in areas like Hilltop Estates. One of Kalita's middle-class interviewees is "taken aback" when asked about the belongingness of Hilltop Estates residents in the ethnoburb. The interviewee sniffs that "those people are different from us. Those of us with businesses [respectable livelihoods] live in our own houses" (89). The interviewee distances himself from "those people," the working poor like Harish, in terms of class and space. He prefers that the internal ghetto of Hilltop Estates were not, and should not be, a part of the ethnoburb, even as he, as a business owner, likely depends on those who live there.

The ethnoburb exists as an ethnoburb because there are low-wage workers to support the projects and lifestyles of its middle and wealthy classes, because there are Patels to support the Kotharis and Sarmas. It is a self-feeding space of ethnic character not only because ethnics live there, but also because there is labor to support ethnic businesses and enterprises, whether they be stores catering to Indian tastes or cultural productions like Navratri that allow residents to participate in their ethnicity. Menial and service workers adapt to costs and social exclusions in the ethnoburb by creating internal ghettos. There are relative advantages to ethnoburbian ghettoization. Despite living in "pockets of poverty," ghettoized ethnoburbians have access to good school districts and safe neighborhoods (even if there are suburban street gangs). They also have access to culture. What is the role of culture in ethnoburb formation?

Culture Corrected

Underwriting the structural reasons for ethnoburb formation is culture. Wealthy immigrants have the wherewithal to settle directly in the suburbs, but this does not fully explain why they congregate in and form ethnic suburbs. Li notes that specific local conditions cause this congregation, such as access to highways, good school systems, and low crime (83). However, there are many other suburbs—white suburbs—that offer these conditions. What is missing from the white suburbs is, of course, ethnicity. Cultural community is the compelling draw that makes Asian Americans, especially if they are wealthy enough to have residential choices, seek to participate in and cultivate ethnic-specific suburban spaces. This is evident in Li's interviewees' explanations of why they moved to Monterey Park. One woman states: "Why? Because in living here we [Chinese Americans] feel just like home. There are so many Chinese people and Chinese stores, restaurants, banks, newspapers, radios and TV, almost everything you need." Another interviewee expresses the same sentiment through an ironic twist of the concept of "foreigner": "Want to know why I moved here? . . . [Because a]ll I see are Chinese, there are no *foreigners* at all!" (qtd. in Li 92, emphasis added by Li).

For low-wage workers, the rationale might be reversed. Specific local conditions, such as good schools, low crime, and so forth are likely to be weighted over culture (after all, cultural community is available in the conventional urban ghetto). Nonetheless, culture is an important precondition that makes it sufferable for these workers to be ghettoized to "pockets of poverty" in the ethnoburb. Because of culture, the ethnoburb is an alternative to ghettoization in the mainstream with no cultural community; or marginalization to urban ghettos with cultural community, but without the local benefits of the suburb.

Suburban Sahibs depicts how culture works vis-à-vis ghettoized as well as wealthy ethnoburbians. As a corrective ethnography, it shows that culture as a draw to ethnoburb settlement has its drawbacks. Showing that Indian culture in Edison is a social construction, *Suburban Sahibs* delineates how culture is manipulated in the ethnoburb. Wealthy residents command these manipulations, which in particular offer culture to low-wage workers as a salve to their ethnoburbian ghettoization.

Suburban Sahibs is framed by culture. It is framed around Navratri, with which the text begins and ends. Kalita describes Navratri as a Hindu religious festival comprised of ritual dancing that celebrates the triumph of good over evil (15). In Edison, it is also a cultural gathering, a chance for diasporics to remember and relive experiences of their homeland: "[T]hose who left India may feel that they never really did [at Navratri]. . . . Tonight, they transport themselves back to those festival nights [in India]. . . . [They] remember laughing at the neighbor's son as he brought [] a cup of sugar cane juice seasoned with salt and spices in between dances" as well as the "scent of Grandmother's sandalwood soap" (16). The festival is as cultural as it is religious. At Navratri, "nostalgia reigns" (17).

The nostalgia that Navratri feeds convenes Edison's Hindus under a literal tent that constructs a cultural tent, that socially constructs some coherent form of Hindu Indian culture. Nostalgia constructs other cultural coherences in Edison. For instance, the Sarmas are perplexed that in the United States Indian ethnic groups self-balkanize: "Gujaratis stuck with Gujaratis, Bengalis with Bengalis, Punjabis with the Punjabis" (28). Recalling much more fluid and interwoven intra-ethnic relationships in India, the Sarmas find that Indians in America are constructed, and self-constructed, as discrete ethnic groups with discrete and bounded cultures. Cultural coherence is also constructed through the blurring of differences. Harish Patel has the opposite experience of the Sarmas. At one point, Harish lives in a cramped apartment of laborers. He is surprised to find that one of his roommates, a Sikh, goes out of his way to prepare vegetarian dishes to accommodate Harish's Hindu practice: "*Such a friendship would have been rare in Gujarat,* Harish thought" (54, emphasis in original). Here, Indian cultural coherence is constructed across lines of ethnicity, religion, and region.

Nostalgia has great power to mask the constructedness of culture, but sometimes Indian culture in Edison feels too manufactured. Some attendees of Pradip's Navratri complain that the festival has lost its religious solemnity, that it has been turned into a "Hindu *Jesus Christ Superstar*" (19). This complaint is part of the larger criticism that Navratri is not a cultural event, but a commercial venture that serves Pradip's class interests. Pradip is accused of using Navratri to preserve his power, his "Godfather" status, within the Hindu Indian community; and also to enrich himself, through the festival's admission charges and his use of the festival to advertise his travel business (18–19). Kalita describes Edison's Navratri, where glow wands replace the traditional wooden sticks used in the ritual dances, as denuded of both culture and religion: "Pradip's name graces everything related to Navratri, from the souvenir program to the advertisements that adorn the hall to the plaques given to politicians and guest artists from India. In the months before the tents go up, his travel agency in the 'Little India' section of town becomes festival headquarters" (19)

That Pradip uses his travel agency as Navratri's central command might be unremarkable and pragmatic if it were not for the ways that his travel business embodies the peddling of cultural nostalgia for profit. Pradip's travel agency specializes in arranging trips for Indian migrants to India, a profitable business given the rapidly growing Indian population in Edison and the surrounding areas and, as Kalita notes, the intense nostalgia that makes Navratri such a success. Besides plane tickets, Pradip's travel business, like Navratri, sells nostalgia, access to the culture left in the homeland. Kalita does not explicitly identify culture-peddling as Pradip's motive for getting into the travel business, but contextualized within his commercialization of Navratri, his business can be read as another use of culture as a commodity.

Incidentally, Pradip's travel business literally capitalizes on diaspora and transnationalism. It profits by fulfilling his customers' transnational dreams, of maintaining physical and cultural connections to their homeland. However, *Suburban Sahibs* calls attention to another form of transnationalism, the "compulsory transnationalism" that is configured not by cultural longing, but by material need. Harish is one of these compulsory transnationals. Within three years of his immigration to the United States, he has returned to India three times—not to indulge his nostalgia, but because he is not able to make a decent living in America (52). *Suburban Sahibs* deromanticizes transnationalism. Individuals like Harish might buy plane tickets from people like Pradip, but their transnationalism is not configured by the consumption of cultural nostalgia.

Pradip's relationship to Indian culture likens the ethnoburb to the ethnic enclave economy. In the latter, the better-off class of business owners peddles culture as a totem of trust and goodwill, enabling the exploitation of co-ethnic employees. Wealthy ethnoburbians' trade in culture is slightly different, but similarly maintains a class divide. In the case of Navratri, Pradip enriches himself by exploiting cultural nostalgia. As discussed, the production of this nostalgia depends on the quiet labor of the working class and working poor (the grocery store clerks, beauty salon workers, and security guards). A successful Navratri, the successful circulation of culture for profit, relies on class stratification. Those who profit from selling cultural nostalgia need a laboring class to materialize it.

The laboring class, however, might be more than willing to purchase the cultural nostalgia on sale in the ethnoburb. For instance, Navratri is a salve for Edison's ghettoized Indians. For Harish's daughter, Kajal, the cultural festival is an escape from the drudgery of her job as a grocery store clerk. Kajal has a sparse and strained life. She sleeps in the living room of her family's apartment because her parents cannot afford a larger place, and she turns over a portion of her Shoprite paycheck to help pay household expenses (25). Attending

Navratri is a rare excursion outside of work and family obligations that allows her to gather with Indian American peers and lose herself in the giddy festival dances. Kajal likely enjoys Navratri for the teenage excitement it provides (scoping out love interests and so forth), but the enjoyment is cultural too. It is a chance for Kajal to wear her "favorite blue lehenga, ornate and dazzling" (24), to inhabit a cultural identity marked through dress, which enables her to be more than a grocery store clerk.

Kajal is represented as being sufficiently succored by culture, but *Suburban Sahibs* ultimately shows that culture is a false salve for ghettoization. Kajal's father has no illusions that Navratri has some transcendental function or edifying cultural effect. Though he allows his daughter to attend, he is uninterested in the festival himself. In fact, he is vocal about the commercialism of the event, how it "taint[s] his religion with US dollars" (24). Critical of Pradip's version of Navratri, Harish does not buy into its cultural nostalgia production.

Post-class, Post-race, and Post-ethnographic Imperative

The paradox of the ethnoburb—that it is an emblem of Asian American class achievement and Asian diasporic class privilege, yet it can only be formed and sustained through the ghettoization of other Asian Americans—qualifies the idea that Asian Americans have "arrived" in terms of class, that they are either model minorities or already moneyed minorities. The constitutively class-divided structure of the ethnoburb unsettles the idea that Asian Americans are a post-class formation and the attendant suggestion that race (at least for Asian Americans) no longer has a negative impact on class. The arrival of a post-class, post-race condition is unsettled by another ethnoburbian paradox—if a central factor behind class inequity is racial difference, claiming a post-class condition via the Asian American ethnoburb does so through a social formation that makes Asian Americans not less, but more visible in terms of race. This paradox can be resolved by the inversion of the race/class dyad that I invoked in the beginning of this study, the positioning of race as having a positive rather than negative impact on class for Asian Americans, as seen in the model minority myth. But this inversion gives rise to another paradox, or at least a constitutive, contradictory polarization. In the class-divided space of the ethnoburb, race and culture have a positive correlation with class, as well as a negative impact on it. These cascades of contradictions are perhaps best made sense of by not driving toward resolution. In *The Woman Warrior*, Maxine Hong Kingston writes: "I learned to make my mind large, as the universe is large, so that there is room for paradoxes" (29). To understand the complexity of Asian American class experiences—especially to acknowledge that they experience class inequity—perhaps it is best to make our minds large.

As a class ethnography, *Suburban Sahibs* corrects the culturalizing obfuscations put forth by the genre of the "Chinatown book." This is not to lionize Kalita's text for its ethical work or to suggest that Asian American literature has arrived, has transcended its political-aesthetic limits to now have free voice to author Asian American lives more complexly. *Suburban Sahibs* is an instructive example of corrective ethnography, but it is not the only direction of Asian American literature. In fact, Asian American literature in some respects has become more deeply obfuscating of class inequity in that it has become less interested in race. I refer to the body of literature that can be described as "postracial," to works that pointedly avoid or dismiss Asian American themes, characters and race overall. Even as Asian American experiences are becoming more racialized and more classed, Asian American literature is turning to the postracial and, implicitly, post-class. To put it another way, even as some Asian American literature trends toward "corrective ethnography," to gainsay the disciplines of the ethnographic imperative, others are disengaged with the imperative—and Asian Americans—altogether. We might think that this makes our minds large, makes the scope of Asian American aesthetic contributions more capacious—this is a plangent argument. But in contracting the visibility of a racial group that is often invisible, when it is a group that offers rich, perplexing convergences of race, class, gender, and sexuality, maybe we are not enlarging our minds, but shrinking them.

Conclusion: The Postracial Aesthetic and Class Visibility

At the Iowa Writers' Workshop, Nam, the narrator of Nam Le's short story, "Love and Honor and Pity and Pride and Compassion and Sacrifice," is surrounded by white classmates who resent ethnic literature. To them, ethnic literature is a sell-out genre. One student remarks: "Faulkner, you know . . . said we should write about the old verities. Love and honor and pity and pride and compassion and sacrifice. . . . [T]hat's why I don't mind your work, Nam. Because you could just write about Vietnamese boat people all the time. . . . You could *totally* exploit the Vietnamese thing" (10). One need only possess an ethnic body that channels an ethnic story in order to gain professional accolades and good sales. His classmates sniff: "I'm sick of ethnic lit. . . . It's full of descriptions of exotic food," and "You can't tell if the language is spare because the author intended it that way, or because he didn't have the vocab" (9). Nam, a Vietnamese Australian, remains quiet vis-à-vis his classmates' assessments. He eschews ethnic writing himself, in tacit agreement that it would be too easy to exploit, in his case, "the Vietnamese thing" (10). Nam's friend teases: "How could you have writer's block? Just write a story about Vietnam" (10). Ethnic literature is not good literature, just expedient literature. Genuinely good writers, Nam's friend opines, hew to the "old verities." rather than "writ[ing] about Vietnamese boat people all the time" (10).[1] Good literature is postracial.

The postracial in Asian American literature can be described as literature written by Asian American writers that does not contain Asian American characters or address Asian American experiences. The absence of ethnic characters or experiences in literature by ethnic authors is not new or particularly alarming. But of interest is postracial literature that is characterized by the deliberate abnegation of ethnic content. This rejection frees the author from the ostensible shackles of ethnic particularity and difference to examine transcendent, universal themes, like "love and honor and pity." For Asian American authors, the postracial more specifically frees them from writing Orientalist caricatures and reductive ethnographies—from the "Chinatown book." The postracial is a mode of freedom from the ethnographic imperative.

The freedom conveyed by the postracial aesthetic is both a problem and a subversion. The problem of the postracial is that it intensifies the effacement of class. Insofar as race and class are inextricable, the absence of race in works by Asian American authors is likely accompanied by the absence of class.[2] In addition, as a form of freedom from the ethnographic imperative, the postracial aesthetic iterates the effacement of class. Freedom from the ethnographic imperative, and its retooling of class as culture, suggests freedom from the class effacements of this retooling. Class is perhaps given the space to be articulated. However, this does not bear out because the postracial aesthetic generally untethers Asian American writers from the ethnographic imperative by simply dropping attention to race and culture. It thereby tends to drop attention to related matters of class. Class is freed from being reconfigured through the ethnographic imperative's culturalizations, but is not necessarily addressed, and more likely forgotten again. Of central concern here is that the postracial aesthetic is misleadingly nonmimetic. If race is poor literary material, the postracial aesthetic suggests that race is immaterial, that race is obsolete as an organizing—and damaging—structure of social life. Class inequity is excised as one of race's obsolete damaging effects. The postracial aesthetic is also a post-class aesthetic that suggests that class inequities produced by race have been surmounted.

At the same time, the postracial makes class more plain, more visible as a constitutive element of ethnic writing and ethnic life. The freedom from the ethnographic imperative that the postracial bestows enables a refusal to write reductive ethnographies. Claiming a postracial aesthetic can be a rejection of the multiculturalist literary market in which the "Chinatown book" so profitably circulates. This profitable circulation has a class inflection—the resentment of ethnic literature is a form of class anxiety. In Le's short story, Nam's classmates resent ethnic literature not only because of chauvinistic aesthetic evaluations, but also because it *sells*. A hot topic of gossip is a "substantial six-figure contract" offered to a Chinese national who writes about immigration (8–9). The Chinese writer is resented not just because she writes ethnic literature, but also because that endeavor reaps her significant material and social capital. Ethnic literature as a commodity in the multiculturalist literary market is a means to class mobility. A postracial aesthetic, then, is a rejection of using ethnicity as means to class mobility. The postracial aesthetic can be a refusal to participate in the logic that racialized ethnicity improves class. This logic bears the idea that class inequity does not exist for Asian Americans, as we have seen in the model minority myth. By refusing to perpetuate the directly proportional relationship between ethnicity and class, the postracial reduces the validity of the idea (or at least makes the idea less accessible) that ethnicity improves class. It thereby undermines the corollary inference, the inference that Asian Americans do not suffer class inequity. In addition, Le's story demonstrates that the absence of race via the postracial aesthetic can be rearticulated as a representation of class inequity. If the ethnographic imperative retools class as culture, the postracial can possibly rearticulate race as class. The postracial, through its lack of treatment of race, paradoxically makes class inequity more visible, or at least fends against its perpetuated effacement.

"Love and Honor and Pity and Pride and Compassion and Sacrifice" illustrates these contradictory modes of the postracial, its obfuscation of class inequity on the one hand, and its mitigation of that obfuscation on the other. Though the narrator, Nam, is not Asian American, his experiences as an author illustrate the dynamics of writing and publishing Asian-ethnic literature within the context of an American literary marketplace. The preceding chapters have mapped a range of Asian American writers' ethical and aesthetic positions in relation to the ethnographic imperative. These positions help and hinder the authoring of Asian American class experiences. They make Asian American ghettoization visible as well as more difficult to see, thereby enabling and hindering the understanding of American life as constitutively disciplined by class. I end here with an account of that ethical variation as it is encoded within one aesthetic, an aesthetic to which Asian American writers are increasingly turning. The postracial makes class invisible— now not because authors are straitened by racial subject matter, that is, by the reductions of the ethnographic imperative, but because they are untethered from racial subject matter, from race as a subject that matters. But the postracial also limns the class inflections of racial subject matter. It does so through absence, through the absence of race as an instrument of upward mobility, suggesting that it is harder to imagine that Asian Americans experience class inequity under race's presence.

Racial Dissonance

The postracial and attendantly post-class aesthetic is an indentifiable trend in Asian American literature. I am not concerned with all Asian American texts that do not engage with Asian American characters or themes, but with those whose authors deliberately reject ethnicity-specific content. This rejection is manifest in the protestations of one of the field's most esteemed authors, Chang-rae Lee. Though Lee's first two novels are undeniably about Asian American experiences, he is careful not to pigeonhole himself as an Asian American writer. An interviewer for the *Telegraph* recounts her conversation with Lee: "I ask whether he now sees himself as a Korean or an American writer. He replies that he is an 'American novelist,' but that this includes being a 'Korean writer.' 'In fact, sometimes, I think being a Korean-American novelist doesn't quite include being an American novelist, which is frustrating'" (Bradbury). The question is baited and muddied by the interviewer's conflation of Korean and Korean American. But Lee's qualified response demonstrates that he is careful not to limit himself to being an ethnic writer, as if ethnicity, as an author's identity and subject matter, is an axiomatic limitation. This sentiment has come to characterize Lee's aesthetic. Min Song calls attention to the entry on Lee in *Asian American Novelists: A Bio-Bibliographical Critical Sourcebook*: Lee "express[es] his concern that a novelist who chooses to focus on his ethnicity or region is too readily categorized as 'ethnic' or 'regional' with both terms suggesting works with less than universal themes and less than lasting import" (Kich 176).

"Love and Honor and Pity and Pride and Compassion and Sacrifice" stages the struggle of an ethnic writer over the sentiment that ethnic literature is substandard literature. Nam tacitly agrees with his white classmates' denigration of ethnic literature, essaying not to "exploit the Vietnamese thing" (10). Ironically, Nam's white classmates' distaste for ethnic literature is based on the same tenets of the *Aiiieeeee!* editors. Nam's classmates echo the editors' signature complaints, that Asian American literature is burdened with "descriptions of exotic food" ("food pornography") and exploits the "[Asian] thing" (reductive cultural ethnography) (Le 9, 10). In other words, Nam's Iowa Workshop classmates and the *Aiiieeeee!* editors alike reject the ethnographic imperative, sharing the view that works that submit to it lack literary integrity and merit.[3] That these two groups share an aesthetic sensibility is ironic. The Asian American *Aiiieeeee!* editors would be surprised that white students at one of the most sanctified American writing programs are critical of the ethnographic imperative, for it is the racial power of whiteness that the editors identify as ghettoizing Asian American literature to the genre of the "Chinatown book." It could be that if there are "yellow white supremacists," sycophants to the ethnographic imperative, there are also white yellow supremacists, white authors and literary producers who advocate the antiracist, politically oppositional "sensibility" that the *Aiiieeeee!* editors mandate (Chan et al. xvi, xxvi). But this is not the case. Though these groups share an aesthetic impulse (rejection of the ethnographic imperative), they desire a different aesthetic product. In mandating an antiracist, politically oppositional aesthetic, the *Aiiieeeee!* editors seek and write literature that is fundamentally racialized, that is centrally concerned with addressing the damages of racism and racialization. Nam's Iowa Workshop classmates desire the opposite. The "sensibility" here desires the denuding of literature of race, the denuding of the literary canon of ethnic literature. They disparage works produced under the ethnographic imperative not because they do not like what the imperative does to representations of race, but because they do not like race.

Freedom from the ethnographic imperative via the postracial is thereby a dubious freedom. It is a freedom that stems from disparaging race. This freedom also suggests that race is no longer disparaging, that it no longer has damaging effects; it is obsolete as an organizing structure of social life. Le's short story shows otherwise. It shows that in contradiction to the postracial aesthetic's implication that race is over, racializations and its attendant class effects have not been roundly surmounted. This contradiction is evident in the dissonance that infuses Nam's venture of writing a postracial story. As he seeks to write less about race, the role of race is heightened in his personal life. Despite Nam's efforts to write a postracial story, race and racializations intrude into and insist upon structuring his life. The erasure of race in literature does not comport with the continuing organization of social experience by race.

Race intrudes into Nam's life through the unwelcome visit of his father. Nam is struggling to write a final story for his end-of-semester portfolio when his father arrives at his apartment. Nam has written one story about Vietnamese boat people based on his and his family's personal experiences, but it appears to be an anomaly in his oeuvre, which he is attempting to cap off with a piece that avoids racial subject matter.

But his father's irksome presence reminds him that race constitutively structures his life. When, hastily cleaning up his desk, he spots a picture of his girlfriend, he hides it in panic under some papers. Nam has not told his father about his girlfriend because she is white. For the same reason, he tells his girlfriend that he will not introduce her to his father during his father's visit (5–7). Nam's father's visit disrupts the equilibrium that Nam has created in his relationship with his girlfriend, the equilibrium of a fiction, that they are in a generic, abstract relationship. His father's presumed displeasure at the relationship reminds Nam that it is an interracial relationship, that his girlfriend is not just a girlfriend, but a white girlfriend, and he is not just a boyfriend, but a Vietnamese one.

Simply put, Nam's father's presence reminds Nam that he is racialized as Vietnamese. More specifically, Nam's father figures the trauma of being racialized as Vietnamese, of the psychical and physical damage of being racialized as dispensable life during the Vietnam War, and the subsequent haunting of both father and son by the brutality of that racialization. Nam's father accosts Nam and others with the trauma of being racialized as Vietnamese. When Nam's father strikes up a conversation with a hobo on a local riverbank, he makes a point of telling the hobo, "*We* are the Vietnamese boat people," impressing upon this stranger that Vietnamese boat people, made into such as a consequence of a racializing war, are not just historical abstractions (13, emphasis in original). Nam's father's sudden presence also unburies his son's implication in the traumatic racialization of being Vietnamese, Nam's psychical inheritance of the war wounds of his father. His father's visit launches Nam into a memory of his childhood, when he had accompanied his father to a drinking party attended by friends who had lived through the Vietnam War. Here he learns that his father was a teenage survivor of the My Lai Massacre. As the gruesome patchwork of memory gels into a coherent narrative, Nam ends his flashback with a declarative realization: "My father grew up in the province of Quang Ngai, in the village of Son My, in the hamlet of Tu Cung, later known to the Americans as My Lai. He was fourteen years old" (17).

This memory effects a shift for Nam. The declarative sentence structure that ends his flashback makes the memory a proclamation. It is a proclamation that a racialization so vicious that it animated and condoned a civilian massacre is not to be excised or effaced from his family's personal history and the public imagination. That Nam is the voice of this declaration signals his acceptance of his racialization and the conditioning influence of race in his life. This is demonstrated by his phrasing, "later known to the Americans," through which he takes on the perspective of a Vietnamese, of a racialized subject.

If Nam has now accepted his racialization, this acceptance does not jibe with his attempts to write a postracial story. We have again a dissonance between the racially denuded aesthetic he seeks to abide by and the racialized experiences and history reinserted into his epistemology of self by his father's visit. Nam resolves this dissonance easily—he abjures the postracial project: "*Fuck it*, I thought. I had two and a half days left. I would write the ethnic story of my Vietnamese father. It was a good story. It was a fucking *great* story. I fed in a sheet of blank paper. At the top of the page, I typed 'ETHNIC STORY' in capital letters. I pushed the carriage return and scrolled down to the next line. The sound of helicopters in a dark sky. The keys hammered the page" (17, emphasis in original).

Nam's father's visit intrudes race and racializations not only into Nam's memory and sense of self, but also into his writing. Nam ultimately concedes, even defiantly taking on that racialization. He will now write an ethnic story, which, despite his white classmates' and his own initial defamations, is "a fucking *great* story."

But "Love and Honor and Pity . . . " does not end with such a pat resolution. Even if Nam abjures the postracial aesthetic, he confronts another obstacle—his father burns the "ETHNIC STORY." Having spent all night writing a draft, Nam wakes up to find the story gone, taken by his father and burned by the riverbank. A shift has taken place not only for Nam, but also for his father. If Nam takes leave of his postracial aesthetic, his father takes leave of embodying the confrontation of racialization. By burning the story, Nam's father extinguishes an important means of making his traumatic racialization known. He extinguishes the writing. He insists that the ethnic story not be written and read, that his racialization not be authored into the social imagination.

It turns out, then, that the postracial author in "Love and Honor and Pity . . ." is not Nam, but Nam's father. As much as he figures the intrusion of racialization into his son's life, Nam's father is ultimately the vehicle of its effacement. He drops the topic of race. He drops race literally, by dropping his son's manuscript into a metal drum fire that warms the riverbank hobo. Nam's father's postracial aesthetic warrants qualification. His rejection of the writing of his racialization into the social imagination does not result from his belief that the damages of race are over, but is a coping strategy. It is a way to repress the traumas of race that indeed continue to structure his psyche and subjectivity. This is evident in the strategy of trivialization that Nam's father and his homeland peers employ to cope with their histories. At the drinking party, after Nam's father finishes recounting his experience of the My Lai Massacre, of how he lay with the "tattered bodies" of his family atop him, "mud filling his lungs," the silence is broken by a heartbreaking quip: "You really *did* have it bad!" (19, 16, emphasis in original). Repression sutures the dissonance between Nam's father's postracial aesthetic and the racializations that structure his life. Nonetheless, by destroying Nam's story, he disables a means of writing race into representations of Asian American experience. Asian American life gets documented as postracial or, to put it another way, it does not get documented all.

Class Dissonance, Class Visibility

If there is a dissonance between Nam's and his father's postracial aesthetic and their racialized lives, there is a dissonance in terms of class too. If the postracial is attendantly post-class, it would not be surprising if the postracial story that Nam initially hopes to write is absent of class. Likewise, Nam's father's destruction of his son's "ETHNIC STORY" bars class, along with anything else, from being articulated from that text. But in the same way that Nam's and his father's effacing of racial writing does not correspond with the continuing racial organization of their lives, their assumedly post-class writing ignores the conditioning of their lives by class. For one, previously a lawyer, Nam has lost social capital, at least in his father's estimation, in leaving a high-paying, respected profession to become a graduate student (23). That loss of social capital is accompanied by a loss of material capital, which reduces Nam to subsisting on cheap junk food and noodles (22). If the postracial is also post-class, Nam's following of this aesthetic would not capture this or other forms of downward mobility, which in Nam's case he experiences in order to be, ironically, a writer who denies, or at least omits, treatments of race.

The downward mobility that Nam experiences by becoming a graduate student is not the most plangent figuration of class inequity in Le's story (moreover, this type of downward mobility, while conferring real material hardship, is not equivalent to the kind of ghettoization of, say, the exploited sweatshop laborers that I have discussed). A more haunting figuration is expressed through a peripheral, but recurring character in the story—the hobo at the riverbank. The hobo appears twice: in a chance meeting with Nam and his father during a stroll along the river, and when Nam's father returns to the riverbank to burn his son's story.

The hobo is a quiet spectacle of class inequity. He is an anomaly in the sanitized, pastoral urbanity of Iowa City. Nam describes: "Next to [his father], a bundled-up, bearded figure stooped over a burning gasoline drum. . . . I smelled animals in him, and fuel, and rain," "Never had I seen anything like it in Iowa City" (12, 13). Nam's surprise at the sight of the hobo bespeaks his psychically bourgeois desire not to see. It is not that homeless tramps do not exist in Iowa City. Rather, they are made invisible.

The hobo is thereby a figure of discord, of dissonance, between empirical experiences of impoverishment and comforting class fantasies. This dissonance shows that class inequity has not been surmounted, as implied by the postracial aesthetic, but continues to organize social life. As Nam initially seeks to make his writing less racial and, attendantly, less concerned with class, empirical experiences do not comport; they are heavily classed. I should note that this is a skewed formulation because it is not likely that the hobo is Asian American (we are not told his race). Not being Asian American, the hobo does not directly figure the dissonance between postracial, post-class Asian American literature and Asian Americans' experiences of class inequity. However, perhaps his not being Asian American is what makes him a signification of Asian Americans' relationship to class. The hobo can figure as a proxy of Asian American class inequity. He can be read as a stand-in for the Asian American class inequity that cannot be voiced under the post-racial aesthetic. That is, the hobo is not identified as Asian American precisely because Asian American class inequity cannot be voiced under the postracial aesthetic. Le's making of the hobo racially nonspecific is an enactment of the erasure of racially specific class inequity under the postracial aesthetic.

That the hobo is not marked as Asian American raises a few issues. It could suggest that other races more keenly suffer class inequity. But again, because the hobo is racially nonspecific, it is difficult to use him to make class comparisons across racial groups. How is it that the hobo exists at all? Isn't the erasure of race accompanied by an erasure of class, as I have been arguing? This is not the case in Le's story. The hobo's existence indicates that class inequity *is* represented (even if not in racially specific form) in negotiations of the postracial aesthetic. The postracial can, counterintuitively, make class inequity visible.

The visibility that the postracial aesthetic gives to class inequity is evident in Nam's father's mode of postracial authorship. Nam's father's figuration as a postracial author suggests that the postracial aesthetic is liberating, perhaps subversive, in that it makes class more visible. I mentioned that the postracial aesthetic disrupts the formula that ethnicity improves class. In "Love and Honor and Pity . . . ," it does so in the realm of the diegetical literary. Nam's classmates bridle that writing about ethnicity yields six-figure publishing contracts (8–9). The postracial disrupts this formulation by refusing to furnish ethnicity as a literary commodity, especially as an instrument of literary (and the accompanying material) upward mobility. Extending this literary effect to social life more generally, we can say that the postracial refuses to perpetuate the model minority myth, which posits Asian ethnicity as improving class and, as a result, has made Asian American experiences of class inequity so difficult to see.

By burning his son's story, Nam's father enacts this liberating facet of the postracial. On the surface, Nam's father burns the story because he does not like how he has been portrayed in it. But by obliterating the story, Nam's father achieves something deeper: he refuses to let ethnicity be circulated in the multiculturalist marketplace as a commodity. Nam's father states as much. He admonishes Nam: "Why do you want to write this [ethnic] story? . . . They [white audiences] will read and clap their hands and forget" (24). Thus, when Nam's father burns his son's story, he is enacting a form of class warfare.[4] Insofar as Nam's father prevents ethnicity from being circulated as a commodity, which leads to the formulation that ethnicity leads to upward mobility, he is preventing that formula from being completed. In doing so, Asian American experiences of class inequity are made more visible, or at least more readily imagined, in that the fiction that ethnicity leads to upward mobility, embodied in the model minority myth, is derailed.

That the postracial can make class inequity more imaginable is expressed through the site of Nam's father's authorship. Nam's father enacts his postracial aesthetic at a kind of altar of class inequity—the hobo's metal drum fire, a fixture in the hobo's riverbank encampment, a space where class inequity is not only visible, but constitutive. Nam's father's postracial aesthetic, rather than erasing class, brings him and the reader into intimate confrontation with class inequity. What we see, then, in Le's short story is that the muffling of race leads to the articulation of class. This articulation is a kind of rearticulation. The flames that burn Nam's racial story cast a bright light on class inequity (imagine the glow on the hobo bent over the metal drum fire), suggesting the representational obstinacy of difference. Difference will be represented. Though Nam's father attempts to efface one kind of difference (race), it emerges as another kind—as class difference (impoverishment as a deviation from the fantasy that the normative American status is middle class). Race, as an axis of difference, is not turned into ash, but is kindled into a representation of class inequity.

Abandonment and Denial

This study has mapped the expression and silencing of Asian American experiences of class inequity. Regarding the silences, it has been centrally concerned with how Asian American writers produce those silences themselves, how they are complicit in preventing the authoring of Asian American ghettoization in the social imagination. "Love and Honor and Pity . . ." provides another narrativization of complicity, in which Nam and his father are postracial authors who try to prevent ethnic and class stories from being written. This is the result of traumatized repression, in Nam's father's case, and more generally reflects the literary traumatization of Asian American writing by the ethnographic imperative, which has engendered a genealogy of literature that is quiet about class. This account of complicity does not signal a hopelessness of crafting a satisfactory Asian American literary ethics, or to demand their uniformity, but it reminds us that there are many class and "ETH-NIC STOR[IES]" that remain untold and continue to be lived.

At the same time, the postracial makes class dynamics more visible, rendering it a potentially liberating and subversive aesthetic. We are left with a quandary—does writing about race make Asian American experiences of class inequity more legible, or does *not* writing about race achieve the same? Though I have demonstrated how the latter can work, I suggest caution in taking up this view. The postracial can break the link between ethnicity and upward mobility, but only if it is positioned as a specific kind of refusal—a refusal of the ethnographic imperative and its commodification of ethnic literature. This would enrich our understanding of both race and class. However, if the postracial aesthetic results from compliance to the kind of resentful harping expressed by Nam's Workshop classmates, the postracial is a denial or abandonment of race and class. This second form of the postracial defuses the subversive potential of this aesthetic and returns it to doing what is more likely expected to do; to erase race and class, and suggest that they have been surmounted as organizing structures of social life. However, an intriguing line of inquiry might pick up the provocative suggestion of Le's short story, the suggestion that the submerging of race results in the rearticulation of difference as class.

There are gaps and dissonances between aesthetic direction and lived experience. Such disjunctions are increasingly pronounced. As literature by Asian American authors is becoming less concerned with race and class, the racialization and class stratification in Asian American lived experience are intensifying. Take, for example, the ethnoburb, which I discussed in chapter 6. The ethnoburb embodies the problematic of the postracial. On the one hand, it is a spatial version of the postracial, post-class aesthetic. It is a space that appears to show that the damages of race and class have been surmounted, insofar as it is a middle-class and wealthy space in which race does not hinder, but in fact helps, the building of wealth. But the ethnoburb is a postracial and post-class formation only if we ignore the ethnoburbian paradox, the paradox that class inequity necessarily structures the ethnoburb even as the ethnoburb is an emblem of Asian American class privilege. Thus, on the other hand, the ethnoburb makes a poor signifier of the postracial, post-class aesthetic. Because the privilege of well-off ethnoburbians is supported by a ghettoized ethnoburbian underclass, a putatively post-race, post-class emblem shows that the damaging effects of racialization, such as class inequity, have not been surmounted, but intensified.[5]

There is a disconnect. As Asian American literature becomes less racialized and classed, Asian American social formations are becoming more racialized and more classed. The paradox I have presented is that through postracial and post-class aesthetics voices that tell of Asian American experiences of racialization and class inequity can be both muted and heard. Our challenge is to understand this paradox, insofar as we seek to hear these voices, in literature as well as in the social world that literature represents and makes imaginable. Our challenge is to listen carefully.

NOTES

1 / Introduction: The Asian American Ghetto

1. The recent U.S. economic crisis has brought class into the forefront of public debate, especially during the campaigns for the 2008 presidential election. Candidates like Barack Obama who foreground the need for greater class parity are accused of inciting "class warfare" or of being dangerous socialists, accusations that deny class inequity or maintain it as a taboo subject. But even as candidates call to attention class, they do so primarily to advocate for the strengthening and returning of power and dignity to the middle class. These candidates use the term "middle class" capaciously and also a bit obfuscatingly. This use of "middle class" as a touchstone of public class discourse glosses over the problems of ghettoization—that in addition to a middle class, there are underclasses—and constructs class in America as a structure of aspiration, of always belonging or imminently belonging to the vaguely defined, but palatably invoked position of middle class.

2. I am indebted to Gandal's *The Virtues of the Vicious* for this diction.

3. Most notable are the opposing views of Wilson, and Massey and Denton. Wilson argues that class or socioeconomic conditions create ghettos, while Massey and Denton argue that race is the primary factor in ghetto formation.

2 / "Like a Slum": Ghettos and Ethnic Enclaves, Ghetto and Genre

1. Ahn Joo's father ultimately makes enough money to settle himself and his daughter in a middle-class Maryland suburb of Washington, D.C. However, I contend that Asian American small business owners like Ahn Joo's father remain delimited by class insofar as they have few alternatives to small business ownership. This is not to equate their difficulties with those Asian Americans who cannot even get this far, but it is to attend to a different form of ghettoization, which, though not the most severe, demonstrates an additional way that Asian Americans are delimited by class. I detail this in chapter 5, in reference to Korean American mom-and-pop shopkeepers.

2. I focus on Park's comments on racialized immigrant groups, but his theories on ghettoization encompass racialized and ethnic white immigrants, as well as African Americans in the postslavery diaspora (*On Social Control* 60, 118–19). Park is criticized for too readily likening these disparate social groups, for instance, in his mapping of the assimilation process of immigrants onto the integration processes of southern blacks migrating north after the Civil War (John Hagedorn 195).

3. This is not to pigeonhole Park's line of thinking. Though his tone is often of great certainty, especially in the assimilationist writings for which he is well known, his work shows a diversity of viewpoints. For instance, Park wrote a foreword for Wirth's *The Ghetto* (Wirth was a student of Park's), in which Park recognizes the potential for community in the ghetto.

4. The Chicago school calls much attention to and relies on the term "ghetto," but its concept is more akin to the concept of the ethnic enclave. I detail this ironic similarity below, but make the point here that though the Chicago school uses the term "ghetto," this is not the concept of the ghetto that I seek to return to or make visible.

5. The secondary sector of the U.S. labor market is defined as being comprised of white-owned firms in which the majority of employees are ethnic, and is characterized by "labor intensity, low profits, low productivity, intensive product market competition, lack of unionization, and low wages." The primary sector is comprised of white-owned firms in which the majority of employees are white and is characterized by "high productivity, high profits, high degree of unionization, and job security" (Gilbertson and Gurak 211).

6. See Sander and Nee, "Limits," for a detailed analysis of this imbalance.

7. This is not to say that Chinatown business owners are the principal villains in the exploitation of Chinatown laborers, even as they are one source of it. Business owners are often only marginally better-off than their workers. This does not absolve them of responsibility for labor exploitation, but it adds another layer of complexity to class relations in the Asian American ghetto. The ghetto is a site of structural class inequity, but there are variations in levels of economic disenfranchisement and levels of relative privilege within that site. I discuss this in more detail in chapter 4.

8. In chapter 5, I discuss this transformation vis-à-vis the 1992 Los Angeles riots when model minority Korean American shopkeepers were turned into invading foreigners.

9. When capitalist development, needing as it does cheap, racialized exploited labor, is at odds with national attempts to forge a unified national identity, that is, white racial-cultural identity, as was the case in the late nineteenth century to World War II as Lisa Lowe points out (13), the yellow peril is a fitting construction for Asian Americans. As the yellow peril, Asian Americans are an alien presence in the nation, thereby always outside of it, outside of any claim to being part of the national racial-cultural identity. Thus, they can be tolerated for their presence as labor—alien labor—as long as they remain otherwise excluded from the polity. The construction of Asian Americans as a racially and culturally alien labor force palliates and naturalizes their labor exploitation: at least the United States does not exploit its native workers, and Asian Americans would be exploited anyway because their primitive culture does not allow them to be more than part of a coolie class. As Vijay Prashad puts it, Asian immigrants are "only wanted here for [their] labor and not to create [meaningful] lives" (*Karma* 80).

10. As the United States turned away from New Deal policies and ethics after World War II and toward those of economic deregulation and free market capitalism, national ideology turned toward a "melting pot" identity and ideals of racial assimilation. However, the civil rights era of the 1960s forced the nation to contend with the failure of the melting pot ideal vis-à-vis the contentiously racially fractured condition of the nation. Mainstream African American civil rights activism sought to achieve the ideal of racial integration by appealing to the entity of government as a welfare state, for instance, by demanding that government programs establish racial-economic parity, which violated the principles of free market capitalism. Not incidentally, the model minority thesis came into parlance at this time. It was a useful counterpoint to defuse African American civil rights demands as well as to reconcile the nation's desires to be both a modern, free market capitalist state as well as a racially integrated one. Asian Americans as model minorities testify to the idea that racial integration need not unsettle free market capitalism, but rather is enabled by it. This is evident in the discourse of the "welfare check" in *U.S. News & World Report*'s articulation of the model minority myth. Asian Americans do not depend on a "welfare check"—much less a welfare state—but "win wealth" by bootstrapping themselves to the "Promised Land" (Peterson 73). The "Promised Land" is implicitly a free market, capitalist land, specifically an American exceptionalist free market state, where conditions of democratic, race-blind, free market capitalism are what makes racialized subjects' virtuous "own efforts" an effective means of economic advancement in the first place. The model minority thesis is also a culturalization in that it posits Asian Americans' model economic behavior as deriving from Asian cultural values of self-reliance. Thus, Asian Americans are claimed to integrate themselves racially into the polity, at least economically, not by violating free market capitalism, but by embodying it.

11. That White, as a member of a law enforcement institution, seeks to rectify Chinatown's ills might suggest a recognition of the need for a public, institutional response to Chinatown's ghetto conditions. However, White, as a representative of the police department, merely seeks to be a catalyst to what is ultimately a private, cultural solution to Chinatown's ills, that is, its assimilation to white cultural norms.

12. See Sui Sin Far, "Her Chinese Husband" and "In the Land of the Free," in Ling and White-Parks edition 78–82, 93–100.

13. See reviews of *Native Speaker* quoted in Song 169–70.

14. The reabsorption of *The Woman Warrior* into an ethnographic frame is also demonstrated in the tussle over the text's genre. Kingston states that she wrote the text as a novel, but her publisher insisted on marketing it as nonfiction so that readers could get a "grasp of the story," that is, so that they could filter the text through the familiar frame of ethnographic consumption (Kubota 2).

3 / The Japanese American Internment: Master Narratives and Class Critique

1. The *San Francisco Chronicle*, quoted on the back cover blurb of the 1996 edition of *Nisei Daughter*.

2. In the author's preface to the 1979 edition, Sone overtly claims that her autobiography protests the injustices of the internment. However, I read this preface, published twenty-six years after the original publication of the autobiography, as a retroactive imprinting of the autobiography as an internment critique. By 1979, Japanese American groups seeking redress and reparations had gained traction. Their efforts bore fruit in

1981, when the Congressional Commission on Wartime Relocation and Internment of Civilians issued a statement that described the Japanese American internment as a "grave injustice" that resulted from "race prejudice, war hysteria and failure of political leadership" (qtd. in Chan 198). In 1987, Congress issued a formal apology for the internment and compensated each camp survivor with twenty thousand dollars. In other words, there was a very different social opinion of the internment in 1979 than in 1953, when *Nisei Daughter* was first published. The different social milieus in which these different texts (the preface and the body of the autobiography) produce the gap between the claims of the preface and the master narrative–supporting body of the autobiography. To read *Nisei Daughter* as incontestably and willfully subversive would be to ignore or discount this gap. We might also say that the preface, though articulating politically oppositional discourse, is a kind of master narrative itself, as it rehearses the redress and reparations discourse that had legitimacy in the 1970s and 1980s.

3. Though I critique Miyamoto's theorizations, they should also be recognized as symptomatic of the anti-Japanese context in which he wrote, when portraying Japanese Americans positively, for instance, through their interesting culture, might have been a strategy to counter racism against them.

4. Predating the ethnic enclave economy theorists, Miyamoto conceptualizes Nihonmachi as an ethnic enclave economy in which co-ethnic bonds are used to aid ghetto dwellers' economic interests, particularly through the laborer–small business owner relationship that is the core unit of the "co-ethnic cooperation" of the ethnic enclave economy theory. However, Miyamoto more readily acknowledges that this culture-based economy can lead to exploitation and economic failure (72–79, 80–81).

5. Miyamoto certainly notes that external structural factors, such as exclusionary laws and racist attitudes, contribute to Nihonmachi's formation, that these lead to "a definite trend towards the establishment of a ghetto" (63). However, culture is still the preeminent force behind Nihonmachi formation, to the extent that ghettoization itself becomes a Japanese cultural characteristic. Miyamoto writes that if Japanese Americans are "ghetto-seekers," it is because they are "[cultural] community builders" (57). This attribution of ghettoization to cultural community building enfolds the externally imposed structural aspects of ghettoization into Japanese culture, ultimately transforming structural ghettoization, though initially recognized as such, into a Japanese cultural practice.

6. It is possible that the Nihonmachi residents had access to organizing Tenchosetsu in Japan because they were class-privileged in Japan, but suffered downward mobility in the United States. However, this is not the case, as shown in the following section. Even if it were, retaining the cultural practices of a privileged class to which they once belonged is a way of denying and compensating for their current class situation as ghettoized immigrants.

7. The Nihonmachi performance of Tenchosetsu can offer the symbolic compensation of claiming Japanese high culture to allay American ghettoization. But this is poor compensation for ongoing experiences of racialized class inequity, and also self-defeatingly diverts attention from redressing that inequity by further suggesting that Nihonmachi is a cultural community rather than a class formation. Vijay Prashad writes of a similar dynamic for South Asian Americans: "The immigrants of South Asia may cloak themselves in a high culture even though on the subcontinent such an act might accord ill with their own class positions. . . . Here [in the United States]

we act as ex officio representatives of a civilization rather than as members of a class community" (*Karma* 117).

8. This is not to essentialize class by suggesting that there is something inherent in Mr. Sakaguchi's body that marks his class situation. Kazuko's description invests Mr. Sakaguchi's body with class meanings, but those meanings are rooted in socially constructed, class-informed practices (for instance, his unfamiliarity with codes of formal dress) that are then cast onto his body.

9. This critique of class racism could suggest that *Nisei Daughter* is a politically oppositional text, as opposed to being a collation of master narratives. However, throughout the text, critical or potentially critical statements are mitigated by opposing accommodationist sentiments, producing a tension between accommodation and opposition, as I discussed in the previous section.

10. In the 1941 Los Angeles/1947 Chicago comparison, Japanese American men in the white-collar workforce nearly quintupled (from 1.7% to 8.4%), but Japanese American female professionals increased by only about half a percentage point (from 2.9% to 3.5%) (Broom and Riemer 40).

11. Even though the majority of the relocatees at the end of 1944 were nisei, the majority of nisei, like the issei, remained in the camps. About 30,000 nisei were relocated, but the remaining 50,000 were not. The population with the highest number of individuals remaining in the camps were female nisei (about 20,000, or 25 percent of the nisei population), further indicating a gender imbalance in the relocation process. This gender imbalance was partially caused by the use of military service as a main route of relocation, which favored nisei men. Nearly half of the relocatees (17,000) at the end of 1944 were nisei men (Thomas, *Salvage* 616).

12. Of nisei, 71 percent of men and 63 percent of women who had professional and semi-professional skills were relocated by the end of 1944. Of professional issei, only 23 percent of men and 21 percent of women relocated in the same time period (Broom and Riemer 36).

13. By the end of 1944, 32,799 out of 38,849 issei remained in the camps (Thomas, *Salvage* 616).

14. In 1942 Los Angeles, there were 360 Japanese American–owned hotels and 250 Japanese American–owned restaurants. In 1946 Los Angeles, only 200 hotels and 30 to 50 restaurants were reestablished (WRA, *People* 87). The drastically reduced Japanese American presence in small business did not always indicate individual economic losses. Many of the internees who did reopen their shops enjoyed brisk business, and in the case of the hotel industry, even though fewer Japanese Americans reentered that niche, individual proprietors were able to charge double the prewar rates. Leaving the small business field could also indicate socioeconomic gain. For instance, hotel owners who were able to retain their property through the internment found that they could sell or lease it for triple the prewar value (WRA, *People* 92, 87). Notwithstanding, Japanese Americans overall suffered devastating economic losses, as reflected by the $74–$400 million estimate of aggregate financial losses.

15. The IRS also destroyed most of the evacuees' income tax returns for 1939–42 (Commission 118).

16. See also WRA, *People* 51–57.

17. I thank Crystal Parikh for calling my attention to the GI Bill as an analogue for the relocation program.

18. Kazuko does experience racism during relocation. She is exploited by her first employer, whose abuse is not explicitly characterized as racist, but whose temper is described as a "white rage"; and she is excluded from a sorority at Wendell College because of "whites only" bylaws (224, 228–29).

19. Kazuko's claim to American culture is freighted with national-political implications. By rejecting Japanese culture, she rejects a soon to be enemy nation and establishes her political allegiance to America. Kazuko's Americanization narrative can thereby be read as internment critique. Pointing out that she is culturally and politically American before the internment calls out that the U.S. government imprisoned subjects who properly belonged to the nation. However, the internment critique of Kazuko's Americanization narrative is mitigated because it supports the WRA's reconfiguration of the internment as a socioeconomic opportunity as I discuss later in this chapter.

4 / Chinese Suicide: Political Desire and Queer Exogamy

1. Nineteenth and early twentieth-century Chinatown in San Francisco was a "bachelor society" because immigration laws favored the entry of male laborers (until the Chinese Exclusion Act of 1882), most Chinese women were prohibited entry under the 1857 Page Law, and antimiscegenation laws prohibited Chinese men from forming new families. See Hing for laws affecting pre-1965 Chinese immigration to the United States (19–27).

2. Saskia Sassen writes that the domination of normative channels of goods, labor, and information by behemoth transnational corporations pushes smaller producers into unregulated, underground economic activity, creating a market for and of itinerant, casual labor that is concentrated in densely racialized spaces like Chinatown (289–305).

5 / Ethnic Entrepreneurs: Korean American Spies, Shopkeepers, and the 1992 Los Angeles Riots

1. The 1990 Census records that one-quarter of Korean Americans was self-employed, a proportion that is double the national average of self-employment and the highest among ethnic groups (Yoon 20–21). The majority of Korean American shops are not in black ghettos, but the small businesses in black ghettos are disproportionately owned by Korean Americans. A 1991 *Korea Times Los Angeles* survey shows that though only 10 percent of Korean American businesses were located in impoverished African American neighborhoods in South Los Angeles, 80 percent of the businesses in that area were owned by Korean Americans (Min 66–67).

2. For instance, in New York City, 20 to 25 percent of Korean American businesses that opened in the 1980s failed, and in 1994, 700 stores were opened, but 900 were shut down (K. Park 47; Prashad, *Everybody* 118). Even when shop revenues indicate economic wealth, this numerical assessment masks the long hours and unpaid family labor usually needed to run a small business.

3. Klinkenborg's review describes *Native Speaker*'s immigrant themes as only a subtext, and some other reviews, as Song discusses, universalize the novel's Korean immigrant themes. The reviews, then, of *Native Speaker* are bifurcated along the lines of denying that the novel is an immigrant story, and thereby denying that race and immigration are important issues in American life and literature; and of claiming that

it is only an immigrant story (Song 170). The former is not a solution to the problem that I pose. My point is not to urge the denuding of immigrant and racial themes from Lee's novel, but to critique how it is limited to being capable of only those themes.

4. Yoon and Park refer to schools of thought that focus on cultural theories of Korean American small business ownership, but both are critical of them, favoring structural explanations.

5. Studies attribute varying centrality to the role of the *ggeh*, some documenting that as many as 40 percent of Korean American small business owners rely on it for start-up capital. Others record a much lower number and posit the *ggeh* as just one of several private resources, such as personal savings and informal loans from friends and family (Lin 46–50; and Yoon 141–45).

6. Jews, of course, were not always considered white, but here Lee equates them with whiteness.

7. I reiterate that not all Korean American shopkeepers in South Los Angeles were wealthy like Henry's father. However, the shopkeepers did function as a symbol of minority upward mobility, especially in contrast to blacks, their relationship to whom I discuss later in this chapter.

8. See especially Abelmann and Lie; and Min. See also Claire Jean Kim; Kim contests the scapegoating thesis, arguing that Korean American shopkeepers are complicit in perpetuating white racial power and the disenfranchisement of African Americans. Kim also argues that the scapegoating thesis represents African American hostility toward Korean American shopkeepers as irrational racism, rather than as a strategic, organized challenge to white racial power (2–6).

9. Min and Kolodny describe the middleman minority position as characterized by: "(1) a concentration in small business, (2) a focus on providing services to minority customers, (3) a dependence on U.S. corporations for supply of merchandise, (4) a strong ethnic cohesion, (5) a subjection to stereotyping, and (6) experiences of hostility from the host society" (132).

10. This is the title of Min's study of Korean American small business owners in New York.

11. For instance, some take issue with Bonacich's assertion that a "sojourning mentality," the immigrant middleman's orientation toward their homeland, is central to their economic behavior (the middleman's willingness to tolerate hostility from groups above and below in exchange for economic gain because they do not see the host country as a permanent place of settlement), as it reinforces the idea that Asian Americans are perpetual foreigners.

12. I am indebted to Gandal's *The Virtues of the Vicious* for this phrase.

13. See Omi and Winant.

14. James Lee points out that the issue for Henry is not that he cannot speak English well, but that he speaks it too well (247). Nonetheless, this overly perfected, labored English flags Henry as racially/culturally different, as lacking a natural ease with the language, marking him as an outsider to white mainstream culture (C. Lee 12).

15. The phrase "Korean of the future" actually describes Henry, specifically what Henry, posing as a volunteer for Kwang's campaign, imagines Kwang must think of him for his interest in political participation. I apply the phrase to Kwang since Henry imagines that this is what Kwang thinks under his (mis)understanding that Henry is a mirror of him.

16. While this kind of bar is common in Korea and Korean American commercial districts in the United States, this is not to say that sex work is an inveterate part of Korean culture. However, Koreans and Korean Americans have certainly argued that it is, in order to justify sex work, that is, to use the excuse of culture to justify the sexual exploitation of women.

6 / Indian Edison: The Ethnoburbian Paradox and Corrective Ethnography

1. I thank Anita Mannur for calling my attention to these advertisements.

2. See Li 45 for a detailed breakdown of the differences among "ghetto," "ethnic enclave," and "ethnoburb." Li conceptualizes the ghetto and the ethnic enclave as different spaces (17–18), while I conceptualize them as the same empirical space, as I discuss below. However, I make a discursive distinction between "ghetto" and "ethnic enclave," which I also discuss later in this chapter.

3. Kalita's account of the Sarmas begins with their "gold-paved entry" to the United States, but proceeds to focus on their "shaky ground" (80), their uncertain job and financial security under H-1B visas and the bursting of the technology bubble. The Sarmas' privilege is thereby as illusory as the image that the ethnoburb is pervasively wealthy. However, I address them as a subject of privilege because they remain, despite their "shaky ground," privileged over the ghettoized ethnoburbian underclass. Lipi herself acknowledges this privilege: She "occasionally thought about how she never had to wash dishes or work as a cashier like some of the older immigrants they were friends with" (84).

Conclusion: The Postracial Aesthetic and Class Visibility

1. The binary that Nam's friend articulates, between the "old verities" or universal humanism on the one hand, and ethnic difference and particularity on the other, constructs a false binary between aesthetics (as in transcendental artistic and formal values) and ethnicity. This is an important topic that is beyond the scope of this discussion, but has been insightfully addressed in the volumes edited by Davis and Lee, as well as Zhou and Najmi.

2. Of course the presence of race in an Asian American text does not guarantee the presence of class, as I have argued throughout this study. In addition, even as race is effaced by the postracial, it might resurface as class, as I discuss below.

3. This was not always the prevalent view at the Iowa Writers' Workshop. When Frank Chin, one of the major figures of the *Aiiieeeee!* group, attended the Workshop, he was encouraged to write Orientalist ethnographies (Nee and Nee 379, 383–84).

4. I am indebted to Daniel Kim for this insight.

5. Postracial, post-class literature of course can claim not to represent any Asian American social formation; it is postracial, after all. However, by not representing any Asian American social formation, the postracial and postclass aesthetic continues to efface the intensification of Asian American racialization and class inequity.

WORKS CITED

Abelmann, Nancy, and John Lie. *Blue Dreams: Korean Americans and the Los Angeles Riots.* Cambridge: Harvard University Press, 1995.

Aero, Rita. *Things Chinese.* New York: Dolphin Books, 1980.

Alba, Richard, and Victor Nee. *Remaking the American Mainstream.* Cambridge: Harvard University Press, 2003.

Baldwin, James. "Negroes Are Anti-Semitic Because They Are Anti-White." 1967. In *Blacks and Jews: Alliances and Arguments*, edited by Paul Berman, 31–41. New York: Delacorte Press, 1994.

Before Columbus Foundation. 2002. *The American Book Awards.* www.ankn. uaf.edu/IEW/BeforeColumbus/index2002.html.

Belluck, Pamela. "Being of Two Cultures and Belonging to Neither: After an Acclaimed Novel, a Korean-American Writer Searches for His Roots." *New York Times*, 10 July 1995.

Berner, Richard C. *Seattle 1921–1940: From Boom to Bust.* Seattle in the 20th Century 2. Seattle: Charles Press, 1991.

———. *Seattle Transformed: World War II to Cold War.* Seattle in the 20th Century 3. Seattle: Charles Press, 1991.

Birkerts, Sven. "In Our House There Were No Chinese Things." Review of *Charlie Chan Is Dead: An Anthology of Contemporary American Fiction*, edited by Jessica Hagedorn. *New York Times* 19 December 1993.

Bradbury, Lorna. "Chang-rae Lee." 20 June 2004. www.telegraph.co.uk/culture/3619233/Chang-rae-Lee.html.

Broom, Leonard, and Ruth Riemer. *Removal and Return: The Socio-Economic Effects of the War on Japanese Americans.* Berkeley and Los Angeles: University of California Press, 1949.

Bonacich, Edna. "A Theory of Middleman Minorities." *American Sociological Review* 38.5 (October 1973): 583–94.

Bourdieu, Pierre. *The Field of Cultural Production*. New York: Columbia University Press, 1993.

Bush, George W. "Statement by the President in His Address to the Nation." 11 September 2001. Office of the Press Secretary. www.whitehouse.gov/news/releases/2001/09/20010911-16.html#.

———. "Address to a Joint Session of Congress and the American People." 20 September 2001. Office of the Press Secretary. www.whitehouse.gov/news/releases/2001/09/20010920-8.html.

Carpenter, John, dir. *Big Trouble in Little China*. 20th Century Fox, 1986.

Caserio, Robert. "The Antisocial Thesis in Queer Theory." *PMLA* 121.3 (May 2006): 819–21.

Cha, Theresa Hak Kyung. *Dictée*. Berkeley: Third Woman Press, 1995.

Chan, Jeffery, Frank Chin, Lawson Inada, and Shawn Wong, eds. *Aiiieeeee! An Anthology of Asian American Writers*. 1989. New York: Meridian, 1997.

Chan, Sucheng. *Asian Americans: An Interpretive History*. New York: Twayne, 1991.

Chang, Juliana. "Melancholic Remains: Domestic and National Secrets in Fae Myenne Ng's *Bone*." *Modern Fiction Studies* 51.1 (Spring 2005): 110–33.

Chen, Tina. *Double Agency: Acts of Impersonation in Asian American Literature and Culture*. Palo Alto: Stanford University Press, 2005.

Cheng, Anne. *The Melancholy of Race: Psychoanalysis, Assimilation, and Hidden Grief*. New York: Oxford University Press, 2001.

Chin, Frank. "Railroad Standard Time." In *The Chinaman Pacific & Frisco R.R. Co.*, 1–7. Minneapolis: Coffee House Press, 1988.

Cho, Sumi K. "Korean Americans vs. African Americans: Conflict and Construction." In *Reading Rodney King, Reading Urban Uprising*, edited by Robert Gooding-Williams, 196–211. New York: Routledge, 1993.

Chuh, Kandice. *Imagine Otherwise: Asian Americanist Critique*. Durham, N.C.: Duke University Press, 2004.

Chuman, Frank. *The Bamboo People: The Law and Japanese-Americans*. Del Mar, Calif.: Publisher's Inc., 1976.

Cimino, Michael, dir. *The Year of the Dragon*. MGM/UA, 1985.

Clifford, James. *The Predicament of Culture: Twentieth-Century Ethnography, Literature, and Art*. Cambridge: Harvard University Press, 1988.

Commission on the Wartime Relocation and Internment of Civilians. *Personal Justice Denied*. Washington, D.C.: Commission on the Wartime Relocation and Internment of Civilians, 1982.

Daniels, Roger, Sandra C. Taylor, and H. L. Kitano, eds. *Japanese Americans: From Relocation to Redress*. Salt Lake City: University of Utah Press, 1986.

Davis, Rocio, and Su-Im Lee, eds. *Literary Gestures: The Aesthetic in Asian American Writing*. Philadelphia: Temple University Press, 2006.

Dean, Tim. "The Antisocial Homosexual." *PMLA* 121.3 (May 2006): 826–28.

Dezell, Maureen. "The Tug of 'Warrior': Stereotypes or True Stories? Huntington Play Provokes a Clash over Chinese Culture." Review of stage adaptation of *The Woman Warrior* by Maxine Hong Kingston. *Boston Globe*, 23 September 1994.

Dirlik, Arif. "Confucius in the Borderlands: Global Capitalism and the Reinvention of Confucianism." *boundary 2* 22.3 (Fall 1995): 229–73.

Dobie, C. C. *San Francisco's Chinatown*. New York: Appleton-Century-Crofts, 1936.

Edelman, Lee. *No Future: Queer Theory and the Death Drive*. Durham, N.C.: Duke University Press, 2004.

Ellison, Ralph. "The World and the Jug," In *Shadow and Act*. New York: Vintage, 1972.

Emerson, Robert, ed. *Contemporary Field Research: Perspectives and Formulations*. 2nd ed. Long Grove, Ill.: Waveland Press, 2001.

Eng, David. *Racial Castration: Managing Masculinity in Asian America*. Durham, N.C.: Duke University Press, 2001.

Eng, David, and Shinhee Han. "A Dialogue on Racial Melancholia." In *Loss*, edited by David Eng and David Kazanjian. Berkeley and Los Angeles: University of California Press, 2003.

Farwell, W. B. *The Chinese at Home and Abroad*. San Francisco: A. L. Bancroft, 1885.

Felski, Rita. "Nothing to Declare: Identity, Shame, and the Lower Middle Class." *PMLA* 115.1 (January 2000): 33–45.

Fong, Timothy. *The First Suburban Chinatown: The Remaking of Monterey Park, California*. Philadelphia: Temple University Press, 1994.

Frank, Thomas. *One Market under God: Extreme Capitalism, Market Populism, and the End of Economic Democracy*. New York: Anchor, 2001.

Fussell, Paul. *Class: A Guide through the American Status System*. New York: Touchstone, 1992.

Gandal, Keith. *The Virtues of the Vicious: Jacob Riis, Stephen Crane, and the Spectacle of the Slum*. New York: Oxford University Press, 1997.

Gilbertson, Greta, and Douglas Gurak. "Broadening the Enclave Debate: The Labor Market Experiences of Dominican and Columbian Men in New York City." *Sociological Forum* 8.2 (June 1993): 205–20.

Goldberg, Jeffrey. "The Soul of the New Koreans." *New York Magazine*, 10 April 1995, 43–51.

Hagedorn, Jessica. *Charlie Chan Is Dead: An Anthology of Contemporary Asian American Fiction*. New York: Penguin, 1993.

Hagedorn, John. "Race Not Space: A Revisionist History of Gangs in Chicago." *Journal of African America History* 91.2 (Spring 2006): 194–208.

Hall, Stuart. "Race, Articulation, and Societies Structured in Dominance." In *Black British Cultural Studies*, edited by Houston Baker, Manthia Diawara, and Ruth Lindeborg, 16–60. Chicago: University of Chicago Press, 1996.

Hattori, Tomo. "Model Minority Discourse and Asian American Jouis-Sense." *differences* 11.2 (1999): 245.

Hayashi, Ann Koto. *Face of the Enemy, Heart of a Patriot: Japanese-American Internment Narratives*. New York: Garland, 1995.

Hing, Bill Ong. *Making and Remaking Asian America through Immigration Policy, 1850–1990*. Stanford: Stanford University Press, 1993.

Hirabayashi, Lane Ryo. "The Impact of Incarceration on the Education of Nisei Schoolchildren." In *Japanese Americans: From Relocation to Redress*, edited by Roger Daniels, Sandra Taylor, Harry Kitano, 44–51. Salt Lake City: University of Utah Press, 1986.

Ice Cube, "Black Korea," *Death Certificate*. Priority Records, 1991.

Kalita, S. Mitra. *Suburban Sahibs: Three Immigrant Families and Their Passage from India to America*. New Brunswick: Rutgers University Press, 2005.

Kaneko, Lonny. "The Shoyu Kid." In *The Big Aiiieeeee! An Anthology of Chinese American and Japanese American Literature*, edited by Jeffery Chan, Frank Chin, Lawson Inada and Shawn Wong, 304–14. New York: Meridian, 1991.

Kich, Martin. "Chang-rae Lee." In *Asian American Novelists: A Bio-Bibliographical Critical Sourcebook*, edited by Emmanuel Nelson, 175–76. Westport, Ct.: Greenwood Press, 2000.

Kikuchi, Charles. *The Kikuchi Diary: Chronicle from an American Concentration Camp*. Edited by John Modell. Chicago: University of Illinois Press, 1973.

Kim, Claire Jean. *Bitter Fruit: The Politics of Black-Korean Conflict in New York City*. New Haven: Yale University Press, 2003.

Kim, Elaine. *Asian American Literature: An Introduction to the Writings and Their Social Context*. Philadelphia: Temple University Press, 1982.

———. "Beyond Railroads and Internment: Comments on the Past, Present, and Future of Asian American Studies." In *Privileging Positions: The Sites of Asian American Studies*, edited by Gary Okihiro, Marilyn Alquizola, Dorothy Fujita Rony, and K. Scott Wong, 11–19. Pullman: Washington State University Press, 1995.

———. "They Armed in Self-Defense." *Newsweek*, 18 May 1992, 10.

Kim, Patti. *A Cab Called Reliable*. New York: St. Martin's-Griffin, 1998.

Kin, Huie. *Reminiscences*. Peiping: San Yu Press, 1932.

Klinkenborg, Verlyn. "Witness to Strangeness, Espionage Is Only One of a Korean-American Hero's Secrets." *New Yorker*, 10 July 1995, 76–77.

Koshy, Susan. "The Fiction of Asian American Literature." *Yale Journal of Criticism: Interpretation in the Humanities* 9:2 (Fall 1996): 315–46.

Kubota, Gary. "Maxine Hong Kingston: Something Comes from Outside onto the Paper." Interview with Kingston in *Conversations with Maxine Hong Kingston*, edited by Skenazy and Martin, 1–4. Jackson: University of Mississippi Press, 1998.

Kwong, Peter. *The New Chinatown*. 1987. New York: Hill and Wang, 1996.

Lahiri, Jhumpa. *Unaccustomed Earth*. New York: Alfred Knopf, 2008.

Lang, Amy Schrager. *The Syntax of Class: Writing Inequality in Nineteenth-Century America*. Ann Arbor: University of Michigan Press, 2006.

Lauter, Paul. "Under Construction." In *New Working-Class Studies*, edited by John Russo and Sherry Lee Linkon, 63–77. Ithaca, N.Y.: ILR–Cornell University Press, 2005.

Lauter, Paul, and Ann Fitzgerald, eds. *Literature, Class and Culture: An Anthology*. New York: Longman, 1999.

Le, Nam. "Love and Honor and Pride and Pity and Compassion and Sacrifice." In *Boat*, 3–28. New York: Vintage, 2008.

Lee, Calvin. *Chinatown, U.S.A.* New York: Doubleday, 1965.

Lee, Chang-rae. *Native Speaker*. New York: Riverhead, 1995.

Lee, James Kyung-Jin. "Where the Talented Tenth Meets the Model Minority: The Price of Privilege in Wideman's *Philadelphia Fire* and Lee's *Native Speaker*." *Novel: A Forum on Fiction* 35:2–3 (Spring-Summer 2002): 231–57.

Lee, Rose Hum. "The Decline of Chinatowns in the United States." *American Journal of Sociology* 54.5 (March 1949): 422–32.

Lee, Yan Phou. *When I Was a Boy in China*. Boston: D. Lothrop, 1887.

Li, Wei. *Ethnoburb*. Honolulu: University of Hawai'i Press, 2009.

Lin, Jan. *Reconstructing Chinatown: Ethnic Enclave, Global Change*. Minneapolis: University of Minnesota Press, 1998.

Lin, Yutang. *Chinatown Family*. New York: J. Day Co., 1948.

———. *My Country and My People*. New York: Reynal and Hitchcock, 1935.

Loke, Margaret. "The Tao Is Up." Review of *The Woman Warrior* by Maxine Hong Kingston. *New York Times Magazine*, 30 April 1989.

Loo, Chalsa. *Chinatown: Most Time, Hard Time*. New York: Praeger-Greenwood, 1991.

Lott, Eric. *Love and Theft: Blackface Minstrelsy and the American Working Class*. New York: Oxford University Press, 1995.

Louie, Miriam Ching Yoon. *Sweatshop Warriors: Immigrant Women Workers Take on the Global Factory*. Cambridge: South End Press, 2001.

Lowe, Lisa. *Immigrant Acts*. Durham, N.C.: Duke University Press, 1996.

Lowe, Lisa, and David Lloyd, eds. *The Politics of Culture in the Shadow of Capital*. Durham, N.C.: Duke University Press, 1997.

Lye, Colleen. *America's Asia: Racial Formation and American Literature*. Princeton, N.J.: Princeton University Press, 2004.

Massey, Douglas, and Nancy Denton. *American Apartheid: Segregation and the Making of the Underclass*. Cambridge: Harvard University Press, 1993.

Min, Pyong Gap. *Caught in the Middle: Korean Communities in New York and Los Angeles*. Berkeley and Los Angeles: University of California Press, 1996.

Min, Pyong Gap, and Andrew Kolodny. "The Middleman Minority Characteristics of Korean Immigrants in the United States." In *Koreans in the Hood:*

Conflict with African Americans, edited by Kwang Chung Kim, 131–54. Baltimore: Johns Hopkins University Press, 1999.

Miyamoto, Frank S. Introduction to *Nisei Daughter*, by Monica Sone, vii–xiv. Seattle: University of Washington Press, 1996.

———. "Social Solidarity among the Japanese in Seattle." *Bulletin: University of Washington Publications in the Social Sciences* 11.2 (December 1939): 57–130.

National Japanese American Student Relocation Council. *How to Help Japanese American Student Relocation*. Philadelphia: National Japanese American Student Relocation Council, 1943.

Nee, Victor, and Brett de Bary Nee. *Longtime Californ': A Documentary Study of an American Chinatown*. Palo Alto: Stanford University Press, 1986.

New York Stock Exchange. *New York Times*, 17 September 2001.

Ng, Fae Myenne. *Bone*. 1993. New York: HarperPerennial, 1994.

Nguyen, Viet. *Race and Resistance: Literature and Politics in Asian America*. New York: Oxford University Press, 2002.

Nisei Student Relocation Commemorative Fund, Inc. "A Short History of the National Japanese American Student Relocation Council.". www.nsrcfund. org/history/history.html.

Okada, John. *No-No Boy*. 1976. Seattle: University of Washington Press, 1988.

Okihiro, Gary. *Margins and Mainstreams: Asians in American History and Culture*. Seattle: University of Washington Press, 1994.

Omi, Michael, and Howard Winant. "The Los Angeles 'Race Riot' and Contemporary U.S. Politics." In *Reading Rodney King, Reading Urban Uprising*, edited by Robert Gooding-Williams, 97–114. New York: Routledge, 1993.

Parikh, Crystal. "Ethnic America Undercover: The Intellectual and Minority Discourse." *Contemporary Literature* 43:2 (Summer 2002): 249–84.

Park, Jung Sun. "Identity Politics: Chicago Korean-Americans and the Los Angeles 'Riots.'" In *Koreans in the Hood: Conflict with African Americans*, edited by Kwang Chung Kim. 202–31. Baltimore: Johns Hopkins University Press, 1999.

Park, Kyeyoung. *The Korean American Dream: Immigrants and Small Business in New York City*. Ithaca, N.Y.: Cornell University Press, 1997.

Park, Robert E. *On Social Control and Collective Behavior: Selected Papers*. Edited by Ralph Turner. Chicago: University of Chicago Press, 1967.

———. *Race and Culture*. Glencoe, Ill.: Free Press, 1950.

Park, Robert E., and Ernest Burgess. "Plant Communities in Animal Societies." In *Introduction to the Science of Sociology*, edited by Park and Burgess, 175–82. 1921. Chicago: University of Chicago Press, 1969.

Park, You-me, and Gayle Wald. "Native Daughters in the Promised Land: Gender, Race, and the Question of Separate Spheres." *American Literature: A Journal of Literary History, Criticism, and Bibliography* 70:3 (September 1998): 607–33.

Peterson, William. "Success Story of One Minority Group in the U.S." *U.S. News & World Report*, 26 December 1966, 73–78.

Polanski, Roman, dir. *Chinatown*. Paramount Pictures, 1974.

Prashad, Vijay. *The Karma of Brown Folk*. Minneapolis: University of Minnesota Press, 2000.

———. *Everybody Was Kung Fu Fighting: Afro-Asian Connections and the Myth of Cultural Purity*. Boston: Beacon Press, 2001.

Reed, Adolph. "The 'Underclass' as Myth and Symbol: The Poverty of Discourse about Poverty." In *Stirrings in the Jug*, 179–98. Minneapolis: University of Minnesota Press, 1999.

Roediger, David. *The Wages of Whiteness: Race and the Making of the American Working Class*. 1991. New York: Verso, 1999.

Russo, John, and Sherry Lee Linkon, eds. *New Working-Class Studies*. Ithaca, N.Y.: ILR–Cornell University Press, 2005.

Said, Edward W. *Orientalism*. New York: Vintage Books, 1979.

Sanders, Jimy, and Victor Nee. "Limits of Ethnic Solidarity in the Enclave Economy." *American Sociological Review* 52.6 (December 1987): 745–73.

———. "Problems in Resolving the Enclave Economy Debate." *American Sociological Review* 57.3 (June 1992): 415–18.

Sassen, Saskia. *The Global City: New York, London, Tokyo*. Princeton, N.J.: Princeton University Press, 2001.

Schocket, Eric. *Vanishing Moments: Class and American Literature*. Ann Arbor: University of Michigan Press, 2006.

Shah, Nayan. *Contagious Divides: Epidemics and Race in San Francisco's Chinatown*. Berkeley and Los Angeles: University of California Press, 2001.

Shiver, Jube, Jr., and Kenneth J. Garcia. "Owners' Lifelong Dreams Were Destroyed in Minutes." *Los Angeles Times*, 3 May 1992.

Smith, Anna Deavere. *Twilight: Los Angeles, 1992*. New York: Anchor-Doubleday, 1994.

Smith, Lynn. "Author Mixes Yin, Yang in Her Writing." Review of *The Woman Warrior*, by Maxine Hong Kingston. *Los Angeles Times*, 27 April 1986.

Sone, Monica. *Nisei Daughter*. 1953. Seattle: University of Washington Press, 1996.

Song, Min. *Strange Future: Pessimism and the 1992 Los Angeles Riots*. Durham, N.C.: Duke University Press, 2005.

Spivak, Gayatri Chakravorty. "Can the Subaltern Speak?" In *Marxism and the Interpretation of Culture*, edited by Lawrence Grossberg and Cary Nelson, 271–313. Urbana: University of Illinois Press, 1988.

Sugimoto, Etsuko. *Daughter of a Samurai*. Garden City, N.Y.: Doubleday, Page, 1925.

Sumida, Steven H. "Protest and Accommodation, Self-Satire and Self-Effacement, and Monica Sone's *Nisei Daughter*." In *Multicultural Autobiography: American Lives*, edited by James R. Payne, 207–9. Knoxville: University of Tennessee Press, 1992.

Sui Sin Far. *Mrs. Spring Fragrance*. Chicago: A. C. McClurg, 1912.

———. *Mrs. Spring Fragrance and Other Writings*. Edited by Amy Ling and Annette White-Parks. Urbana: University of Illinois Press, 1995.

Taylor, Quintard. *The Forging of a Black Community: Seattle's Central District from 1870 through the Civil Rights Era*. Seattle: University of Washington Press, 1994.

Thomas, Dorothy Swaine. *The Spoilage*. Berkeley and Los Angeles: University of California Press, 1946.

———. *The Salvage*. Berkeley and Los Angeles: University of California Press, 1952.

Watanna, Onoto. *Tama*. New York: Harper Brothers, 1910.

Williams, Raymond. *Keywords: A Vocabulary of Culture and Society*. 1976. New York: Oxford University Press, 1983.

———. *The Sociology of Culture*. New York: Schocken Books, 1982.

Wilson, Kenneth, and Alejandro Portes. "Immigrant Enclaves: An Analysis of the Labor Market Experiences of Cubans in Miami." *American Journal of Sociology* 86.2 (September 1980): 295–319.

Wilson, William Julius. *The Truly Disadvantaged: The Inner City, the Underclass, and Public Policy*. Chicago: University of Chicago Press, 1987.

Wirth, Louis. *The Ghetto*. Chicago: University of Chicago Press, 1960.

Wong, Jade Snow. *Fifth Chinese Daughter*. New York: Harper, 1950.

Wong, Sau-Ling. *Reading Asian American Literature: From Necessity to Extravagance*. Princeton, N.J.: Princeton University Press, 1993.

———. "Sugar Sisterhood." In *The Ethnic Canon: Histories, Institutions and Interventions*, edited by David Palumbo-Liu, 174–210. Minneapolis: University of Minnesota Press, 1995.

WRA (War Relocation Authority). *Education Program in Relocation Centers*. Washington, D.C.: U.S. Department of the Interior, 1945.

———. *The Evacuated People: A Quantitative Description*. 1946. Vol. 3. New York: AMS Press, 1975.

———. *Myths and Facts about the Japanese Americans: Answering Common Misconceptions Regarding Americans of Japanese Ancestry*. Washington, D.C.: U.S. Department of the Interior, 1935.

———. *People in Motion: The Postwar Adjustment of the Evacuated Japanese Americans*. 1947. Vol. 5. New York: AMS Press, 1975.

———. *Relocation of Japanese Americans*. Washington, D.C.: War Relocation Authority, 1942.

———. *The Relocation Program*. 1946. Vol. 7. New York: AMS Press, 1975.

———. *The Relocation Program: A Guidebook for the Residents of Relocation Centers*. 1943. Vol. 6. New York: AMS Press, 1975.

———. *Uprooted Americans in Your Community*. Washington, D.C.: U.S. Department of the Interior, 1945.

———. *WRA: A Story of Human Conservation*. 1946. Vol. 9. New York: AMS Press, 1975.

Yoon, In-Jin. *On My Own: Korean Businesses and Race Relations in America*. Chicago: University of Chicago Press, 1997.

Yudice, George. *The Expediency of Culture: Uses of Culture in the Global Era.* Durham, N.C.: Duke University Press, 2004.

Yun, Leong Gor. *Chinatown Inside and Out.* New York: B. Mussey, 1936.

Zhou, Min. *Chinatown: The Socioeconomic Potential of an Urban Enclave.* Philadelphia: Temple University Press, 1992.

Zhou, Xiaojing, and Samina Najmi, eds. *Form and Transformation in Asian American Literature.* Seattle: University of Washington Press, 2005.

Zia, Helen. *Asian American Dreams: The Emergence of an American People.* New York: Farrar, Straus and Giroux, 2000.

Index

About the Author

Yoonmee Chang is an assistant professor of English and cultural studies at George Mason University. Her research focuses on how class shapes Asian American literature and culture. She is currently working on two projects: an investigation of the State Department papers of Jade Snow Wong, and an examination of the postracial aesthetic in Asian American literature. Chang's work has been published in the *Journal of Asian American Studies* and *Modern Fiction Studies*.

Breinigsville, PA USA
29 October 2010
248291BV00002B/2/P